HYBRID MICROCIRCUIT
RELIABILITY DATA

Some Pergamon Books of Interest

ABRAHAMS & PRIDHAM	Semiconductor Circuits: Theory, Design and Experiments
ABRAHAMS & PRIDHAM	Semiconductor Circuits: Worked Examples
BINDMANN	Dictionary of Semiconductor Physics and Electronics: English/German, German/English
BOWDLER	Measurements in High-Voltage Test Circuits
BROOKES	Basic Electric Circuits, 2nd Edition
DUMMER	Electronic Components, Tubes and Transistors
DUMMER & GRIFFIN	Electronic Reliability: Calculation and Design
DUMMER & GRIFFIN	Environmental Testing Techniques for Electronics and Materials
DUMMER & ROBERTSON	Electronic Connection Techniques and Equipment 1968–69
DUMMER & ROBERTSON	Fluidic Components and Equipment 1968–69
DUMMER & ROBERTSON	German Microelectronics Data 1968–69
FAGOT & MAGNE	Frequency Modulation Theory
FISHER & GATLAND	Electronics: From Theory into Practice, 2nd Edition
GATLAND	Electronic Engineering Applications of Two Port Networks
HARRIS & ROBSON	The Physical Basis of Electronics
HOLBROOK	Laplace Transforms for Electronic Engineers, 2nd Edition
HOWSON	Mathematics for Electrical Circuit Analysis
JENKINS & JARVIS	Principles of Electronics— Volume 1: Thermionics Volume 2: Semiconductors
MURPHY	Thyristor Control of AC Motors
NEIDHARDT	Dictionary of Electronics: English/German/French/Russian
PRIDHAM	Electronic Devices and Circuits Volumes 1, 2 and 3
PRIDHAM	Solid State Circuits
RODDY	Introduction to Microelectronics

HYBRID MICROCIRCUIT RELIABILITY DATA

Prepared by:
IIT RESEARCH INSTITUTE

PERGAMON PRESS

OXFORD · NEW YORK · TORONTO
SYDNEY · PARIS · FRANKFURT

OXFORD	Pergamon Press Ltd., Headington Hill Hall, Oxford OX3 0BW, England
U.S.A.	Pergamon Press Inc., Maxwell House, Fairview Park, Elmsford, New York 10523, U.S.A.
CANADA	Pergamon of Canada Ltd., P.O. Box 9600, Don Mills M3C 2T9, Ontario, Canada
AUSTRALIA	Pergamon Press (Aust.) Pty. Ltd., 19a Boundary Street, Rushcutters Bay, N.S.W. 2011, Australia
FRANCE	Pergamon Press SARL, 24 rue des Ecoles, 75240 Paris, Cedex 05, France
WEST GERMANY	Pergamon Press GmbH, 6242 Kronberg-Taunus, Pferdstrasse 1, Frankfurt-am-Main, West Germany

First edition 1975; reprinted 1976

Library of Congress Catalog Card No. 75-29637

Printed in Great Britain by A. Wheaton & Co., Exeter

ISBN 0 08 0205356 (Flexi)

TABLE OF CONTENTS

Table of Contents (con't)

Table of Contents (con't)

Table of Contents (con't)

INTRODUCTION

This first edition of the Hybrid Microcircuit Reliability Data contains test and operational data in both highly summarized and detailed format to provide maximum utilization. Functions which may benefit from this unique publication include: part selection, failure rate predictions, screening decisions, environmental test specification preparation, failure modes and effects analysis and corrective action decisions.

Data for HMRD is collected, verified, and reduced by the Reliability Analysis Center Engineering Staff to provide objective information for government and industry use. Qualifying codes and descriptors are included in the detailed data presentations to allow the user to select specific subsets of the data for specialized analyses.

Analyzed data presentations consist of device experienced versus predicted failure rates, screening fallout summary, and a failure classification.

SECTION 1

EXPERIENCED vs PREDICTED FAILURE RATES

Figure 1 presents a comparison of hybrid device users' experienced failure rate with predicted failure rate based on MIL-HDBK-217B, 20 September, 1974. A summary of the supporting data is given in Table 1. In each case, any assumptions which were necessary to complete the prediction calculations are shown. This analysis was limited to users data where device operating hours were sufficient to yield long term reliability information. Burn-in data were not included.

Intervals in Figure I are between the upper and lower 75% confidence levels of the chi-square distribution, assuming an exponential failure distribution. Lower and upper limits are computed for 2r and 2(r + 1) degrees of freedom respectively.

Although not specifically considered by the MIL-HDBK-217B hybrid prediction model, multichip devices were included in this analysis and are identified on Figure 1 by the dashed interval lines.

The maximum likelihood estimator (point estimate) is given wherever failures occurred.

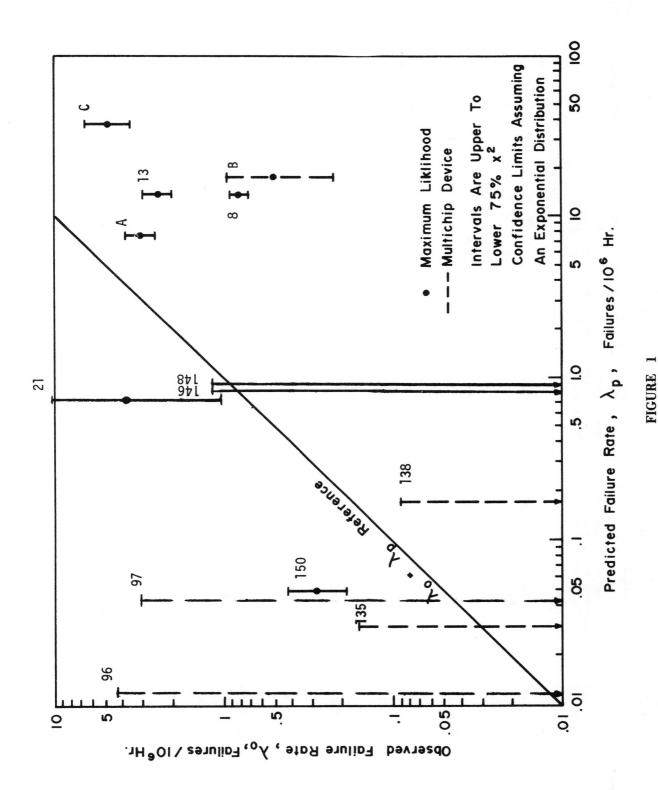

FIGURE 1

USER EXPERIENCE VS. PREDICTED FAILURE RATES

TABLE 1

USER DATA

Entry No.	Circuit Function	Pertinent Data Not Reported	Test Environment	Test Temp	Part Hours (Hrs)	No. of Failures	λ_p (F/10⁶Hrs)	λ_σ Min λ Max (F/10⁶Hrs)		Maximum Likelihood (F/10⁶Hrs)
96	Quad Driver	Transistor Type	Satellite Orbit	50°C	3.31E5	0	.01	0	4.2	N/A
97	Adjustable Positive D.C. Voltage Regulator	Transistor Type	Satellite Orbit	50°C	5.0E5	0	.05	0	2.8	N/A
135	Combination of 135 Entries	N/A	N/A	N/A	7.71E6	0	.03	0	.18	N/A
135	Driver	Transistor Type	Satellite Orbit	50°C	2.78E6	0	.03	0	.5	
135	Driver	Transistor Type Orbit	Satellite Orbit	50°C	3.07E6	0	.03	0	.45	
135	Driver	Transistor Type	Satellite Orbit	50°C	1.86E6	0	.03	0	.75	
150	FET Switch	Transistor Diode Type Resistor Tol.	AirInhb	30°C	17.5E6	5	.05	.19	.42	.28
138	Quad Driver *	Transistor Type	Satellite Orbit	50°C	1.5E7	0	.17	0	.09	N/A
21	Input Interface	Transistor Type	AirInhb	30°C	2.64E5	1	.75	1.1	10.2	3.8
146	Emitter Follower **	Transistor Type	Lab	25°C	1.14E6	0	.77	0	1.22	N/A
148	Clamped Differential**	Transistor Diode Type	Lab	25°C	1.14E6	0	.92	0	1.22	N/A

User Data (con't)
Table 1

Entry No.	Circuit Function	Pertinent Data Not Reported	Test Environment	Test Temp	Part Hours (Hrs)	No. of Failures	λ_p (F/10⁶Hrs)	λ o Min λo Max (F/10⁶Hrs)		Maximum Likelihood (F/10⁶Hrs)
A	Combination of Entries 11 & 16	N/A	N/A	N/A	5.4E6	17	8.0	2.6	3.8	3.1
11	Quad Buffer/ Driver	Transistor Type	AirInhb	30°C	5.07E6	17	7.86	2.77	4.07	
16	Triple Signal Conditioner		AirInhb	30°C	3.56E5	0	9.17	0	3.9	
8	Analog Gate		AirInhb	30°C	56.2E6	45	13.9	.72	.90	0.8
13	Demodulator	Transistor Type, I.C. Part. No.	Air Inhb	30°C	9.04E6	22	14.3	2.1	2.9	2.4
B	Combination of 154 Entries *	N/A	N/A	N/A	4.0E6	2	18	.24	.97	0.5
154	Diode Array	Substrate Size	Air Inhb	30°C	6.1E5	1	18	.5	4.4	
154	Diode Array	Substrate Size	Air Inhb	30°C	3.4E6	1	18	.09	.79	
C	Combination of 106 Entries	N/A	N/A	N/A	1.66E6	8	38.5	3.6	6.5	4.8
106	Signal Processor	Transistor Type, I.C. Part No. Resistor No.	Air Inhb	30°C	1.41E6	7	38.5	3.6	6.9	
106	Signal Processor	Transistor Type, I.C. Part No. Resistor Tol.	Air Inhb	30°C	2.54E5	1	38.5	.63	5.9	

* Multichip Devices
** Beam Lead Device

-5-

SECTION 2

SCREENING SUMMARY

Tables 2 through 7 summarize the fallout results for hybrid devices which were subjected to screening sequences approximately equivalent to MIL-STD-883, Method 5004 Class B or C. Data were taken from the detailed listings in Section 5.

Table 2 is a summary of the rejects detected by each test in the B and C sequence. In general, parts failing during Bake, Temperature Cycling, Thermal Shock and Constant Acceleration, are detected during Fine and Gross Leak (Hermeticity) or Electrical Measurements (EM 1) Similarly, those failing during an unmonitored Burn-In are detected at EM2. Large variations in the number tested are due to the variety of screening sequences, especially in Class C. The Hermeticity test method entries are sums of the fine and gross leak values.

Table 3 shows the relative distribution of the rejects from Table 2. Again, the percentages are higher for the detector tests than for the stress tests. Combining these data by major sequence phase produced Tables 4 and 5. This grouping includes the appropriate detection tests with each stress test. Both tables indicate that the environmental portion of the screening sequence precipitated the greatest proportion of failures. The combined total, however, is somewhat biased by the small number tested in the burn-in phase of the Class C equivalent sequence.

Table 6 shows the fallout experienced for various stress levels applied during an environmental sequence consisting of high temperature bake, temperature cycling, and constant acceleration. Failure detection occurred during hermeticity testing, first electrical measurements, or electrical measurements following burn-in. An absence of correlation between higher stress levels and percentage rejected is attributed to the diverse complexities of the devices.

Table 7 summarizes the screening results in the most general form and indicates that the lumped total percentage removed by the various screening sequences is 15%.

TABLE 2

SCREENING FALLOUT REJECTED / TESTED

TEST METHOD	- Class B Eqv -			- Class C Eqv -			Combined	%
	DIG	LIN	TOTAL	TOTAL	DIG	LIN	TOTAL	
Int Visual	219 / 4508	438 / 13883	657 / 18391	77 / 6210	35 / 3280	42 / 2930	734 / 24601	3
Bake	0 / 4289	0 / 13268	0 / 17557	1 / 6246	1 / 3358	0 / 2888	1 / 23803	0
Temp Cyc	1 / 4287	0 / 13338	1 / 17625	0 / 3960	0 / 1072	0 / 2888	1 / 45388	0
Therm Shk	—	0 / 293	0 / 293	0 / 2285	0 / 2285	—	0 / 2578	0
Const Acc	2 / 4288	13 / 13445	15 / 17733	5 / 6245	3 / 3357	2 / 2888	20 / 23978	.08
Hermeticity	149 / 4286	618 / 13432	767 / 17718	344 / 16195	120 / 3314	224 / 2881	1111 / 23913	4.6
Fine Leak	60 / 4286	221 / 13432	281 / 17718	78 / 6195	34 / 3314	44 / 2881	359 / 23913	1.5
Gross Leak	89 / 4227	397 / 13212	486 / 17439	266 / 6119	86 / 3280	180 / 2839	752 / 23558	3.2
EM 1	162 / 2918	494 / 12708	656 / 15626	258 / 5460	112 / 2980	146 / 2480	914 / 21086	4.3
Burn-In	10 / 3975	5 / 12320	15 / 16295	0 / 917	0 / 738	0 / 179	15 / 17212	.08
EM 2	223 / 3965	592 / 12315	815 / 16280	27 / 917	22 / 738	5 / 179	842 / 17197	4.9
Ext Visual	8 / 3711	35 / 10335	43 / 14046	18 / 4631	7 / 2307	11 / 2324	61 / 18677	.3

TABLE 3

DISTRIBUTION OF FALLOUTS BY TEST METHOD (%)

TEST MTHD	Class B Eqv DIG	Class B Eqv LIN	Class B Eqv TOTAL	Class C Eqv TOTAL	Class C Eqv DIG	Class C Eqv LIN	Combined TOTAL
Int Visual	28.3	20.0	22.1	10.6	11.8	9.8	19.9
Bake	0	0	0	0.1	0.3	0	0
Temp Cyc	0.1	0	0	0	0	0	0
Therm Shk	–	0	0	0	0	–	0
Const Acc	0.3	0.6	0.5	0.7	1.0	0.5	0.5
Hermeticity	19.3	28.2	25.9	47.1	40.0	52.1	30.0
Fine Leak	7.8	10.1	9.5	10.7	11.3	10.2	9.7
Gross Leak	11.5	18.1	16.4	36.4	28.7	41.9	20.3
EM 1	20.9	22.5	22.2	35.3	37.3	34.0	24.7
Burn-In	1.3	0.2	0.5	0	0	0	0.4
EM 2	28.8	26.9	27.5	5.7	7.3	1.1	22.8
Ext Visual	1.0	1.6	1.4	2.5	2.3	2.5	1.7

SCREENING FALLOUT BY MAJOR SEQUENCE PHASE

TABLE 4   Rejected / Tested

PHASE	Class B Eqv. DIG	LIN	TOTAL	Class C Eqv. TOTAL	DIG	LIN	Combined TOTAL	%
Internal Visual	219 / 4508	438 / 13883	657 / 18391	77 / 6210	35 / 3280	42 / 2930	734 / 24601	3.0
Environmental	314 / 4289	1126 / 13445	1440 / 17734	603 / 6059	236 / 3358	367 / 2701	2043 / 23793	8.6
Burn—In (EM2)	233 / 3975	597 / 12320	830 / 16295	27 / 917	22 / 738	5 / 179	857 / 17212	5.0
External Visual	8 / 3711	35 / 10448	43 / 14159	18 / 4631	7 / 2307	11 / 2324	61 / 18790	0.3

TABLE 5   Normalized Distribution of Fallout %

PHASE	Class B Eqv DIG	LIN	TOTAL	Class C Eqv TOTAL	DIG	LIN	Combined TOTAL
Internal Visual	28.3	19.9	22.1	10.6	11.7	9.9	19.9
Environmental	40.6	51.3	48.5	83.2	78.7	86.3	55.3
Burn—In (EM2)	30.1	27.2	27.9	3.7	7.3	1.2	23.2
External Visual	1.0	1.6	1.5	2.5	2.3	2.6	1.6

TABLE 6

ENVIRONMENTAL SEQUENCE RESULTS

| TEST SEQUENCE | | | HERMETICITY | | | | EM1 | | | | BURN–IN | | | |
HIGH TEMP (HRS)	TMPCYC (°C)	CNSTACC (KG)	Class B Eqv	%	Class C Eqv	%	Class B Eqv	%	Class C Eqv	%	Class B Eqv	%	Class C Eqv	%
24	-65/150	20	30/931	3.2	-	-	28/101	3.1	-	-	30/873	3.4	-	-
24	-65/150	30	-	-	60/526	11.4	-	-	39/466	8.4	-	-	16/427	3.7
32	-55/125	5	54/866	6.2	-	-	47/812	5.8	-	-	93/765	12.2	-	-
32	-55/125	10	40/433	9.2	-	-	11/393	2.8	-	-	21/382	5.5	-	-
32	-55/125	20	60/1581	3.8	2/318	0.6	28/1469	1.9	5/282	1.8	36/1493	2.4	6/311	1.9
32	-55/125	30	110/4180	2.6	-	-	120/4070	2.9	-	-	172/3950	4.4	-	-
32	-65/150	5	51/1149	4.4	-	-	9/1098	0.8	-	-	71/1089	6.5	-	-
32	-65/150	10	-	-	14/310	4.5	N/R	-	34/296	11.5	60/1243	5.6	-	-
32	-65/150	20	45/1286	3.5	26/513	5.1	29/297	9.8	22/487	4.5	12/268	4.5	-	-
32	-65/150	30	6/303	2.0	-	-	-	-	-	-	-	-	-	-
48	-55/125	20	41/1245	3.3	56/2288	2.4	131/1080	12.1	68/2232	3.0	129/1077	12.0	-	-
48	-65/150	20	213/3591	5.9	0/69	0.0	142/3378	4.2	-	-	135/3236	4.2	-	-
48	-65/150	30	-	-	2/113	1.8	-	-	-	-	-	-	-	-
60	-65/150	20	-	-	8/187	4.3	-	-	-	-	-	-	5/179	2.8
100	-65/150	20	-	-	176/1873	9.4	-	-	90/1697	5.3	-	-	-	-

-10-

TABLE 7

SUMMARY OF SCREENING RESULTS

	Class B Eqv			Class C Eqv			
	DIG	LIN	TOTAL	TOTAL	DIG	LIN	TOTAL
Sample Size	4508	13883	18391	6323	3393	2930	24714
No. Survivors	3731	11688	15419	5580	3093	2487	20999
No. Failures	774	2195	2969	733	300	433	3702
No. Unaccounted	3	0	3	10	0	10	13
% Failure	17.2	15.8	16.1	11.6	8.8	14.8	15

SECTION 3

FAILURE CLASSIFICATIONS

Tables 8 and 9 summarize the failure analyses performed on malfunctioning devices. These reports do not appear in the Section 5 details due to a lack of constructional and statistical information. Since the analyses were conducted by various organizations, the level of detail varies from four classifications down to the case where only an indicator is known.

COLUMN HEADING DEFINITIONS

Indicator	The external manifestation of failure
Failure Mode/Mech/Cause	Internal failure site, mechanism, and cause of defect when known
No. Occur.	Total number of devices with a particular failure description
%	Percentage of total malfunctions having a particular failure description
Dev. RPTS	Number of separate documents in which the occurrences were reported

THIN FILM

Digital

Indicator	Failure Mode/Mech/Cause	No. Occur	%	Dev. RPTS
Open	Lifted Wire Bond	8	15.7	8
Open	Lifted Metallization	2	3.92	2
Open	Collector Resistor	2	3.92	2
Open	Contamination	2	3.92	2
Open	Poor Chip Attach; Process Control	5	9.80	4
Open	Lifted Wire Bond; Process Defect	1	1.96	1
Open	Wire Bond; Smeared Metal; Metal Process Defect	1	1.96	1
Open	N/R	1	1.96	1
Short	Emitter-Collector	1	1.96	1
Short	Base-Collector	2	3.92	1
Short	Lifted Bond to Cover	1	1.96	1
Short	Foreign Particles	3	5.88	3
Short	Metal Defect	5	9.80	1
Short	Pin/Package Cover	5	9.80	4
Short	Pin Orientation	2	3.92	2
Short	Metal Corrosion; Package Leak	1	1.96	1
Intermittent Output	Shorted Transistor	1	1.96	1
Electrical Reject	Chip Attach Failure	4	7.84	4
Degradation; Diode Junction	Contamination	2	3.92	1
Output Defective	Poor Attach; Resistor Block	1	1.96	1
Loss of Channel; Diode Replaced	Poor Ball Bond Process	1	1.96	1
		51	100.0	43

Linear

Indicator	Failure Mode/Mech/Cause	No. Occur	%	Dev. RPTS
Open	Lifted Au Wire	1	11.1	1
Open	Metal Defect; Package Failure	1	11.1	1
Open	Wire Bond; Metal Defect; Surf. Inversion	1	11.1	1
Open	Film Resistor; Metal Defect	1	11.1	1
HiI_{LK}	Contaminated Bulk Oxide	1	11.1	1
Improper Switching	Open Metal in Oxide Step	1	11.1	1
Elect Reject	Open Header Bond	1	11.1	1
V_{OH}	Poor Lead Bond; Metal Defect; Corrosion Metallization	1	11.1	1
N/R	Defect; Poor Solder Reflow	1	11.1	1
		9	100.0	9

TABLE 8 THIN FILM FAILURE ANALYSIS SUMMARY

THICK FILM

Digital

Indicator	Failure Mode/Mech/Cause	No. Occur	%	Dev. RPTS
Open	Wire to Pad Resistor. detached Wire Bond	1	1.11	1
Short	Base-Emitter; Gold Particle	1	1.11	1
Short	Metal Particles	20	22.2	3
Short	Smeared Metal Contact	1	1.11	1
No Output	Metal Particles	1	1.11	1
Inoperative	Chip Attach Failure	1	1.11	1
Intermittent	Contamination	1	1.11	1
Degraded Diode Junction of Transistors	Contamination	2	2.22	1
N/R	Substrate Attach	59	65.6	1
N/R	Voids; Substrate Attach Material	1	1.11	1
N/R	Surface Film on Transistor; Dicing Fault on Chip; Poor Lead Dress	1	1.11	1
N/R	Contamination	1	1.11	1
		90	100.0	14

Linear

Indicator	Failure Mode/Mech/Cause	No. Occur	%	Dev. RPTS
Short	Capacitor Breakdown; Porous Dielectric	2	11.8	2
No Output;	Lifted Pads Process Control	1	5.88	1
Output to Zero;	Elect Stress; Resistor Trim Process	1	5.88	1
Electrical Reject	Broken Au Wedge Bond	1	5.88	1
Electrical Reject	Cracked Resistor	1	5.88	1
N/R	Chip Defects	1	5.88	1
N/R	Ag Migration; Moisture in Package	4	23.5	1
N/R	Package Leak; Glass Seal Damage	2	11.8	1
N/R	Poor Lead Dress; Foreign Particles; Corrosion Between Leads and Chip	2	11.8	1
N/R	Contamination; Al Metal Erroded; Poor Cover Seal	1	5.88	1
Erroneous Output @ Elevated Temp	Excessive I_{OLK}	1	5.88	1
		17	100.0	12

TABLE 9   THICK FILM FAILURE ANALYSIS SUMMARY

SECTION 4

CROSS REFERENCE INDEX

Constituents of the detailed device descriptors are indexed by line entry number from Section 5. This provides a means of locating data on devices having constructional features of particular interest.

CROSS REFERENCE INDEX

CONDUCTORS (con't)

Palladium Silver (PdAg)

1	5	16	142
2	6	88	150
4			

Platinum Gold (PtAu)

87   115

CROSSOVER

148

DIODE

Ceramic

92

Germanium, General Purpose (Ge)

4

High Voltage (HiV)

69

Silicon, General Purpose (Si)

All entires except where
otherwise noted

Varactor

4   92   93

Zener Avalanche (ZenAv)

1	91	109	144
2	97	128	158
73			

INDUCTORS

Thin Film

90   155

Toroid

92   93   153   156

INTEGRATED CIRCUITS

Cermet Switch

159

Comparator (Compar)

72

Driver

64   66   72

FET Regulator (FET Reg)

158

Flip Flop (FlFl)

36	64	66	107
63	65		

Gate

36	72	127	138
64	95	130	139
65	107	131	142
66	109	135	149
70	117	137	

Inverter

109

Operational Amplifier (OpAmp)

69	109	122	158
72	111	125	159
106	112		

Voltage Comparator (Volt Comp)

71

Voltage Regulator (Volt Reg)

109

INTERCONNECT SYSTEMS

Aluminum Wire (AlWire)

111	119	122	155
112	120	132	156
118	121	133	

Gold Paste (AuPaste)

13	108	132	151
106	111	144	154

Gold Wire (AuWire)

All entries except where otherwise noted

Silver Paste (AgPaste)

15	18	24	121

Solder Tab (Sldr Tab)

80	158

LEADLESS INVERTED DEVICES

Lid

89	115

FET SWITCHES

129

PACKAGES

Can

All entries except where otherwise noted

Ceramic DIP (C-DIP)

101	114	132	159

Ceramic Metal (CM-DIP)

46	110	129	157

PACKAGES (con't)

Ceramic Metal in Line (CMInLn)

153	156

Epoxy in Line (E-ILn)

4	5	6	79

Flat Pack Ceramic (FPCm)

1	66	71	105
2	67	72	107
63	68	95	127
64	69	96	138
65	70	100	152

Flat Pack Glass (FPG1)

136	139	140	141

Flat Pack Metal (FPM1)

All entries except where otherwise noted

Flat Pack Metal Ceramic (FPM1Cm)

19	23	112	131
21	111	130	137

Flat Pack Plastic (FPP1)

55	56	76

Metal in Line (MInLn)

155

Plastic in Line (P-InLn)

36	52

Silicon DIP (S-DIP)

3	84	115	133
78			

PACKAGE SEAL

Epoxy

52	105	138	152
96	114	139	154
100	127	140	156
101	136	141	159
104			

Silicon (Silic)

78	84	115	133

Silver Epoxy (AgEpoxy)

1	2

Solder

111	112	149

Weld

All entries except where otherwise noted

RESISTOR

Carbon

85	87	88	111
86			

Cermet

All entries except where otherwise noted

Nickel Alloy (NiA)

79

Nickel Chrome (NiCr)

81	109	119	144
83	116	120	152
84	118	141	156

RESISTOR (con't)

Silicon Chrome (SiCr)

98	99	100	101

Tantalum (Ta)

145

Tantalum Nitride (TaNi)

141	153	155

Tantalum Oxide (TaO)

109	121

Thick Film

All entries except where otherwise noted

Thin Film

13	147	148	154
146			

SUBSTRATE MATERIAL

Alumina (Al_2O_3)

All entries except where otherwise noted

Berylia (BeO)

8	39	46	52
12	39	48	53
30	41	49	55
36			

Chromium/Nickel/Gold (Cr-Ni-Au)

73	74

Coppter/Tin (Cu/Sn)

79

SUBSTRATE MATERIAL (con't)

Glass (PsG)

98	100	149	156
99	101		

Molybdemic Manganese (MoMn)

120   130   131

Substrate Metallization

(See Conductors)

Vitreous Glass (VitGl)

128

TRANSISTOR

Silicon NPN (SiNPN)

All entries except where
otherwise noted

Silicon PNP (SiPNP)

8	73	112	124
29	74	114	126
30	89	116	128
68	97	121	151
69	111	123	158
71			

Field Effect Transistor (FET)

8   74

Unijunction (Unij)

97	118	128	145
114			

SECTION 5

DETAILED TEST DATA TABULATION

The detailed data is tabulated in a format which provides device constructional features compatible with MIL-HDBK-217B, test specifications and stress levels, failure statistics, and failure analysis information. The organization is by device manufacturer and device type to consolidate all data on file for each device. Descriptive code interpretations are found in the appendix.

DEVICE SECTION

MANUFACTURER: BECKMAN INST. INC.
TECHNOLOGY: THICK FILM

FUNCTIONAL CATEGORY: LINEAR
DEVICE FUNCTION: VOLTAGE REGULATOR

HYBRID MICROCIRCUIT RELIABILITY DATA

RELIABILITY ANALYSIS CENTER

ENTRY NO.	PKG/ NO. PINS	SIZE OP TEMP	PKG MFG	PKG SEAL	SUBSTR MTL/ BOND	SUBSTR SIZE	NO. COND LYR	SUBSTR METAL #/BONDS	IC NO./TYPE	IC CHP ATCH/ INTERCON	TRANSISTOR NO./TYPE	TRANSISTOR CHP ATCH/ INTERCON	DIODE NO./TYPE	DIODE CHP ATCH/ INTERCON	CAPACITOR NO./TYPE	CAPACITOR CHP ATCH/ INTERCON	RESISTOR NO./TYPE	RESISTOR CHP ATCH/ INTERCON	RES TOL (%)	ELMT ATCH/ INTERCON NO./TYPE
1	FPCm 3	0.50x 1.00x 0.13 -55/ 125C		Ag Epoxy	Al$_2$O$_3$ N/A	.5x1.0 x.010	1	PdAu/ Au 28	0		6 SiNPN	AgEpoxy AuWire	2 ZenAv	AgEpoxy AuWire	1 Thick	Dep PdAg.	8 Thick	Fired PdAg	N/R	

LIFE / ENVIRONMENTAL EXPERIENCE

DATA SRCE	SCR CLS	TST SRC	TEST TYP/ APP ENV	STR LVL/ EQP TYPE	TEST STD MTD/COND	NO. TSTD	TEST DUR.	PART HRS.	NO. FLD	FAILURE CLASSIFICATION IND; MODE; MECH; CAUSE (NO. FAILED / EVENT)	% DEF	TEST DATE	REMARKS
U	SSD	Env	VisInsp		MS750 2071	159			0			7/69	
U	N	Scr/SSD	TempCyc	-65/200C 5/5 min	MS750 1051C	22						7/69	
			ThrmStr	0/100C 5/15 sec	MS750 1056A	22							
			Moistr	-10/65C 98%RH	MS750 1021	22			2	V_oZero; Q Open; Short Resistor Due to Moisture	9.09		
U	N	Scr/SSD	MechShk	1.5KG 0.5 msec	MS750 2016	22							
			VibFtg	60HZ 20G	MS750 2046	22							
			VbVrFq	.1/2KHZ 20G	MS750 2056	22							
			CnstAcc	20KG 6 AXES	MS750 2006	22			0				
U	SSD	Env	TrmStr		MS750 2036E	11			0				
U	SSD	Env	SltAtmos	35C 20%NACl	MS202 101B	11			0				
U	SSD	Lab	StgLife	150C	MS750 1031	38		38000	1	$V_o >$ Spec; Faulty Zener Diode			

SYSTEM / EQUIPMENT	PART HISTORY	SCR CLS	DATE CODE	FAILURE ANALYSIS / CORRECTIVE ACTION

MALFUNCTION DATA

SYSTEM / EQUIPMENT	PART HISTORY	SCR CLS	DATE CODE	FAILURE ANALYSIS / CORRECTIVE ACTION

DEVICE SECTION

FUNCTIONAL CATEGORY: LINEAR

MANUFACTURER: BECKMAN INST. INC.

DEVICE FUNCTION: VOLTAGE REGULATOR

TECHNOLOGY: THICK FILM

ENTRY NO.	PKG/ NO. PINS	SIZE OP TEMP	PKG MFG	PKG SEAL	SUBSTR MTL/ BOND	SUBSTR SIZE	NO. COND LYR	SUBSTR METAL #BONDS	IC NO./ TYPE	IC CHP ATCH/ INTERCON	TRANSISTOR NO./ TYPE	TRANSISTOR CHP ATCH/ INTERCON	DIODE NO./ TYPE	DIODE CHP ATCH/ INTERCON	CAPACITOR NO./ TYPE	CAPACITOR CHP ATCH/ INTERCON	RESISTOR NO./ TYPE	RESISTOR CHP ATCH/ INTERCON	RES TOL (%)	ELMT ATCH/ INTERCON NO./ TYPE
1 (Cntd)																				

LIFE / ENVIRONMENTAL EXPERIENCE (con't)

DATA SRCE	SCR CLS	TST SRC	TEST TYP/ APP ENV	STR LVL/ EQP TYPE	TEST STD MTD/COND	NO. TSTD	TEST DUR.	PART HRS.	NO. FLD	FAILURE CLASSIFICATION IND; MODE; MECH; CAUSE (NO. FAILED / EVENT)	% DEF	TEST DATE	REMARKS
U	SSD	Lab	OpCnst	25C	MS750 1026	77		77000	0				
U	SSD	Env	Solder		MS750 2026								

MALFUNCTION DATA

SYSTEM/ EQUIPMENT	PART HISTORY	SCR CLS	DATE CODE	FAILURE ANALYSIS / CORRECTIVE ACTION

SYSTEM/ EQUIPMENT	PART HISTORY	SCR CLS	DATE CODE	FAILURE ANALYSIS / CORRECTIVE ACTION

RELIABILITY ANALYSIS CENTER

HYBRID MICROCIRCUIT
RELIABILITY DATA

DEVICE SECTION

MANUFACTURER: BECKMAN INST. INC.   FUNCTIONAL CATEGORY: LINEAR
TECHNOLOGY: THICK FILM   DEVICE FUNCTION: DC VOLTAGE REGULATOR

ENTRY NO.	PKG/ NO. PINS	SIZE OP TEMP	PKG MFG	PKG SEAL	SUBSTR MTL/ BOND	SUBSTR SIZE	NO. COND LYR	SUBSTR METAL/ #BONDS	IC NO./ TYPE	IC CHP ATCH/ INTERCON	TRANSISTOR NO./ TYPE	TRANSISTOR CHP ATCH/ INTERCON	DIODE NO./ TYPE	DIODE CHP ATCH/ INTERCON	CAPACITOR NO./ TYPE	CAPACITOR CHP ATCH/ INTERCON	RESISTOR NO./ TYPE	RESISTOR CHP ATCH/ INTERCON	RES TOL (%)	ELMT ATCH/ INTERCON NO./ TYPE
2	FPCm 5	0.50x 0.17	Ag Epoxy	Al₂O₃ N/A	0.50x 1.00x 0.01	1	PdAu/ Au 36	0		7 SiNPN	AgEpoxy AuWire	3 ZenAv	AgEpoxy AuWire	2 Thick	Dep PdAg	10 Thick	Fired PdAg	N/R	

LIFE / ENVIRONMENTAL EXPERIENCE

DATA SRCE CLS	SCR CLS	TST SRC	TEST TYP/ APP ENV	STR LVL/ EQP TYPE	TEST STD MTD/COND	NO. TSTD	TEST DUR.	PART HRS.	NO. FLD	FAILURE CLASSIFICATION IND; MODE; MECH; CAUSE (NO. FAILED / EVENT)	% DEF	TEST DATE	REMARKS

MALFUNCTION DATA

SYSTEM / EQUIPMENT	PART HISTORY	SCR CLS	DATE CODE	FAILURE ANALYSIS / CORRECTIVE ACTION
Satellite	Incoming Inspection -10/40C	B		Short; Silver Migration Path Between Bond Sites Caused By Moisture in Packages/4

PAGE 24

DEVICE SECTION

MANUFACTURER: CENTRALAB (DIV GLOBE UNION)

TECHNOLOGY: THICK FILM

FUNCTIONAL CATEGORY: RESISTOR ARRAY

DEVICE FUNCTION: THICK FILM

HYBRID MICROCIRCUIT
RELIABILITY DATA

RELIABILITY ANALYSIS CENTER

ENTRY NO.	PKG/ NO. PINS	SIZE OP TEMP	PKG MFG	PKG SEAL	SUBSTR MTL/ BOND	SUBSTR SIZE	NO. COND LYR	SUBSTR METAL #BONDS	IC NO./ TYPE	IC CHP ATCH/ INTERCON	TRANSISTOR NO./ TYPE	TRANSISTOR CHP ATCH/ INTERCON	DIODE NO./ TYPE	DIODE CHP ATCH/ INTERCON	CAPACITOR NO./ TYPE	CAPACITOR CHP ATCH/ INTERCON	RESISTOR NO./ TYPE	RESISTOR CHP ATCH/ INTERCON	RES TOL (%)	ELM ATCH/ INTERCON NO./ TYPE
3	S-DIP 14	TO-116 15/85C	CENT- RALAB		Al_2O_3	.78x .28	1	N/A 0	0		0		0		0		8 Thick	Fired N/A	N/R	

LIFE / ENVIRONMENTAL EXPERIENCE

DATA SRCE NO.	SCR CLS	TST SRC	TEST TYP/ APP ENV	STR LVL/ EQP TYPE	TEST STD MTD/COND	NO. TSTD	TEST DUR.	PART HRS.	NO. FLD	FAILURE CLASSIFICATION IND; MODE; MECH; CAUSE (NO. FAILED / EVENT)	% DEF	TEST DATE	REMARKS
I	SSD	Scr	TempCyc	-35/85C 10/10 min		5266						4/74	
			Temp	70C 168 Hrs									
			VisInsp	Ext		5266			68	EM Rej/15 VisInsp/40 N/R/13	0.28 0.76 0.25		

MALFUNCTION DATA

SYSTEM / EQUIPMENT	PART HISTORY	SCR CLS	DATE CODE	FAILURE ANALYSIS / CORRECTIVE ACTION

SYSTEM / EQUIPMENT	PART HISTORY	SCR CLS	DATE CODE	FAILURE ANALYSIS / CORRECTIVE ACTION

RELIABILITY ANALYSIS CENTER

DEVICE SECTION

MANUFACTURER: (CENTRALAB (GLOBE UNION)

TECHNOLOGY: THICK FILM

ENTRY NO.	PKG/ NO. PINS	SIZE OP TEMP	TST SRC	PKG MFG	PKG SEAL	SUBSTR MTL/ BOND	SUBSTR SIZE	NO. COND LYR	SUBSTR METAL #BONDS	IC NO./TYPE	IC CHP ATCH/ INTERCON	TRANSISTOR NO./TYPE	TRANSISTOR CHP ATCH/ INTERCON	DIODE NO./TYPE	DIODE CHP ATCH/ INTERCON	CAPACITOR NO./TYPE	CAPACITOR CHP ATCH/ INTERCON	RESISTOR NO./TYPE	RESISTOR CHP ATCH/ INTERCON	RES TOL (%)	ELMT ATCH/ INTERCON NO./TYPE
4	E-11n 10	0.50x 1.00x 0.25.. 0/70C	N	N/R	N/A	Al₂O₃ N/A	0.50x 1.00x 0.01	1	PdAg 36	0		4 SiNPN	Eutect AuWire	4 GeGP	Eutect AuWire	4 Thin	Sldr PdAg	15 Thick	Fired PdAg	+ 5.00	

LIFE / ENVIRONMENTAL EXPERIENCE

DATA SRCE SRC	SCR CLS	TST SRC	TEST TYP/ APP ENV	STR LVL/ EQP TYPE	TEST STD MTD/COND	NO. TSTD	TEST DUR.	PART HRS.	NO. FLD	FAILURE CLASSIFICATION IND; MODE; MECH; CAUSE (NO. FAILED / EVENT)	% DEF	TEST DATE	REMARKS
V	N	Scr/C	VisInsp		MS883 2010B	70			0				
			Temp	150C 48 Hr	MS883 1008	70			1	$I_{ceo} >$ Spec; Transistor Junction Defect	1.43	12/69	
			TempCyc	-65/150C 10/10 min	MS883 1010	69							
			CnstAcc	20KG	MS883 2001								
			FineLk	6 AXES	MS883 1014A								
			GrossLk	90 psia Fluoro	MS883 1014C								
			VisInsp		MS883 2009	69			0				

MALFUNCTION DATA

SYSTEM / EQUIPMENT	PART HISTORY	SCR CLS	DATE CODE	FAILURE ANALYSIS / CORRECTIVE ACTION	SYSTEM / EQUIPMENT	PART HISTORY	SCR CLS	DATE CODE	FAILURE ANALYSIS / CORRECTIVE ACTION

RELIABILITY
ANALYSIS
CENTER

FUNCTIONAL CATEGORY: DIGITAL

DEVICE FUNCTION: TRIGGERING CIRCUIT

DEVICE SECTION

MANUFACTURER: CENTRALAB
(DIV GLOBE UNION)

TECHNOLOGY: THICK FILM

ENTRY NO.	PKG/ NO. PINS	SIZE OP TEMP	PKG MFG	PKG SEAL	SUBSTR MTL/ BOND	SUBSTR SIZE	NO. COND LYR	SUBSTR METAL #BONDS	IC NO./ TYPE	IC CHP ATCH/ INTERCON	TRANSISTOR NO./ TYPE	TRANSISTOR CHP ATCH/ INTERCON	DIODE NO./ TYPE	DIODE CHP ATCH/ INTERCON	CAPACITOR NO./ TYPE	CAPACITOR CHP ATCH/ INTERCON	RESISTOR NO./ TYPE	RESISTOR CHP ATCH/ INTERCON	RES TOL (%)	ELMT ATCH/ INTERCON NO./ TYPE
5	E-ILn 10	0.50x 1.00x 0.25 0/70C	N/R	N/A	Al₂O₃ N/A	0.50x 1.00x 0.01	1	PdAg 24	0	0	4 SiNPN	Eutect PdAg	0		2 Ceramic	Sldr PdAg	10 Thick	Fired PdAg	+5	

LIFE / ENVIRONMENTAL EXPERIENCE

DATA SRCE	SCR CLS	TST SRC	TEST TYP/ APP ENV	STR LVL/ EQP TYPE	TEST STD MTD/COND	NO. TSTD	TEST DUR.	PART HRS.	NO. FLD	FAILURE CLASSIFICATION IND; MODE; MECH; CAUSE (NO. FAILED / EVENT)	% DEF	TEST DATE
V	N	Scr/C	VisInsp		MS883 2010B	40			0			12/69
			Temp	150C 48 Hrs	MS883 1008							
			ThrmShk	0/100C H₂O 15 cyc	MS883 1011							
			MechShk	1.5KG 6 AXES	MS883 2002	40						
			CnstAcc	30KG 6 AXES	MS883 2001	40						
			VisInsp		MS883 2009	40			1	Base Collector Short	10.0	

REMARKS

MALFUNCTION DATA

SYSTEM / EQUIPMENT	PART HISTORY	SCR CLS	DATE CODE	FAILURE ANALYSIS / CORRECTIVE ACTION

SYSTEM / EQUIPMENT	PART HISTORY	SCR CLS	DATE CODE	FAILURE ANALYSIS / CORRECTIVE ACTION

DEVICE SECTION

MANUFACTURER: CENTRALAB (DIV GLOBE UNION)
TECHNOLOGY: THICK FILM

FUNCTIONAL CATEGORY: DIGITAL
DEVICE FUNCTION: SWITCHING CIRCUIT

HYBRID MICROCIRCUIT
RELIABILITY DATA

 RELIABILITY ANALYSIS CENTER

ENTRY NO.	PKG/ NO. PINS	SIZE OP TEMP	PKG MFG	PKG SEAL	SUBSTR MTL/ BOND	SUBSTR SIZE	NO. COND LYR	SUBSTR METAL #BONDS	IC NO./ TYPE	IC CHP ATCH/ INTERCON	TRANSISTOR NO./ TYPE	TRANSISTOR CHP ATCH/ INTERCON	DIODE NO./ TYPE	DIODE CHP ATCH/ INTERCON	CAPACITOR NO./ TYPE	CAPACITOR CHP ATCH/ INTERCON	RESISTOR NO./ TYPE	RESISTOR CHP ATCH/ INTERCON	RES TOL (%)	ELMT ATCH/ INTERCON NO./ TYPE
6	E-ILn 10	0.50x 1.00x 0.25 0/70C	N/R	N/A	Al$_2$O$_3$ N/A	0.50x 1.00x 0.01	1	PdAg 10	0		1 SiNPN	Eutect AuWire	0		0		2 Cermet	Fired PdAg	± 5	

LIFE / ENVIRONMENTAL EXPERIENCE

DATA SRCE	SCR CLS	TST SRC	TEST TYP/ APP ENV	STR LVL/ EQP TYPE	TEST STD MTD/COND	NO. TSTD	TEST DUR.	PART HRS.	NO. FLD	FAILURE CLASSIFICATION IND; MODE; MECH; CAUSE (NO. FAILED / EVENT)	% DEF	TEST DATE	REMARKS
V	N	Brn	OpDyn	125C		36	100 Hrs	3600	0			10/70	

MALFUNCTION DATA

SYSTEM / EQUIPMENT	PART HISTORY	SCR CLS	DATE CODE	FAILURE ANALYSIS / CORRECTIVE ACTION	SYSTEM / EQUIPMENT	PART HISTORY	SCR CLS	DATE CODE	FAILURE ANALYSIS / CORRECTIVE ACTION

HYBRID MICROCIRCUIT
RELIABILITY DATA

DEVICE SECTION

MANUFACTURER: CIRCUIT TECHNOLOGY INC. FUNCTIONAL CATEGORY: DIGITAL

TECHNOLOGY: THICK FILM DEVICE FUNCTION: DUAL SWITCH

ENTRY NO.	PKG/ NO. PINS	SIZE OP TEMP	PKG MFG	PKG SEAL	SUBSTR MTL/ BOND	SUBSTR SIZE	NO. COND LYR	SUBSTR METAL #BONDS	IC NO./TYPE	IC CHP ATCH/INTERCON	TRANSISTOR NO./TYPE	TRANSISTOR CHP ATCH/INTERCON	DIODE NO./TYPE	DIODE CHP ATCH/INTERCON	CAPACITOR NO./TYPE	CAPACITOR CHP ATCH/INTERCON	RESISTOR NO./TYPE	RESISTOR CHP ATCH/INTERCON	RES TOL (%)	ELMT ATCH/INTERCON NO./TYPE
7	Can 8	TO-5 -55/ 125C		Weld	Header	N/A	1	Kov/Au 16	0		4 N/R	Eutect AuWire	0		0		16 Thick	Eutect Kov/Au		

LIFE / ENVIRONMENTAL EXPERIENCE

DATA SRCE NO.	SCR CLS	TST SRC	TEST TYP/ APP ENV	STR LVL/ EQP TYPE	TEST STD MTD/COND	NO. TSTD	TEST DUR.	PART HRS.	NO. FLD	FAILURE CLASSIFICATION IND; MODE; MECH; CAUSE (NO. FAILED / EVENT)	% DEF	TEST DATE
V	39	Scr/C	VisInsp			249			0			6/72
			Temp	150C			32 Hrs					
			TempCyc	-55/125C								
			CnstAcc	5/5 min 20KG Y1								
			FineLk	5x10−8 cc/sec		249			1	N/R	0.40	
			GrossLk	Fluoro		248			1	N/R	2.42	
			EM	25C		247			5	N/R	2.02	
			Burn-In	25C		242	168 Hrs		5	N/R	2.07	
			EM			242						

MALFUNCTION DATA

SYSTEM / EQUIPMENT	PART HISTORY	SCR CLS	DATE CODE	FAILURE ANALYSIS / CORRECTIVE ACTION

SYSTEM / EQUIPMENT	PART HISTORY	SCR CLS	DATE CODE	FAILURE ANALYSIS / CORRECTIVE ACTION

REMARKS

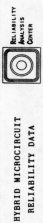
RELIABILITY ANALYSIS CENTER

HYBRID MICROCIRCUIT
RELIABILITY DATA

DEVICE SECTION

MANUFACTURER: CIRCUIT TECHNOLOGY INC. FUNCTIONAL CATEGORY: DIGITAL

TECHNOLOGY: THICK FILM DEVICE FUNCTION: ANALOG GATE

ENTRY NO.	PKG/ NO. PINS	SIZE OP TEMP	PKG MFG	PKG SEAL	SUBSTR MTL/ BOND	SUBSTR SIZE	NO. COND LYR	SUBSTR METAL #BONDS	IC NO./ TYPE	IC CHP ATCH/ INTERCON	TRANSISTOR NO./ TYPE	TRANSISTOR CHP ATCH/ INTERCON	DIODE NO./ TYPE	DIODE CHP ATCH/ INTERCON	CAPACITOR NO./ TYPE	CAPACITOR CHP ATCH/ INTERCON	RESISTOR NO./ TYPE	RESISTOR CHP ATCH/ INTERCON	RES TOL (%)	ELMT ATCH/ INTERCON NO./ TYPE
8	Can 8	TO-5 -55/ 125C		Weld	Al₂O₃ BeO	N/A	1	AuCond 30	0		6 Fet (2) SiNPN (2) SiPNP (2)	Eutect AuWire	2 SiGP	Eutect AuWire	0		6 Cermet	Fired AuCond	±10	

LIFE / ENVIRONMENTAL EXPERIENCE

DATA SRCE	SCR CLS	TST SRC	TEST TYP/ APP ENV	STR LVL/ EQP TYPE	TEST STD MTD/COND	NO. TSTD	TEST DUR.	PART HRS.	NO. FLD	FAILURE CLASSIFICATION IND; MODE; MECH; CAUSE (NO. FAILED / EVENT)	% DEF	TEST DATE	REMARKS
U	C	Fld	AirInhab	Navgtn/ Operate 30C		398		56.2E6	45	Electrical Malfunction/4 N/R/41		5/73	Used In Flight Guidance System

MALFUNCTION DATA

SYSTEM / EQUIPMENT	PART HISTORY	SCR CLS	DATE CODE	FAILURE ANALYSIS / CORRECTIVE ACTION	SYSTEM / EQUIPMENT	PART HISTORY	SCR CLS	DATE CODE	FAILURE ANALYSIS / CORRECTIVE ACTION

HYBRID MICROCIRCUIT
RELIABILITY DATA

RELIABILITY
ANALYSIS
CENTER

DEVICE SECTION

MANUFACTURER: CIRCUIT TECHNOLOGY INC.

FUNCTIONAL CATEGORY: DIGITAL

DEVICE FUNCTION: TRIGGER CIRCUIT

TECHNOLOGY: THICK FILM

ENTRY NO.	PKG/ NO. PINS	SIZE OP TEMP	PKG MFG	PKG SEAL	SUBSTR MTL/ BOND	SUBSTR SIZE	NO. COND LYR	SUBSTR METAL #BONDS	IC NO./TYPE	IC CHP ATCH/INTERCON	TRANSISTOR NO./TYPE	TRANSISTOR CHP ATCH/INTERCON	DIODE NO./TYPE	DIODE CHP ATCH/INTERCON	CAPACITOR NO./TYPE	CAPACITOR CHP ATCH/INTERCON	RESISTOR NO./TYPE	RESISTOR CHP ATCH/INTERCON	RES TOL (%)	ELMT ATCH/INTERCON NO./TYPE
9	Can 10	TO-5 -55/ 125C		Weld	Header	N/A	N/A	Kov/Au N/R	0		2 N/R	Eutect AuWire	2 N/R	Eutect AuWire	0		0			

LIFE / ENVIRONMENTAL EXPERIENCE

DATA SRCE	SCR CLS	TST SRC	TEST TYP/ APP ENV	STR LVL/ EQP TYPE	TEST STD MTD/COND	NO. TSTD	TEST DUR.	PART HRS.	NO. FLD	FAILURE CLASSIFICATION IND; MODE; MECH; CAUSE (NO. FAILED / EVENT)	% DEF	TEST DATE
V	N	Scr/SSA	VisInsp	150C		1203			370	N/R	30.8	1/73
			Bake	-65/150C		833			0			
			TempCyc	5/5 min		833			0			
			EM	25C		833			4	N/R	0.48	
			Burn-In	125C		829	240 Hrs		1	N/R	0.12	
			CnstAcc	20KG Y₁		829						
			EM	25		828			6	N/R	0.72	
			EM	125		822			13	N/R	1.58	
			EM	-55		809			3	N/R	0.37	
			FineLk	5x10⁻⁸		806			17	N/R	2.11	
			GrossLk	cc/sec		789			10	N/R	1.27	
			X-Ray	Min Oil		779			0			
			VisInsp			779			0			

REMARKS

MALFUNCTION DATA

SYSTEM / EQUIPMENT	PART HISTORY	SCR CLS	DATE CODE	FAILURE ANALYSIS / CORRECTIVE ACTION

SYSTEM / EQUIPMENT	PART HISTORY	SCR CLS	DATE CODE	FAILURE ANALYSIS / CORRECTIVE ACTION

PAGE 31

DEVICE SECTION

MANUFACTURER: CIRCUIT TECHNOLOGY INC. FUNCTIONAL CATEGORY: DIGITAL
TECHNOLOGY: THICK FILM DEVICE FUNCTION: SWITCHING CIRCUIT

HYBRID MICROCIRCUIT
RELIABILITY DATA

RELIABILITY ANALYSIS CENTER

ENTRY NO.	PKG/NO. PINS	SIZE OP TEMP	PKG MFG	PKG SEAL	SUBSTR MTL/BOND	SUBSTR SIZE	NO. COND LYR	SUBSTR METAL #BONDS	IC NO./TYPE	IC CHP ATCH/INTERCON	TRANSISTOR NO./TYPE	TRANSISTOR CHP ATCH/INTERCON	DIODE NO./TYPE	DIODE CHP ATCH/INTERCON	CAPACITOR NO./TYPE	CAPACITOR CHP ATCH/INTERCON	RESISTOR NO./TYPE	RESISTOR CHP ATCH/INTERCON	RES TOL (%)	ELMT ATCH/INTERCON NO./TYPE
10	Can 10	TO-74 -55/ 125C		Weld	Header N/A	N/A	N/A	Kov/Au 18	0		3 N/R	Eutect AuWire	2 N/R	Eutect AuWire	0		2 Thick	Eutect Kov/Au	N/R	

LIFE / ENVIRONMENTAL EXPERIENCE

DATA SRCE NO.	SCR CLS	TST SRC	TEST TYP/ APP ENV	STR LVL/ EQP TYPE	TEST STD MTD/COND	NO. TSTD	TEST DUR.	PART HRS.	NO. FLD	FAILURE CLASSIFICATION IND; MODE; MECH; CAUSE (NO. FAILED/EVENT)	% DEF	TEST DATE	REMARKS
V	N	Scr/B	VisInsp			996			39	N/R	4.3	1/73	
			Bake	150C		867	48 Hrs		0				
			TempCyc	-65/150C 5/10 min		867	10 Cyc		0				
			Burn-In	125C		867	240 Hrs		33	N/R	3.81		
			CnstAcc	20KG Y_1		834			1	N/R	0.12		
						833			0				
			EM	25C		833			7	N/R	0.84		
			EM	125C		826			2	N/R	0.24		
			EM	-55		824			1	N/R	0.12		
			FineLk	5x10-8		823			1	N/R	0.12		
			GrossLk	Fluoro		822			4	N/R	0.49		
			X-Ray			818			4	N/R	0.12		
			VisInsp			814			1	N/R			

MALFUNCTION DATA

SYSTEM / EQUIPMENT	PART HISTORY	SCR CLS	DATE CODE	FAILURE ANALYSIS / CORRECTIVE ACTION	SYSTEM / EQUIPMENT	PART HISTORY	SCR CLS	DATE CODE	FAILURE ANALYSIS / CORRECTIVE ACTION

PAGE 32

RELIABILITY ANALYSIS CENTER

HYBRID MICROCIRCUIT
RELIABILITY DATA

DEVICE SECTION

FUNCTIONAL CATEGORY: DIGITAL

MANUFACTURER: CIRCUIT TECHNOLOGY INC.

DEVICE FUNCTION: QUAD BUFFER/DRIVER

TECHNOLOGY: THICK FILM

ENTRY NO.	PKG/ NO. PINS	SIZE OP TEMP	PKG MFG	PKG SEAL	SUBSTR MTL/ BOND	SUBSTR SIZE	NO. COND LYR	SUBSTR METAL /BONDS	IC NO./TYPE	IC CHP ATCH/INTERCON	TRANSISTOR NO./TYPE	TRANSISTOR CHP ATCH/INTERCON	DIODE NO./TYPE	DIODE CHP ATCH/INTERCON	CAPACITOR NO./TYPE	CAPACITOR CHP ATCH/INTERCON	RESISTOR NO./TYPE	RESISTOR CHP ATCH/INTERCON	RES TOL (%)	ELMT ATCH/INTERCON NO./TYPE
11	Can 12	TO-8 -55/ 125C		Weld	Al₂O₃ Eutect	.44D	1	AuCond 32	0		6 SiNPN	Eutect AuWire	0		0		6 Cermet	Fired AuCond	±10	

LIFE / ENVIRONMENTAL EXPERIENCE

DATA SRCE	SCR CLS	TST SRC	TEST TYP/ APP ENV	STR LVL/ EQP TYPE	TEST STD MTD/COND	NO. TSTD	TEST DUR.	PART HRS.	NO. FLD	FAILURE CLASSIFICATION IND; MODE; MECH; CAUSE (NO. FAILED / EVENT)	% DEF	TEST DATE	REMARKS
U	C	Fld	AirInhab	Navgtn/ Operate 30C		36		5.07E6	17	N/R		5/73	Used In Flight Guidance System

MALFUNCTION DATA

SYSTEM / EQUIPMENT	PART HISTORY	SCR CLS	DATE CODE	FAILURE ANALYSIS / CORRECTIVE ACTION		SYSTEM / EQUIPMENT	PART HISTORY	SCR CLS	DATE CODE	FAILURE ANALYSIS / CORRECTIVE ACTION	

DEVICE SECTION

RELIABILITY ANALYSIS CENTER

MANUFACTURER: CIRCUIT TECHNOLOGY INC.
TECHNOLOGY: THICK FILM
FUNCTIONAL CATEGORY: DIGITAL
DEVICE FUNCTION: CAPACITOR CONTROL FIRE CIRCUIT

HYBRID MICROCIRCUIT
RELIABILITY DATA

ENTRY NO.	PKG/NO. PINS	SIZE OP TEMP	PKG SEAL	SUBSTR MTL/BOND	SUBSTR SIZE	NO. COND LYR	SUBSTR METAL #BONDS	IC NO./TYPE	IC CHP ATCH/INTERCON	TRANSISTOR NO./TYPE	TRANSISTOR CHP ATCH/INTERCON	DIODE NO./TYPE	DIODE CHP ATCH/INTERCON	CAPACITOR NO./TYPE	CAPACITOR CHP ATCH/INTERCON	RESISTOR NO./TYPE	RESISTOR CHP ATCH/INTERCON	RES TOL (%)	ELMT ATCH/INTERCON NO./TYPE
12	Can 12	TO-8 -55/125C	Weld	Al$_2$O$_3$/.44D BeO Eutect	.44D	1	AuCond N/R	0		4 N/R	Eutect AuWire	2 N/R	Eutect AuWire	0		6 Cermet	Fired AuCond	±10	

LIFE / ENVIRONMENTAL EXPERIENCE

DATA SRCE	SCR CLS	TST SRC	TEST TYP/APP ENV	STR LVL/EQP TYPE	TEST STD MTD/COND	NO. TSTD	TEST DUR.	PART HRS.	NO. FLD	FAILURE CLASSIFICATION IND;MODE;MECH;CAUSE (NO. FAILED/EVENT)	% DEF	TEST DATE	REMARKS
V	SSD	Scr/A	VisInsp	-40/71C		1279	5 cyc		23	N/R	1.79	12/71	
			TempCyc	0/71C		1256	5 cyc		7	N/R	0.56		
			TempCyc	20KGY$_1$		1249			48	N/R			
			CnstAcc	71C		1249				N/R			
			Temp	He		1201	100 Hrs		40	N/R	3.84		
			FineLk	Min Oil		1161			25	N/R	3.33		
			GrossLk	He		1136			41	N/R	2.15		
			VbVrfq	.02/2KHZ		296	4 min		0	N/R	3.61		
			FineLk	He		296			0				
			GrossLk	Min Oil		1095			3		0.27		
			X-Ray			1092			15		1.37		
			VisInsp			1279			23	N/R	1.79		
			VisInsp	-40/70C		1256	5 cyc		7	N/R	0.56		
			TempCyc	0/70C		1249	5 cyc		0	N/R			
			ThmShk	20KGY$_1$		1201			48	N/R	3.84		
			CnstAcc										
			Burn-In	70C		1201	100 Hrs		40		3.33		
			EM	25C		1161			25	N/R	2.15		
			FineLk	1x10^{-6}		1136			41	N/R	3.61		
			GrossLk	MinOil		296			0	N/R			
			VbVrfq	.2/2KHZ		296			0				
			FineLk	1x10^{-6}		296			0				
			GrossLk	MinOil		296			3	N/R	0.27		
			X-Ray			1095			0				
			EM	25C		296			3				
			VisInsp			1092			15	N/R	1.37		

MALFUNCTION DATA

SYSTEM/EQUIPMENT	PART HISTORY	SCR CLS	DATE CODE	FAILURE ANALYSIS / CORRECTIVE ACTION						SYSTEM/EQUIPMENT	PART HISTORY	SCR CLS	DATE CODE	FAILURE ANALYSIS / CORRECTIVE ACTION

DEVICE SECTION

MANUFACTURER: CIRCUIT TECHNOLOGY INC. **FUNCTIONAL CATEGORY:** DIGITAL

TECHNOLOGY: THICK FILM **DEVICE FUNCTION:** DEMODULATOR

RELIABILITY ANALYSIS CENTER

HYBRID MICROCIRCUIT
RELIABILITY DATA

ENTRY NO.	PKG/ NO. PINS	SIZE OP TEMP	PKG MFG	PKG SEAL	SUBSTR MTL/ BOND	SUBSTR SIZE	NO. COND LYR	SUBSTR METAL #BONDS	IC NO./ TYPE	IC CHP ATCH/ INTERCON	TRANSISTOR NO./ TYPE	TRANSISTOR CHP ATCH/ INTERCON	DIODE NO./ TYPE	DIODE CHP ATCH/ INTERCON	CAPACITOR NO./ TYPE	CAPACITOR CHP ATCH/ INTERCON	RESISTOR NO./ TYPE	RESISTOR CHP ATCH/ INTERCON	RES TOL (%)	ELMT ATCH/ INTERCON NO./ TYPE
13	Can 12	TO-8 -55/ 125C		Weld	Al$_2$O$_3$ Eutect	.47D	2	AuPst 36	1 OpAmp	Eutect AuWire	2 N/R	Eutect AuWire	0		0		8 Cermet 1 Thin Film	Fired AuPst Eutect AuWire	±10	

LIFE / ENVIRONMENTAL EXPERIENCE

DATA SRCE NO.	SCR CLS	TST SRC	TEST TYP/ APP ENV	STR LVL/ EQP TYPE	TEST STD MTD/COND	NO. TSTD	TEST DUR.	PART HRS.	NO. FLD	FAILURE CLASSIFICATION IND; MODE; MECH; CAUSE (NO. FAILED / EVENT)	% DEF	TEST DATE	REMARKS
U	C	Fld	AirInhab	Navgtn/ Operate 30C		64		9.04E6	22	Electrical Malfunction		1/73	Used In Flight Guidance System

MALFUNCTION DATA

SYSTEM / EQUIPMENT	PART HISTORY	SCR CLS	DATE CODE	FAILURE ANALYSIS / CORRECTIVE ACTION	SYSTEM / EQUIPMENT	PART HISTORY	SCR CLS	DATE CODE	FAILURE ANALYSIS / CORRECTIVE ACTION

RELIABILITY ANALYSIS CENTER

DEVICE SECTION

MANUFACTURER: CIRCUIT TECHNOLOGY INC. FUNCTIONAL CATEGORY: DIGITAL
TECHNOLOGY: THICK FILM DEVICE FUNCTION: LINE DRIVER

ENTRY NO.	PKG/ NO. PINS	SIZE OP TEMP	PKG MFG	PKG SEAL	SUBSTR MTL/ BOND	SUBSTR SIZE	NO. COND LYR	SUBSTR METAL #BONDS	IC NO./ TYPE	IC CHP ATCH/ INTERCON	TRANSISTOR NO./ TYPE	TRANSISTOR CHP ATCH/ INTERCON	DIODE NO./ TYPE	DIODE CHP ATCH/ INTERCON	CAPACITOR NO./ TYPE	CAPACITOR CHP ATCH/ INTERCON	RESISTOR NO./ TYPE	RESISTOR CHP ATCH/ INTERCON	RES TOL (%)	ELMT ATCH/ INTERCON NO./ TYPE
14	Can 12	TO-8 -55/ 125C		Weld	Header	N/A	N/A	Kov/Au 29	0		11 N/R	Eutect AuWire	2 N/R	Eutect AuWire	1 SiO_2 Chip	Eutect AuWire	0			

LIFE / ENVIRONMENTAL EXPERIENCE

DATA SRCE	SCR CLS	TST SRC	TEST TYP/ APP ENV	STR LVL/ EQP TYPE	TEST STD MTD/COND	NO. TSTD	TEST DUR.	PART HRS.	NO. FLD	FAILURE CLASSIFICATION IND; MODE; MECH; CAUSE (NO. FAILED / EVENT)	% DEF	TEST DATE	REMARKS
V	N	Scr/C	VisInsp Temp TempCyc CnstAcc FineLk GrossLk EM EM VisInsp	150C -55/125C 5/10 min 20KGY 1x10^{-6} cc/sec Fluoro 25C 80C		44 44 44 44	48 Hrs 5 Cyc	2112	0 0 0 0			1/73	

MALFUNCTION DATA

SYSTEM / EQUIPMENT	PART HISTORY	SCR CLS	DATE CODE	FAILURE ANALYSIS / CORRECTIVE ACTION

SYSTEM / EQUIPMENT	PART HISTORY	SCR CLS	DATE CODE	FAILURE ANALYSIS / CORRECTIVE ACTION

RELIABILITY ANALYSIS CENTER

DEVICE SECTION

MANUFACTURER: CIRCUIT TECHNOLOGY INC. FUNCTIONAL CATEGORY: DIGITAL

TECHNOLOGY: THICK FILM DEVICE FUNCTION: LINE DRIVER

ENTRY NO.	PKG/ NO. PINS	SIZE OP TEMP	PKG MFG	PKG SEAL	SUBSTR MTL/ BOND	SUBSTR SIZE	NO. COND LYR	SUBSTR METAL #BONDS	IC NO./TYPE	IC CHP ATCH/INTERCON	TRANSISTOR NO./TYPE	TRANSISTOR CHP ATCH/INTERCON	DIODE NO./TYPE	DIODE CHP ATCH/INTERCON	CAPACITOR NO./TYPE	CAPACITOR CHP ATCH/INTERCON	RESISTOR NO./TYPE	RESISTOR CHP ATCH/INTERCON	RES TOL (%)	ELMT ATCH/INTERCON NO./TYPE
15	Can 12	TO-8 -55/ 125C		Weld	Header	0.40D	N/A	Kov/Au 29	0		11 N/R	Eutect AuWire	2 N/R	Eutect AuWire	1 Ta	Solder AgPst	10 N/R	N/R Kov/Au	N/R	

LIFE / ENVIRONMENTAL EXPERIENCE

DATA SRCE NO.	SCR CLS	TST SRC	TEST TYP/ APP ENV	STR LVL/ EQP TYPE	TEST STD MTD/COND	NO. TSTD	TEST DUR.	PART HRS.	NO. FLD	FAILURE CLASSIFICATION IND; MODE; MECH; CAUSE (NO. FAILED / EVENT)	% DEF	TEST DATE	REMARKS
V	N	Brn/SSD	EM	26C		1587	168 Hrs		26		1.64	1/73	
			Burn-In	125C		1561			34		2.18		
			EM	25C		1561							

MALFUNCTION DATA

SYSTEM / EQUIPMENT	PART HISTORY	SCR CLS	DATE CODE	FAILURE ANALYSIS / CORRECTIVE ACTION	SYSTEM / EQUIPMENT	PART HISTORY	SCR CLS	DATE CODE	FAILURE ANALYSIS / CORRECTIVE ACTION

RELIABILITY ANALYSIS CENTER

HYBRID MICROCIRCUIT
RELIABILITY DATA

DEVICE SECTION

MANUFACTURER: CIRCUIT TECHNOLOGY INC. **FUNCTIONAL CATEGORY:** DIGITAL

TECHNOLOGY: THICK FILM **DEVICE FUNCTION:** TRIPLE SIGNAL CONDITIONER

ENTRY NO.	PKG/ NO. PINS	SIZE OP TEMP	PKG MFG	PKG SEAL	SUBSTR MTL/ BOND	SUBSTR SIZE	NO. COND LYR	SUBSTR METAL #BONDS	IC NO./ TYPE	IC CHP ATCH/ INTERCON	TRANSISTOR NO./ TYPE	TRANSISTOR CHP ATCH/ INTERCON	DIODE NO./ TYPE	DIODE CHP ATCH/ INTERCON	CAPACITOR NO./ TYPE	CAPACITOR CHP ATCH/ INTERCON	RESISTOR NO./ TYPE	RESISTOR CHP ATCH/ INTERCON	RES TOL (%)	ELMT ATCH/ INTERCON NO./ TYPE
16	Can 16	TO-8 -55/ 125C		Weld	Al$_2$O$_3$ Eutect	.50D	2	PdAg N/R	1 9 Gate	Eutect AuWire	2 SiNPN	Eutect AuWire	0		0		4 Cermet	Fired PdAg	+10	

LIFE / ENVIRONMENTAL EXPERIENCE

DATA SRCE	SCR CLS	TST SRC	TEST TYP/ APP ENV	STR LVL/ EQP TYPE	TEST STD MTD/COND	NO. TSTD	TEST DUR.	PART HRS.	NO. FLD	FAILURE CLASSIFICATION IND; MODE; MECH; CAUSE (NO. FAILED / EVENT)	% DEF	TEST DATE	REMARKS
U	C	Fld	AirInhab	Navgtn/ Operate 30C		14		3.56E5	0			3/72	Used In Flight Guidance System

MALFUNCTION DATA

SYSTEM / EQUIPMENT	PART HISTORY	SCR CLS	DATE CODE	FAILURE ANALYSIS / CORRECTIVE ACTION	SYSTEM / EQUIPMENT	PART HISTORY	SCR CLS	DATE CODE	FAILURE ANALYSIS / CORRECTIVE ACTION

DEVICE SECTION

MANUFACTURER: CIRCUIT TECHNOLOGY INC. **FUNCTIONAL CATEGORY:** DIGITAL

TECHNOLOGY: THICK FILM **DEVICE FUNCTION:** DATA LINE DRIVER

ENTRY NO.	PKG/ NO. PINS	SIZE OP TEMP	PKG MFG	PKG SEAL	SUBSTR MTL/ BOND	SUBSTR SIZE	NO. COND LYR	SUBSTR METAL #BONDS	IC NO./ TYPE	IC CHP ATCH/ INTERCON	TRANSISTOR NO./ TYPE	TRANSISTOR CHP ATCH/ INTERCON	DIODE NO./ TYPE	DIODE CHP ATCH/ INTERCON	CAPACITOR NO./ TYPE	CAPACITOR CHP ATCH/ INTERCON	RESISTOR NO./ TYPE	RESISTOR CHP ATCH/ INTERCON	RES TOL (%)	ELMT ATCH/ INTERCON NO./ TYPE	REMARKS
17	FPM1 10	TO-5 -55/ 125C		Weld	Header	N/A	1	Kov/Au 16	0		2 N/R	Eutect AuWire			0		3 Thick	Eutect Kov/Au			

LIFE / ENVIRONMENTAL EXPERIENCE

DATA SRCE	SCR CLS	TST SRC	TEST TYP/ APP ENV	STR LVL/ EQP TYPE	TEST STD MTD/COND	NO. TSTD	TEST DUR.	PART HRS.	NO. FLD	FAILURE CLASSIFICATION IND; MODE; MECH; CAUSE (NO. FAILED / EVENT)	% DEF	TEST DATE
V	N	Scr/SSB	VisInsp			717	32 Hrs 5 Cyc		10	N/R	1.39	6/72
			Bake	150C		707			9		1.27	
			TempCyc	0/100C								
			CnstAcc	5/15 sec 20KGY 1		707	76 Hrs		12	N/R	1.72	
			FineLk	1×10^{-8} cc/sec		698			10	N/R	1.46	
			GrosLk	Fluoro		686			0			
			Burn-IN	100C		676			14	N/R	2.07	
			VisInsp			676				N/R		
			EM									

MALFUNCTION DATA

SYSTEM / EQUIPMENT	PART HISTORY	SCR CLS	DATE CODE	FAILURE ANALYSIS / CORRECTIVE ACTION

SYSTEM / EQUIPMENT	PART HISTORY	SCR CLS	DATE CODE	FAILURE ANALYSIS / CORRECTIVE ACTION

DEVICE SECTION

MANUFACTURER: CIRCUIT TECHNOLOGY INC.
TECHNOLOGY: THICK FILM

FUNCTIONAL CATEGORY: DIGITAL
DEVICE FUNCTION: LAMP DRIVER

HYBRID MICROCIRCUIT
RELIABILITY DATA

RELIABILITY ANALYSIS CENTER

ENTRY NO.	PKG/NO. PINS	SIZE OP TEMP	PKG MFG	PKG SEAL	SUBSTR MTL/BOND	SUBSTR SIZE	NO. COND LYR	SUBSTR METAL #BONDS	IC NO./TYPE	IC CHP ATCH/INTERCON	TRANSISTOR NO./TYPE	TRANSISTOR CHP ATCH/INTERCON	DIODE NO./TYPE	DIODE CHP ATCH/INTERCON	CAPACITOR NO./TYPE	CAPACITOR CHP ATCH/INTERCON	RESISTOR NO./TYPE	RESISTOR CHP ATCH/INTERCON	RES TOL (%)	ELMT ATCH/INTERCON NO./TYPE
18	FPM1 12	TO-87 -55/ 125C		Weld	Header	N/A	1	Kov/Au N/R 23	0		7 N/R	Eutect AuWire	3 N/R	Eutect AuWire	0 SiO$_2$ Chip	Solder AgPst	17 Thick	Eutect Kov/Au		

LIFE / ENVIRONMENTAL EXPERIENCE

DATA SRCE	SCR CLS	TST SRC	TEST TYP/APP ENV	STR LVL/EQP TYPE	TEST STD MTD/COND	NO. TSTD	TEST DUR.	PART HRS.	NO. FLD	FAILURE CLASSIFICATION IND; MODE; MECH; CAUSE (NO. FAILED / EVENT)	% DEF	TEST DATE
V	N	Scr/C	VisInsp Bake TempCyc CnstAcc FineLk GrossLk Burn-In EM VisInsp	150C -55/125C 5/10 min 20KGY 1 5x10^{-7} cc/sec Fluoro 55C 25C		34 34	32 Hrs 5 Cyc 168 Hrs		0 0 0			12/72

REMARKS

MALFUNCTION DATA

SYSTEM / EQUIPMENT	PART HISTORY	SCR CLS	DATE CODE	FAILURE ANALYSIS / CORRECTIVE ACTION	SYSTEM / EQUIPMENT	PART HISTORY	SCR CLS	DATE CODE	FAILURE ANALYSIS / CORRECTIVE ACTION

HYBRID MICROCIRCUIT
RELIABILITY DATA

DEVICE SECTION

MANUFACTURER: CIRCUIT TECHNOLOGY INC. FUNCTIONAL CATEGORY: DIGITAL

TECHNOLOGY: THICK FILM DEVICE FUNCTION: N/R

ENTRY NO.	PKG/ NO. PINS	SIZE OP TEMP	PKG MFG	PKG SEAL	SUBSTR MTL/ BOND	SUBSTR SIZE	NO. COND LYR	SUBSTR METAL/ BONDS	IC NO./ TYPE	IC CHP ATCH/ INTERCON	TRANSISTOR NO./ TYPE	TRANSISTOR CHP ATCH/ INTERCON	DIODE NO./ TYPE	DIODE CHP ATCH/ INTERCON	CAPACITOR NO./ TYPE	CAPACITOR CHP ATCH/ INTERCON	RESISTOR NO./ TYPE	RESISTOR CHP ATCH/ INTERCON	RES TOL (%)	ELMT ATCH/ INTERCON NO./ TYPE
19	FPM1Cm TO-87 14	-55/ 125C		Weld	Al₂O₃ Eutect	.23x .35	1	N/R	1 N/R	Eutect AuWire	4 N/R	Eutect AuWire	0		0		0			

LIFE / ENVIRONMENTAL EXPERIENCE

DATA SRCE NO.	SCR CLS	TST SRC	TEST TYP/ APP ENV	STR LVL/ EQP TYPE	TEST STD MTD/COND	NO. TSTD	TEST DUR.	PART HRS.	NO. FLD	FAILURE CLASSIFICATION IND; MODE; MECH; CAUSE (NO. FAILED / EVENT)	% DEF	TEST DATE	REMARKS
U	B	Fld	AirInhab	Combin 30C		5		66000	1	N/R		3/74	

MALFUNCTION DATA

SYSTEM / EQUIPMENT	PART HISTORY	SCR CLS	DATE CODE	FAILURE ANALYSIS / CORRECTIVE ACTION

SYSTEM / EQUIPMENT	PART HISTORY	SCR CLS	DATE CODE	FAILURE ANALYSIS / CORRECTIVE ACTION

HYBRID MICROCIRCUIT RELIABILITY DATA

RELIABILITY ANALYSIS CENTER

DEVICE SECTION

MANUFACTURER: CIRCUIT TECHNOLOGY INC. FUNCTIONAL CATEGORY: DIGITAL

DEVICE FUNCTION: BIT LINE CURRENT DRIVER

TECHNOLOGY: THICK FILM

ENTRY NO.	PKG/ NO. PINS	SIZE OP TEMP	PKG SEAL	SUBSTR MTL/ BOND	SUBSTR SIZE	NO. COND LYR	SUBSTR METAL #BONDS	IC NO./ TYPE	IC CHP ATCH/ INTERCON	TRANSISTOR NO./ TYPE	TRANSISTOR CHP ATCH/ INTERCON	DIODE NO./ TYPE	DIODE CHP ATCH/ INTERCON	CAPACITOR NO./ TYPE	CAPACITOR CHP ATCH/ INTERCON	RESISTOR NO./ TYPE	RESISTOR CHP ATCH/ INTERCON	RES TOL (%)	ELMT ATCH/ INTERCON NO./ TYPE
20	FPML 14	TO-87 -55/ 125C	Weld	Al_2O_3	N/A	1	AuCond 26	0		8 N/R	Eutect AuWire	0		0		8 Thick	Eutect AuWire		

LIFE / ENVIRONMENTAL EXPERIENCE

DATA SRCE NO.	SCR CLS	TST SRC	TEST TYP/ APP ENV	STR LVL/ EQP TYPE	TEST STD MTD/COND	NO. TSTD	TEST DUR.	PART HRS.	NO. FLD	FAILURE CLASSIFICATION IND; MODE; MECH; CAUSE (NO. FAILED / EVENT)	% DEF	TEST DATE	REMARKS
V	N	Scp/B	EM VisInsp	25C		89			1	N/R	1.1	2/73	
			Bake	150C		232			37	N/R	15.9		
			TempCyc	-55/125C 5/10 min		195	10 Cyc		0				
			CnstAcc	20KGY1									
			FineLk	5x10-8 cc/sec		195			1	N/R	0.51		
			GrossLk	Fluoro		194			3				
			EM	25C		191			3	N/R	1.57		
			Burn-In	125C		188	240 Hrs		0				
			EM	25C		188			1	N/R	0.53		
			LeadFtg	N/R		187			0				
			FineLk	N/R		187			0				
			GrossLk			187			1	N/R	0.53		
			VisInsp										

MALFUNCTION DATA

SYSTEM / EQUIPMENT	PART HISTORY	SCR CLS	DATE CODE	FAILURE ANALYSIS / CORRECTIVE ACTION	CORRECTIVE ACTION

SYSTEM / EQUIPMENT	PART HISTORY	SCR CLS	DATE CODE	FAILURE ANALYSIS / CORRECTIVE ACTION	CORRECTIVE ACTION

DEVICE SECTION

MANUFACTURER: CIRCUIT TECHNOLOGY INC. FUNCTIONAL CATEGORY: DIGITAL

TECHNOLOGY: THICK FILM

DEVICE FUNCTION: INPUT INTERFACE CIRCUIT

ENTRY NO.	PKG/ NO. PINS	SIZE OP TEMP	PKG MFG	PKG SEAL	SUBSTR MTL/ BOND	SUBSTR SIZE	NO. COND LYR	SUBSTR METAL #BONDS	IC NO./ TYPE	IC CHP ATCH/ INTERCON	TRANSISTOR NO./ TYPE	TRANSISTOR CHP ATCH/ INTERCON	DIODE NO./ TYPE	DIODE CHP ATCH/ INTERCON	CAPACITOR NO./ TYPE	CAPACITOR CHP ATCH/ INTERCON	RESISTOR NO./ TYPE	RESISTOR CHP ATCH/ INTERCON	RES TOL (%)	ELMT ATCH/ INTERCON NO./ TYPE
21	FPM1Cm 14	TO-87 -55/ 125C		Weld	Al$_2$O$_3$ Eutect	.23X .35	1	N/R 32	0		4 SiNPN	Eutect AuWire	8 SiGP	Eutect AuWire	0		16 Cermet	Fired N/R	±10	

LIFE / ENVIRONMENTAL EXPERIENCE

DATA SRCE	SCR CLS	TST SRC	TEST TYP/ APP ENV	STR LVL/ EQP TYPE	TEST STD MTD/COND	NO. TSTD	TEST DUR.	PART HRS.	NO. FLD	FAILURE CLASSIFICATION IND; MODE; MECH; CAUSE (NO. FAILED / EVENT)	% DEF	TEST DATE	REMARKS
U	B	Fld	AirInhab	Combin/ Operate 30C		20		2.64E5	1	N/R		3/74	

MALFUNCTION DATA

SYSTEM / EQUIPMENT	PART HISTORY	SCR CLS	DATE CODE	FAILURE ANALYSIS / CORRECTIVE ACTION

SYSTEM / EQUIPMENT	PART HISTORY	SCR CLS	DATE CODE	FAILURE ANALYSIS / CORRECTIVE ACTION

RELIABILITY ANALYSIS CENTER

RELIABILITY ANALYSIS CENTER

HYBRID MICROCIRCUIT
RELIABILITY DATA

DEVICE SECTION

MANUFACTURER: CIRCUIT TECHNOLOGY INC.   FUNCTIONAL CATEGORY: DIGITAL

TECHNOLOGY: THICK FILM   DEVICE FUNCTION: RELAY DRIVER

ENTRY NO.	PKG/ NO. PINS	SIZE/ OP TEMP	PKG SEAL	PKG MFG	SUBSTR MTL/ BOND	SUBSTR SIZE	NO. COND LYR	SUBSTR METAL/ BONDS	IC NO./ TYPE	IC CHP ATCH/ INTERCON	TRANSISTOR NO./ TYPE	TRANSISTOR CHP ATCH/ INTERCON	DIODE NO./ TYPE	DIODE CHP ATCH/ INTERCON	CAPACITOR NO./ TYPE	CAPACITOR CHP ATCH/ INTERCON	RESISTOR NO./ TYPE	RESISTOR CHP ATCH/ INTERCON	RES TOL (%)	ELMT ATCH/ INTERCON NO./ TYPE
22	FPM1 14	TO-87 -55/ 125C	Weld		Al_2O_3	N/A	1	AuCond 25	0		12 N/R	Eutect AuWire	0		0		8 Thick	Eutect AuWire	N/R	

LIFE / ENVIRONMENTAL EXPERIENCE

DATA SRCE	SCR CLS	TST SRC	TEST TYP/ APP ENV	STR LVL/ EQP TYPE	TEST STD MTD/COND	NO. TSTD	TEST DUR.	PART HRS.	NO. FLD	FAILURE CLASSIFICATION IND; MODE; MECH; CAUSE (NO. FAILED / EVENT)	% DEF	TEST DATE	REMARKS
V	N	Scr/B	Em VisInsp	25C		749			40			2/73	
			Bake	150C		709			100	N/R	5.34		
			TempCyc	-55/125C 5/10 min		609	32 Hrs		0		14.1		
			CnstAcc	20KGY 1									
			FineLk	$1x10^{-8}$ cc/sec		609			14	N/R	2.30		
			GrossLk	Fluoro		595			10	N/R	1.68		
			EM	25C		585			11	N/R	1.88		
			Burn-In	125C		574	240 Hrs		7		1.22		
			EM	25C		574			0				
			LeadFtg			567			0				
			FineLk			567			3	N/R	0.53		
			GrossLk			567			2	N/R	0.35		
			VisInsp			564							

MALFUNCTION DATA

SYSTEM/ EQUIPMENT	PART HISTORY	SCR CLS	DATE CODE	FAILURE ANALYSIS / CORRECTIVE ACTION	SYSTEM/ EQUIPMENT	PART HISTORY	SCR CLS	DATE CODE	FAILURE ANALYSIS / CORRECTIVE ACTION

DEVICE SECTION

MANUFACTURER: CIRCUIT TECHNOLOGY INC.   FUNCTIONAL CATEGORY: DIGITAL

TECHNOLOGY: THICK FILM   DEVICE FUNCTION: DELAY DRIVER

ENTRY NO.	PKG/NO. PINS	SIZE/OP TEMP	PKG MFG	PKG SEAL	SUBSTR MTL/BOND	SUBSTR SIZE	NO. COND LYR	SUBSTR METAL/BONDS	IC NO./TYPE	IC CHP ATCH/INTERCON	TRANSISTOR NO./TYPE	TRANSISTOR CHP ATCH/INTERCON	DIODE NO./TYPE	DIODE CHP ATCH/INTERCON	CAPACITOR NO./TYPE	CAPACITOR CHP ATCH/INTERCON	RESISTOR NO./TYPE	RESISTOR CHP ATCH/INTERCON	RES TOL (%)	ELMT ATCH/INTERCON NO./TYPE
23	FPM1Cm 14	TO-87 -55/ 125C		Weld	Al_2O_3 Eutect	.23x .35	1	AuCond N/R	1 N/R	Eutect AuWire	12 SiNPN	Eutect AuWire	0		4 SiO_2	Eutect AuWire	12 Cermet	Fixed AuCond	± 10	

LIFE / ENVIRONMENTAL EXPERIENCE

DATA SRCE NO.	SCR CLS	TST SRC	PART HISTORY	TEST TYP/APP ENV	DATE CODE	STR LVL/EQP TYPE	TEST STD MTD/COND	NO. TSTD	TEST DUR.	PART HRS.	NO. FLD	FAILURE CLASSIFICATION IND; MODE; MECH; CAUSE (NO. FAILED / EVENT)	% DEF	TEST DATE	REMARKS
U	B	Fld		AirInhab		Combin 30C		10	1.32E5		12	N/R		3/74	

MALFUNCTION DATA

SYSTEM/EQUIPMENT	PART HISTORY	SCR CLS	DATE CODE	FAILURE ANALYSIS / CORRECTIVE ACTION	SYSTEM/EQUIPMENT	PART HISTORY	SCR CLS	DATE CODE	FAILURE ANALYSIS / CORRECTIVE ACTION

DEVICE SECTION

MANUFACTURER: CIRCUIT TECHNOLOGY INC.   FUNCTIONAL CATEGORY: DIGITAL

TECHNOLOGY: THICK FILM   DEVICE FUNCTION: LINE RECEIVER

RELIABILITY
ANALYSIS
CENTER

HYBRID MICROCIRCUIT
RELIABILITY DATA

ENTRY NO.	PKG/ NO. PINS	SIZE OP TEMP	PKG MFG	PKG SEAL	SUBSTR MTL/ BOND	SUBSTR SIZE	NO. COND LYR	SUBSTR METAL #BONDS	IC NO./ TYPE	IC CHP ATCH/ INTERCON	TRANSISTOR NO./ TYPE	TRANSISTOR CHP ATCH/ INTERCON	DIODE NO./ TYPE	DIODE CHP ATCH/ INTERCON	CAPACITOR NO./ TYPE	CAPACITOR CHP ATCH/ INTERCON	RESISTOR NO./ TYPE	RESISTOR CHP ATCH/ INTERCON	RES TOL (%)	ELMT ATCH/ INTERCON NO./ TYPE
24	FPM1 16	TO-87 -55/ 125C		Weld	Al_2O_3	N/R	1	AuCond 24	0		8 N/R	Eutect AuWire	4 N/R	Eutect AuWire	4 SiO_2 Chip	AgPst AuWire	2 Thick	Fired AuCond	N/R	

LIFE / ENVIRONMENTAL EXPERIENCE

DATA SRCE	SCR CLS	TST SRC	TEST TYP/ APP ENV	STR LVL/ EQP TYPE	TEST STD MTD/COND	NO. TSTD	TEST DUR.	PART HRS.	NO. FLD	FAILURE CLASSIFICATION IND; MODE; MECH; CAUSE (NO. FAILED / EVENT)	% DEF	TEST DATE
V	N	Scr/SSC	VisInsp			36			1	N/R	2.78	11/72
			Bake	150C		35	32 Hrs					
			TempCyc	-55/125C 5/10 min			5 Cyc					
			CnstAcc	20KGY₁								
			FineLk	5x10⁻⁸ cc/sec								
			GrossLk	Fluoro		35			0			
			EM	25C		35			1	N/R	2.86	
			Burn-In	125C		35	168 Hrs					
			EM	25C								

REMARKS

MALFUNCTION DATA

SYSTEM / EQUIPMENT	PART HISTORY	SCR CLS	DATE CODE	FAILURE ANALYSIS / CORRECTIVE ACTION

SYSTEM / EQUIPMENT	PART HISTORY	SCR CLS	DATE CODE	FAILURE ANALYSIS / CORRECTIVE ACTION

PAGE 46

RELIABILITY
ANALYSIS
CENTER

DEVICE SECTION

MANUFACTURER: CIRCUIT TECHNOLOGY INC. FUNCTIONAL CATEGORY: DIGITAL

DEVICE FUNCTION: CAUTION LOGIC AND LAMP DRIVER

TECHNOLOGY: THICK FILM

ENTRY NO.	SCR CLS	PKG/ NO. PINS	SIZE OP TEMP	PKG MFG	PKG SEAL	SUBSTR MTL/ BOND	SUBSTR SIZE	NO. COND LYR	SUBSTR METAL/ #BONDS	IC NO./TYPE	IC CHP ATCH/ INTERCON	TRANSISTOR NO./TYPE	TRANSISTOR CHP ATCH/ INTERCON	DIODE NO./TYPE	DIODE CHP ATCH/ INTERCON	CAPACITOR NO./TYPE	CAPACITOR CHP ATCH/ INTERCON	RESISTOR NO./TYPE	RESISTOR CHP ATCH/ INTERCON	RES TOL (%)	ELMT ATCH/ INTERCON NO./TYPE
25	N	FPM1 15	TO-87 -55/ 125C		Weld	Header	N/A	1	AuCond 100	2 8 Gate	Eutect AuWire	25 N/R	Eutect AuWire	18 N/R	Eutect AuWire	7 SiO_2 Chip	Epoxy AuWire	43 Thick	Eutect AuWire		

LIFE / ENVIRONMENTAL EXPERIENCE

DATA SRCE	SCR CLS	TST SRC	TEST TYP/ APP ENV	STR LVL/ EQP TYPE	TEST STD MTD/COND	NO. TSTD	TEST DUR.	PART HRS.	NO. FLD	FAILURE CLASSIFICATION IND; MODE; MECH; CAUSE (NO. FAILED / EVENT)	% DEF	TEST DATE	REMARKS
V	N	Scr/SSC	VisInsp	150C		541			13	N/R	2.40	4/73	
			Bake	-65/150C		528	24 Hrs		0				
			TempCyc	5/10 min			10 Cyc						
			CnstAcc	30KGY		528			2	N/R	0.38		
			FineLk	5×10^{-7} cc/sec		526			7	N/R	1.33		
			GrossLk	Fluoro		519			53	N/R	10.2		
			EM	25C		466	96 Hrs		39		8.37		
			Burn-In	125C		427			0				
			EM	25C		427			16		3.75		

MALFUNCTION DATA

SYSTEM / EQUIPMENT	PART HISTORY	SCR CLS	DATE CODE	FAILURE ANALYSIS / CORRECTIVE ACTION	SYSTEM / EQUIPMENT	PART HISTORY	SCR CLS	DATE CODE	FAILURE ANALYSIS / CORRECTIVE ACTION

DEVICE SECTION

RELIABILITY
ANALYSIS
CENTER

HYBRID MICROCIRCUIT
RELIABILITY DATA

MANUFACTURER: CIRCUIT TECHNOLOGY INC.   FUNCTIONAL CATEGORY: DIGITAL

TECHNOLOGY: THICK FILM   DEVICE FUNCTION: DUAL LINE DRIVER

ENTRY NO.	PKG/ NO. PINS	SIZE OP TEMP	PKG MFG	PKG SEAL	SUBSTR MTL/ BOND	SUBSTR SIZE	NO. COND LYR	SUBSTR METAL #BONDS	IC NO./ TYPE	IC CHP ATCH/ INTERCON	TRANSISTOR NO./ TYPE	TRANSISTOR CHP ATCH/ INTERCON	DIODE NO./ TYPE	DIODE CHP ATCH/ INTERCON	CAPACITOR NO./ TYPE	CAPACITOR CHP ATCH/ INTERCON	RESISTOR NO./ TYPE	RESISTOR CHP ATCH/ INTERCON	RES TOL (%)	ELMT ATCH/ INTERCON NO./ TYPE
26	FPM1 16	TO-87 -55/ 125C		Weld	Header	N/A	1	AuCond 35	1 N/R	Eutect AuWire	6 N/R	Eutect AuWire	6	Eutect AuWire	2 Ceram	Epoxy AuWire	10 Thick	Eutect AuWire	N/R	

LIFE / ENVIRONMENTAL EXPERIENCE

DATA SRCE	SCR CLS	TST SRC	TEST TYP/ APP ENV	STR LVL/ EQP TYPE	TEST STD MTD/COND	NO. TSTD	TEST DUR.	PART HRS.	NO. FLD	FAILURE CLASSIFICATION IND; MODE; MECH; CAUSE (NO. FAILED / EVENT)	% DEF	TEST DATE
V	N	Scr/SSB	VisInsp	150C		224		7104	2	N/R	0.89	10/72
			Bake	-65/150C		222	32 Hrs		0	N/R		
			TempCyc	5/15 min		222	100 Cyc		1		0.45	
			CnstAcc	20MGY 1		221			0			
			FineLk	5x10⁻⁷ cc/sec		221			6	N/R	2.71	
			GrossLk	Fluoro		215			1	N/R	0.47	
			Burn-In	100C		214	168 Hrs		17	N/R	7.94	
			EM	25C		214			1	N/R		
			VisInsp			197			1	N/R	0.51	

REMARKS

MALFUNCTION DATA

SYSTEM / EQUIPMENT	PART HISTORY	SCR CLS	DATE CODE	FAILURE ANALYSIS / CORRECTIVE ACTION

SYSTEM / EQUIPMENT	PART HISTORY	SCR CLS	DATE CODE	FAILURE ANALYSIS / CORRECTIVE ACTION

DEVICE SECTION

MANUFACTURER: CIRCUIT TECHNOLOGY INC.

TECHNOLOGY: THICK FILM

FUNCTIONAL CATEGORY: DIGITAL

DEVICE FUNCTION: RS FLIP FLOP

ENTRY NO.	PKG/ NO. PINS	SIZE OP TEMP	PKG MFG	PKG SEAL	SUBSTR MTL/ BOND	SUBSTR SIZE	NO. COND LYR	SUBSTR METAL #BONDS	IC NO./ TYPE	IC CHP ATCH/ INTERCON	TRANSISTOR NO./ TYPE	TRANSISTOR CHP ATCH/ INTERCON	DIODE NO./ TYPE	DIODE CHP ATCH/ INTERCON	CAPACITOR NO./ TYPE	CAPACITOR CHP ATCH/ INTERCON	RESISTOR NO./ TYPE	RESISTOR CHP ATCH/ INTERCON	RES TOL (%)	ELMT ATCH/ INTERCON NO./ TYPE
27	Can 16	TO-87 -55/ 125C		Weld	Header	N/A	1	AuCond 16	0		8 N/R	Eutect AuWire	3 N/R	Eutect AuWire	5 SiO$_2$ Chip	Epoxy AuWire	20 Thick	Eutect AuWire	N/R	

LIFE / ENVIRONMENTAL EXPERIENCE

DATA SRCE NO.	SCR CLS	TST SRC	TEST TYP/ APP ENV	STR LVL/ EQP TYPE	SUBSTR SIZE	NO. TSTD	TEST DUR.	PART HRS.	NO. FLD	FAILURE CLASSIFICATION IND; MODE; MECH; CAUSE (NO. FAILED / EVENT)	% DEF	TEST DATE
V	N	Scr/B	VisInsp					0	0			10/72
			Bake	150C		52	32 Hrs					
			TempCyc	-55/125C 5/10 min			5 Cyc					
			CnstAcc	20KGY$_1$								
			FineLk	5x10^{-7} cc/sec								
			GrossLk	Fluoro								
			Burn-In	125C		52	168 Hrs		0			
			EM	25C		52			0			
			VisInsp									

REMARKS

MALFUNCTION DATA

SYSTEM / EQUIPMENT	PART HISTORY	SCR CLS	DATE CODE	FAILURE ANALYSIS / CORRECTIVE ACTION

SYSTEM / EQUIPMENT	PART HISTORY	SCR CLS	DATE CODE	FAILURE ANALYSIS / CORRECTIVE ACTION

RELIABILITY ANALYSIS CENTER

HYBRID MICROCIRCUIT
RELIABILITY DATA

DEVICE SECTION

MANUFACTURER: CIRCUIT TECHNOLOGY INC. FUNCTIONAL CATEGORY: DIGITAL

TECHNOLOGY: THICK FILM DEVICE FUNCTION: WRITE CONTROL CIRCUIT

ENTRY NO.	PKG/ NO. PINS	SIZE OP TEMP	SUBSTR MTL/ BOND	SUBSTR SIZE	PKG SEAL	PKG MFG	NO. COND LYR	SUBSTR METAL #BONDS	IC NO./ TYPE	IC CHP ATCH/ INTERCON	TRANSISTOR NO./ TYPE	TRANSISTOR CHP ATCH/ INTERCON	DIODE NO./ TYPE	DIODE CHP ATCH/ INTERCON	CAPACITOR NO./ TYPE	CAPACITOR CHP ATCH/ INTERCON	RESISTOR NO./ TYPE	RESISTOR CHP ATCH/ INTERCON	RES TOL (%)	ELMT ATCH/ INTERCON
28	FPM1 22	TO-87 -55/ 125C	Al$_2$O$_3$	N/A	Weld		1	AuCond 35	0		8 N/R	Eutect AuWire	3 N/R	Eutect AuWire	0		15 Thick	Fired AuCond	N/R	

LIFE / ENVIRONMENTAL EXPERIENCE

DATA SRCE	SCR CLS	TST SRC	TEST TYP/ APP ENV	STR LVL/ EQP TYPE	TEST STD MTD/COND	NO. TSTD	TEST DUR.	PART HRS.	NO. FLD	FAILURE CLASSIFICATION IND; MODE; MECH; CAUSE (NO. FAILED / EVENT)	% DEF	TEST DATE
V	N	Scr/SSB	VisInsp			948			28	N/R	2.95	3/73
			Temp	150C		920	32 Hrs					
			TempCyc	-55/125C			5 Cyc					
			CnstAcc	5/10 min 20KGY$_1$								
			FineLk	5x10^{-7} cc/sec		920			6	N/R	0.65	
			GrossLk	Fluoro		914			30	N/R	3.28	
			EM	25C		884			17	N/R	1.92	
			Burn-In	125C		867	168 Hrs		29	N/R	3.34	
			EM	25C		867						
			VisInsp			838			0			

REMARKS

MALFUNCTION DATA

SYSTEM / EQUIPMENT	PART HISTORY	SCR CLS	DATE CODE	FAILURE ANALYSIS / CORRECTIVE ACTION

SYSTEM / EQUIPMENT	PART HISTORY	SCR CLS	DATE CODE	FAILURE ANALYSIS / CORRECTIVE ACTION

PAGE 50

DEVICE SECTION

MANUFACTURER: CIRCUIT TECHNOLOGY INC. **FUNCTIONAL CATEGORY:** DIGITAL

TECHNOLOGY: THICK FILM **DEVICE FUNCTION:** DUAL HIGHSIDE CURRENT DRIVER

HYBRID MICROCIRCUIT RELIABILITY DATA

RELIABILITY ANALYSIS CENTER

ENTRY NO.	PKG/ NO. PINS	SIZE OP TEMP	PKG MFG	PKG SEAL	SUBSTR MTL/ BOND	SUBSTR SIZE	NO. COND LYR	SUBSTR METAL #BONDS	IC NO./TYPE	IC CHP ATCH/ INTERCON	TRANSISTOR NO./TYPE	TRANSISTOR CHP ATCH/ INTERCON	DIODE NO./TYPE	DIODE CHP ATCH/ INTERCON	CAPACITOR NO./TYPE	CAPACITOR CHP ATCH/ INTERCON	RESISTOR NO./TYPE	RESISTOR CHP ATCH/ INTERCON	RES TOL (%)	ELMT ATCH/ INTERCON NO./TYPE
29	FPM1 22	TO-87 -55/ 125C	Isotronics	Isotrcweld	Al$_2$O$_3$ Eutect	.25x .54x .01	1	AuCond N/R $\approx$46	0		8 SiNPN (6) SiPNP (2)	Eutect AuWire	12 SiSig	Eutect AuWire	0		14 Cermet	Fixed AuCond	±10	

LIFE / ENVIRONMENTAL EXPERIENCE

DATA SRCE	SCR CLS	TST SRC	TEST TYP/ APP ENV	STR LVL/ EQP TYPE	TEST STD MTD/COND	NO. TSTD	TEST DUR.	PART HRS.	NO. FLD	FAILURE CLASSIFICATION IND; MODE; MECH; CAUSE (NO. FAILED / EVENT)	% DEF	TEST DATE	REMARKS
V/I	SSD	Lab	RevBias	150C		15	240 Hrs		8	Electrical Rejects	53.3	9/73	
V/I	SSD	Lab	OpCnst	70C		15	240 Hrs		0				
V/I	SSD	Env	TempCyc	-65/150C	MS883 1010	5	40 Cyc		0				
V/I	SSD	Stp	ThrmShk	4 stps 0/100C -55/125C -65/150C -65/200C 5/5 min	MS883 1011	5			0				Devices were immersed in Ethylene Glycol Baths in hot and cold chambers They were washed and dried after each Step
	SSD	Stp	OpDyn	4 stps 50, 70 100, 125C3.1.5	MS883 5006	5	24 Hrs e stp		0				$V_{CC} = 5.0V$ $V_L = 28.0V$ $I_O = 100MA$
V/I	SSD	Stp	OpDyn	4 stp 50, 70 100, 150C3.1.5	MS883 5006	5	24 Hr e stp		0				$V_{CC} = 5V$ $V_L = 28V$ $I_O = 100MA$ $V_{IN} = 0$ PRR = 1 KHZ Y_I
	SSD	Stp	MechShk	5 stp 1.5, 3 10, 20 30KG	MS883 5006	5	5blo 1.0msec e blo		0				
	SSD	Stp	CnstAcc	3 stp 50, 50 75Kg	MS883 2001	5	1 min		1	Substrate Smashed; Gold Plating Pulled Up From Base of Package	20.0		

MALFUNCTION DATA

SYSTEM/ EQUIPMENT	PART HISTORY	SCR CLS	DATE CODE	FAILURE ANALYSIS / CORRECTIVE ACTION

SYSTEM/ EQUIPMENT	PART HISTORY	SCR CLS	DATE CODE	FAILURE ANALYSIS / CORRECTIVE ACTION

DEVICE SECTION

MANUFACTURER: CIRCUIT TECHNOLOGY INC. **FUNCTIONAL CATEGORY:** DIGITAL

TECHNOLOGY: THICK FILM **DEVICE FUNCTION:** DUAL HIGHSIDE CURRENT DRIVER

HYBRID MICROCIRCUIT
RELIABILITY DATA

RELIABILITY ANALYSIS CENTER

ENTRY NO.	PKG/NO. PINS	SIZE	OP TEMP	PKG MFG	PKG SEAL	SUBSTR MTL/BOND	SUBSTR SIZE	NO. COND LYR	SUBSTR METAL #BONDS	IC NO./TYPE	IC CHP ATCH/INTERCON	TRANSISTOR NO./TYPE	TRANSISTOR CHP ATCH/INTERCON	DIODE NO./TYPE	DIODE CHP ATCH/INTERCON	CAPACITOR NO./TYPE	CAPACITOR CHP ATCH/INTERCON	RESISTOR NO./TYPE	RESISTOR CHP ATCH/INTERCON	RES TOL (%)	ELMT ATCH/INTERCON NO./TYPE
29 (cont'd)																					

LIFE / ENVIRONMENTAL EXPERIENCE (con't)

DATA SRCE	SCR CLS	TST SRC	TEST TYP/APP ENV	STR LVL/EQP ENV	TEST STD MTD/COND	NO. TSTD	TEST DUR.	PART HRS.	NO. FLD	FAILURE CLASSIFICATION IND; MODE; MECH; CAUSE (NO. FAILED/EVENT)	% DEF	TEST DATE	REMARKS
V/I	N	Scr/SSC	Temp	150C	MS883 1008C	113	48 Hrs	0	0				
			TempCyc	-65/150C 10/10 min	1010C		10 Cyc						
			CnstAcc	30KG 6 AXES	MS883 2001								
			FineLk	He 40 psia	MS883 1014A	113	2 Hrs	0	2	N/R	100.0		
			GrossLk	FC78 125C	MS883 1014C	111			0				
			X-Ray	40 psia		111			3	Substrate Lifted Off Header with Eutectic Attached	2.70		
V/I	Env	VisInsp		MS883 2008A	5			0					
		Solder	230C	MS883 2003	6			0					
		TrmStr		MS883 2011	192			0					
		LeadFtg		MS883 2004	110			0					
		FineLk	He 40 psia	MS883 1014A	5	2 Hrs		0					
		GrossLk	FC78 40 psia	MS883 1014C	5			0					Suspended over boiling H$_2$O, 1 Hour Immersed in Mil-F-14256 Flux 10 sec

MALFUNCTION DATA

SYSTEM/EQUIPMENT	PART HISTORY	SCR CLS	DATE CODE	FAILURE ANALYSIS / CORRECTIVE ACTION

SYSTEM/EQUIPMENT	PART HISTORY	SCR CLS	DATE CODE	FAILURE ANALYSIS / CORRECTIVE ACTION

DEVICE SECTION

MANUFACTURER: CIRCUIT TECHNOLOGY INC. FUNCTIONAL CATEGORY: DIGITAL

TECHNOLOGY: THICK FILM

DEVICE FUNCTION: DUAL HIGHSIDE CURRENT DRIVER

HYBRID MICROCIRCUIT
RELIABILITY DATA

RELIABILITY ANALYSIS CENTER

ENTRY NO.	PKG/ NO. PINS	SIZE OP TEMP	PKG MFG	PKG SEAL	SUBSTR MTL/ BOND	SUBSTR SIZE	NO. COND LYR	SUBSTR METAL # BONDS	IC NO./TYPE	IC CHP ATCH/INTERCON	TRANSISTOR NO./TYPE	TRANSISTOR CHP ATCH/INTERCON	DIODE NO./TYPE	DIODE CHP ATCH/INTERCON	CAPACITOR NO./TYPE	CAPACITOR CHP ATCH/INTERCON	RESISTOR NO./TYPE	RESISTOR CHP ATCH/INTERCON	RES TOL (%)	ELMT ATCH/INTERCON NO./TYPE
29 (cntd)																				

LIFE / ENVIRONMENTAL EXPERIENCE (con't)

DATA SRCE	SCR CLS	TST SRC	TEST TYP/ APP ENV	STR LVL/ EQP TYPE	TEST STD MTD/COND	NO. TSTD	TEST DUR.	PART HRS.	NO. FLD	FAILURE CLASSIFICATION IND; MODE; MECH; CAUSE (NO. FAILED / EVENT)	% DEF	TEST DATE	REMARKS
V/I	SSD	Env	ThrmShk	-55/125C 5/5 min	MS883 1011B	7							
			TempCyc	-65/150C 10/10 min	MS883 1010		10 Cyc		0				
			Moistr	-10/65C 98%RH	MS883 1004	7	5 Blo						
			MechShk	0.5KG 0.5msec	MS883 2002	7	1 Cyc						
			VbVrFq	.02/2KHZ X,Y,Z	MS883 2007								
			CnstAcc	30KG 6 AXES	MS883 2001	7			0				
V/I	SSD	Lab	StgLife	150C		8	1000 Hrs	8000	0				
			OpDyn	100C	MS883 1005D	78	2000	1.56E5	7	Short, Output to Ground, Solder Particle Short, Overstress, Solder Bridge Resistive Wire Bonds Shorted Transistor Overstressed/2	8.97		X_1,X_2,Y_1,Y_2,Z_1,Z_2 100HZ +5V Pulse

MALFUNCTION DATA

SYSTEM / EQUIPMENT	PART HISTORY	SCR CLS	DATE CODE	FAILURE ANALYSIS / CORRECTIVE ACTION

SYSTEM / EQUIPMENT	PART HISTORY	SCR CLS	DATE CODE	FAILURE ANALYSIS / CORRECTIVE ACTION

PAGE 53

DEVICE SECTION

MANUFACTURER: CIRCUIT TECHNOLOGY INC.
TECHNOLOGY: THICK FILM

FUNCTIONAL CATEGORY: DIGITAL
DEVICE FUNCTION: DUAL HIGH SIDE CURRENT DRIVER

HYBRID MICROCIRCUIT
RELIABILITY DATA

RELIABILITY ANALYSIS CENTER

ENTRY NO.	PKG/ NO. PINS	SIZE OP TEMP	PKG MFG	PKG SEAL	SUBSTR MTL/ BOND	SUBSTR SIZE	NO. COND LYR	SUBSTR METAL #BONDS	IC NO./ TYPE	IC CHP ATCH/ INTERCON	TRANSISTOR NO./ TYPE	TRANSISTOR CHP ATCH/ INTERCON	DIODE NO./ TYPE	DIODE CHP ATCH/ INTERCON	CAPACITOR NO./ TYPE	CAPACITOR CHP ATCH/ INTERCON	RESISTOR NO./ TYPE	RESISTOR CHP ATCH/ INTERCON	RES TOL (%)	ELMT ATCH/ INTERCON NO./ TYPE
30	FPM1 22	TO-87 -55/ 125C		Weld	Al_2O_3/ BeO	.23x .35	1	AuCond ≈ 30	0		8 SiNPN (6) SiPNP (2)	Eutect AuWire	12 SiSig	Eutect AuWire	0		14 Cermet	Fixed AuCond	±10	

LIFE / ENVIRONMENTAL EXPERIENCE

DATA SRCE NO.	SCR CLS	TST SRC	TEST TYP/ APP ENV	STR LVL/ EQP TYPE	TEST STD MTD/COND	NO. TSTD	TEST DUR.	PART HRS.	NO. FLD	FAILURE CLASSIFICATION IND; MODE; MECH; CAUSE (NO. FAILED / EVENT)	% DEF	TEST DATE	REMARKS
V	N	Scr/SSB	VisInsp			1136			33	N/R	2.90	2/72	
			Bake	150C		1103	48 Hrs 5 Cyc						
			TempCyc	-55/125C 5/10 min									
			CnstAcc	20KGY									
			FineLk	5×10^{-8} cc./sec		1103			18	N/R	1.63		
			GrossLk	Fluoro		1085			16	N/R	1.48		
			X-Ray			1069			0	N/R	2.17		
			EM	25C		942			127	N/R	13.4		
			Burn-In	125C		942	240 Hrs		0				
			EM	25C		942			123	N/R	14.9		
			VisInsp			819			1	N/R	0.14		

MALFUNCTION DATA

SYSTEM / EQUIPMENT	PART HISTORY	SCR CLS	DATE CODE	FAILURE ANALYSIS / CORRECTIVE ACTION	SYSTEM / EQUIPMENT	PART HISTORY	SCR CLS	DATE CODE	FAILURE ANALYSIS / CORRECTIVE ACTION

PAGE 54

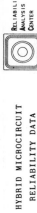

RELIABILITY ANALYSIS CENTER

HYBRID MICROCIRCUIT
RELIABILITY DATA

DEVICE SECTION

MANUFACTURER: CIRCUIT TECHNOLOGY INC.   FUNCTIONAL CATEGORY: DIGITAL

TECHNOLOGY: THICK FILM   DEVICE FUNCTION: DATA STORAGE

ENTRY NO.	PKG/ NO. PINS	SIZE OP TEMP	PKG MFG	PKG SEAL	SUBSTR MTL/ BOND	SUBSTR SIZE	NO. COND LYR	SUBSTR METAL #BONDS	IC NO./ TYPE	IC CHP ATCH/ INTERCON	TRANSISTOR NO./ TYPE	TRANSISTOR CHP ATCH/ INTERCON	DIODE NO./ TYPE	DIODE CHP ATCH/ INTERCON	CAPACITOR NO./ TYPE	CAPACITOR CHP ATCH/ INTERCON	RESISTOR NO./ TYPE	RESISTOR CHP ATCH/ INTERCON	RES TOL (%)	ELMT ATCH/ INTERCON NO./ TYPE
31	FPM1 24	TO-87 -55/ 125C		Weld	Header N/A	N/A	1	AuCond 60	3 N/R	Eutect AuWire	0		6 N/R	Eutect AuWire	0		0			

LIFE / ENVIRONMENTAL EXPERIENCE

DATA SRCE NO.	SCR CLS	TST SRC	TEST TYP/ APP ENV	STR LVL/ EQP TYPE	TEST STD MTD/COND	NO. TSTD	TEST DUR.	PART HRS.	NO. FLD	FAILURE CLASSIFICATION IND; MODE; MECH; CAUSE (NO. FAILED / EVENT)	% DEF	TEST DATE	REMARKS
V	N	Scr/SSB	VisInsp			58			4	N/R	7.00	8/72	
			Bake	150C		54	32 Hrs		0				
			TempCyc	-65/150C 5/10 min									
			CnstAcc	5KGY 1									
			FineLk	5x10⁻⁷ cc/sec		54			1	N/R	1.85		
			GrossLk	Fluoro		53			3	N/R	5.66		
			EM	25C		50			0				
			Burn-In	70C		50	168 Hrs		0				
			EM	25C		50			0				
			VisInsp			50			0				

MALFUNCTION DATA

SYSTEM / EQUIPMENT	PART HISTORY	SCR CLS	DATE CODE	FAILURE ANALYSIS / CORRECTIVE ACTION

SYSTEM / EQUIPMENT	PART HISTORY	SCR CLS	DATE CODE	FAILURE ANALYSIS / CORRECTIVE ACTION

DEVICE SECTION

MANUFACTURER: CIRCUIT TECHNOLOGY INC. FUNCTIONAL CATEGORY: DIGITAL

TECHNOLOGY: THICK FILM DEVICE FUNCTION: 2 BIT LOW SPEED D/A SWITCH

HYBRID MICROCIRCUIT
RELIABILITY DATA

RELIABILITY ANALYSIS CENTER

| ENTRY NO. | PKG NO. PINS | SIZE OP TEMP | SUBSTR MTL/BOND | SUBSTR SIZE | NO. COND LYR | SUBSTR METAL BONDS | IC | | TRANSISTOR | | DIODE | | CAPACITOR | | RESISTOR | | | ELMT ATCH/INTERCON |
							NO./TYPE	CHP ATCH/INTERCON	NO./TYPE	CHP ATCH/INTERCON	NO./TYPE	CHP ATCH/INTERCON	NO./TYPE	CHP ATCH/INTERCON	NO./TYPE	CHP ATCH/INTERCON	RES TOL (%)	NO./TYPE
32	FPM1 28	.625x .375 -55/ 125C	Al$_2$O$_3$	N/A	N/A	AuCond 25	0		4 N/R	Eutect AuWire	2 N/R	Eutect AuWire	0		8 Thick	Fired AuCond	N/R	

LIFE / ENVIRONMENTAL EXPERIENCE

DATA SRCE	SCR CLS	TST SRC	TEST TYP/APP ENV	STR LVL/EQP TYPE	TEST STD MTD/COND	NO. TSTD	TEST DUR.	PART HRS.	NO. FLD	FAILURE CLASSIFICATION IND; MODE; MECH: CAUSE (NO. FAILED / EVENT)	% DEF	TEST DATE
V	N	Scr/C	VisInsp			2266	48 Hrs		21	N/R	0.93	11/72
			Bake	150C		2245	15 Cyc		0			
			ThrmShk	-55/125C		2245			0			
			CnstAcc	20KGY		2245			1	N/R	0.45	
			FineLk	1x10^{-6} cc/sec		2244			24	N/R	1.07	
			GrossLk	Fluoro		2220			32	N/R	1.44	
			EM	25C		2188			68	N/R	3.11	
			VisInsp			2120			6	N/R	0.28	

MALFUNCTION DATA

SYSTEM / EQUIPMENT	PART HISTORY	SCR CLS	DATE CODE	FAILURE ANALYSIS / CORRECTIVE ACTION	SYSTEM / EQUIPMENT	PART HISTORY	SCR CLS	DATE CODE	FAILURE ANALYSIS / CORRECTIVE ACTION	CORRECTIVE ACTION

HYBRID MICROCIRCUIT RELIABILITY DATA

DEVICE SECTION

MANUFACTURER: CIRCUIT TECHNOLOGY INC. FUNCTIONAL CATEGORY: DIGITAL

TECHNOLOGY: THICK FILM DEVICE FUNCTION: SWEEP SERIES GATE

ENTRY NO.	PKG/NO. PINS	SIZE/OP TEMP	PKG SEAL	PKG MFG	SUBSTR MTL/BOND	SUBSTR SIZE	NO. COND LYR	SUBSTR METAL/#BONDS	IC NO./TYPE	IC CHP ATCH/INTERCON	TRANSISTOR NO./TYPE	TRANSISTOR CHP ATCH/INTERCON	DIODE NO./TYPE	DIODE CHP ATCH/INTERCON	CAPACITOR NO./TYPE	CAPACITOR CHP ATCH/INTERCON	RESISTOR NO./TYPE	RESISTOR CHP ATCH/INTERCON	RES TOL (%)	ELMT ATCH/INTERCON NO./TYPE
33	FPM1 30	.38x .63x .13 -55/125C	Weld		Al_2O_3	N/A	N/A	AuCond 30	0		7 N/R	Eutect AuWire	0		1 Ta	Epoxy AuCond	11 Thick	Fired AuCond	N/R	

LIFE / ENVIRONMENTAL EXPERIENCE

DATA SRCE NO.	SCR CLS	TST SRC	TEST TYP/APP ENV	STR LVL/EQP TYPE	TEST STD MTD/COND	NO. TSTD	TEST DUR.	PART HRS.	NO. FLD	FAILURE CLASSIFICATION IND; MODE; MECH; CAUSE (NO. FAILED / EVENT)	% DEF	TEST DATE	REMARKS
V	N	Scr/B	VisInsp			144			2	N/R	1.38	2/73	
			Bake	150C		142	48 Hrs	6816	0				
			TempCyc	-55/150C 5/10 min			10 Cyc						
			CnstAcc	20KGY1									
			FineLk	5×10^{-8} cc/sec		142			2	N/R	1.41		
			GrossLk	Fluoro		140			1	N/R			
			EM	25C		139			4	N/R	3.57		
			Burn-In	125C		135	168 Hrs		0	N/R			
			EM	25C		135			2	N/R			
			VisInsp			133			0				

MALFUNCTION DATA

SYSTEM/EQUIPMENT	PART HISTORY	SCR CLS	DATE CODE	FAILURE ANALYSIS / CORRECTIVE ACTION	SYSTEM/EQUIPMENT	PART HISTORY	SCR CLS	DATE CODE	FAILURE ANALYSIS / CORRECTIVE ACTION

H.M.R.D.—C

DEVICE SECTION

MANUFACTURER: CIRCUIT TECHNOLOGY INC. FUNCTIONAL CATEGORY: DIGITAL

TECHNOLOGY: THICK FILM DEVICE FUNCTION: DUAL LINE RECEIVER

HYBRID MICROCIRCUIT RELIABILITY DATA

RELIABILITY ANALYSIS CENTER

ENTRY NO.	PKG/ NO. PINS	SIZE/ OP TEMP	PKG SEAL	PKG MFG	SUBSTR MTL/ BOND	SUBSTR SIZE	NO. COND LYR	SUBSTR METAL /BONDS	IC NO./ TYPE	IC CHP ATCH/ INTERCON	TRANSISTOR NO./ TYPE	TRANSISTOR CHP ATCH/ INTERCON	DIODE NO./ TYPE	DIODE CHP ATCH/ INTERCON	CAPACITOR NO./ TYPE	CAPACITOR CHP ATCH/ INTERCON	RESISTOR NO./ TYPE	RESISTOR CHP ATCH/ INTERCON	RES TOL (%)	ELMT ATCH/ INTERCON
34	FPM1 30	TO-87 -55/ 125C	Weld		Al$_2$O$_3$	N/A	1	AuCond 30	2 N/R	Eutect AuWire	2 N/R	Eutect AuWire	0		3 SiO$_2$ Chip	Epoxy AuCond	23 Thick	Fired AuCond		

LIFE / ENVIRONMENTAL EXPERIENCE

DATA SRCE	SCR CLS	TST SRC	TEST TYP/ APP ENV	STR LVL/ EQP TYPE	TEST STD MTD/COND	NO. TSTD	TEST DUR.	PART HRS.	NO. FLD	FAILURE CLASSIFICATION IND; MODE; MECH; CAUSE (NO. FAILED / EVENT)	% DEF	TEST DATE	REMARKS
V	N	Scr/SSB	VisInsp	150C		239			1	N/R	0.42	3/73	
			Bake			238			0				
			TempCyc	-65/150C 5/15 min			32 Hrs 100 Cyc	7616					
			CnstAcc	20KGY1									
			FineLk	5x10^{-7} cc/sec		238			2	N/R	0.84		
			GrossLk	Fluoro		236			13	N/R	5.51		
			Burn-In	100C		223	168 Hrs		28	N/R	12.6		
			EM	25C		223				N/R	1.54		
			VisInsp			195			3	N/R			

MALFUNCTION DATA

SYSTEM / EQUIPMENT	PART HISTORY	SCR CLS	DATE CODE	FAILURE ANALYSIS / CORRECTIVE ACTION			SYSTEM / EQUIPMENT	PART HISTORY	SCR CLS	DATE CODE	FAILURE ANALYSIS / CORRECTIVE ACTION

DEVICE SECTION

HYBRID MICROCIRCUIT
RELIABILITY DATA

MANUFACTURER: CIRCUIT TECHNOLOGY INC. FUNCTIONAL CATEGORY: DIGITAL

TECHNOLOGY: THICK FILM DEVICE FUNCTION: TIMING LOGIC

ENTRY NO.	PKG/ NO. PINS	SIZE OP TEMP	PKG MFG	PKG SEAL	SUBSTR MTL/ BOND	SUBSTR SIZE	NO. COND LYR	SUBSTR METAL #BONDS	IC NO./ TYPE	IC CHP ATCH/ INTERCON	TRANSISTOR NO./ TYPE	TRANSISTOR CHP ATCH/ INTERCON	DIODE NO./ TYPE	DIODE CHP ATCH/ INTERCON	CAPACITOR NO./ TYPE	CAPACITOR CHP ATCH/ INTERCON	RESISTOR NO./ TYPE	RESISTOR CHP ATCH/ INTERCON	RES TOL (%)	ELMT ATCH/ INTERCON NO./ TYPE
35	FPM1 32	TO-87 -55/ 125C		Weld	Header N/A		1	AuCond 128	AuCond 12 N/R	Eutect AuWire	0		0		0		0			

LIFE / ENVIRONMENTAL EXPERIENCE

DATA SRCE NO.	SCR CLS	TST SRC	TEST TYP/ APP ENV	STR LVL/ EQP TYPE	TEST STD MTD/COND	NO. TSTD	TEST DUR.	PART HRS.	NO. FLD	FAILURE CLASSIFICATION IND; MODE; MECH; CAUSE (NO. FAILED / EVENT)	% DEF	TEST DATE
V	N	Scr./SSB	VisInsp			31			0		6.45	3/72
			Bake	150C		31	32 Hrs		2	N/R		
			CnstAcc	5KGY₁		29			0			
			TempCyc	N/R								
			GrossLk	Fluoro								
			FineLk	5x10-7 cc/sec								
			Burn-In	70C		29	168 Hrs		0			
			EM	25C		29			0			

REMARKS

MALFUNCTION DATA

SYSTEM / EQUIPMENT	PART HISTORY	SCR CLS	DATE CODE	FAILURE ANALYSIS / CORRECTIVE ACTION

SYSTEM / EQUIPMENT	PART HISTORY	SCR CLS	DATE CODE	FAILURE ANALYSIS / CORRECTIVE ACTION

DEVICE SECTION

MANUFACTURER: CIRCUIT TECHNOLOGY INC.   FUNCTIONAL CATEGORY: DIGITAL

TECHNOLOGY: THICK FILM   DEVICE FUNCTION: STORAGE CONTROL CIRCUIT

RELIABILITY ANALYSIS CENTER

HYBRID MICROCIRCUIT
RELIABILITY DATA

ENTRY NO.	PKG/ NO. PINS	SIZE OP TEMP	PKG MFG	PKG SEAL	SUBSTR MTL/ BOND	SUBSTR SIZE	NO. COND LYR	SUBSTR METAL #BONDS	IC NO./ TYPE	IC CHP ATCH/ INTERCON	TRANSISTOR NO./ TYPE	TRANSISTOR CHP ATCH/ INTERCON	DIODE NO./ TYPE	DIODE CHP ATCH/ INTERCON	CAPACITOR NO./ TYPE	CAPACITOR CHP ATCH/ INTERCON	RESISTOR NO./ TYPE	RESISTOR CHP ATCH/ INTERCON	RES TOL (%)	ELMT ATCH/ INTERCON NO./ TYPE
36	P-InLn 32	1.00x 1.00 70/ 100C		N/A	Al_2O_3/ Be O	1.00x 1.00	1	AuCond N/R	15 JKFF (6) 8 Gate (9)	Eutect AuWire	0		0		0		0			

LIFE / ENVIRONMENTAL EXPERIENCE

DATA SRCE NO.	SCR CLS	TST SRC	TEST TYP/ APP ENV	STR LVL/ EQP TYPE	TEST STD MTD/COND	NO. TSTD	TEST DUR.	PART HRS.	NO. FLD	FAILURE CLASSIFICATION IND; MODE; MECH; CAUSE (NO. FAILED / EVENT)	% DEF	TEST DATE	REMARKS
V	N	Scr/SSB	VisInsp	150C		18			2	N/R	11.1	1/72	
			Bake	20KGY		16	50 Hrs	800	0				
			CnstAcc				10 Cyc						
			TempCyc	-55/85C									
			GrossLk	10/5 min									
			FineLk	Fluoro $5x10^{-7}$ cc/sec		16			1	N/R	6.25		
			Burn-In	70C		15	168 Hrs	2520	2	N/R	13.3		
			EM	25C		15							

MALFUNCTION DATA

SYSTEM / EQUIPMENT	PART HISTORY	SCR CLS	DATE CODE	FAILURE ANALYSIS / CORRECTIVE ACTION	SYSTEM / EQUIPMENT	PART HISTORY	SCR CLS	DATE CODE	FAILURE ANALYSIS / CORRECTIVE ACTION

PAGE 60

DEVICE SECTION

MANUFACTURER: CIRCUIT TECHNOLOGY INC.   **FUNCTIONAL CATEGORY:** LINEAR

TECHNOLOGY: THICK FILM   **DEVICE FUNCTION:** MIC CURRENT AMPLIFIER

HYBRID MICROCIRCUIT
RELIABILITY DATA

ENTRY NO.	PKG/ NO. PINS	SIZE OP TEMP	PKG MFG	PKG SEAL	SUBSTR MTL/ BOND	SUBSTR SIZE	NO. COND LYR	SUBSTR METAL #BONDS	IC NO./TYPE	IC CHP ATCH/INTERCON	TRANSISTOR NO./TYPE	TRANSISTOR CHP ATCH/INTERCON	DIODE NO./TYPE	DIODE CHP ATCH/INTERCON	CAPACITOR NO./TYPE	CAPACITOR CHP ATCH/INTERCON	RESISTOR NO./TYPE	RESISTOR CHP ATCH/INTERCON	RES TOL (%)	NO./TYPE	ELM ATCH/INTERCON
37	Can 10	TO-5 -55/ 125C		Weld	Al_2O_3/ BeO	.35D	1	AuCond 14	0		4 N/R	Eutect AuWire	0		0		2 Cermet	Fired AuCond	± 10		

LIFE / ENVIRONMENTAL EXPERIENCE

DATA SRCE	SCR CLS	TST SRC	TEST TYP/ APP ENV	STR LVL/ EQP TYPE	TEST STD MTD/COND	NO. TSTD	TEST DUR.	PART HRS.	NO. FLD	FAILURE CLASSIFICATION IND; MODE; MECH; CAUSE (NO. FAILED / EVENT)	% DEF	TEST DATE
V	N	Scy/SSB	VisInsp									2/72
			TempCyc	-65/150C 5/10 min		70	10 Cyc		0			
			CnstAcc	20KGY								
			GrossLk	Fluoro								
			FineLk	5×10^{-8} cc/sec								
			Burn-In	125C		70	168 Hrs	11760	2	N/R	2.86	
			EM	25C		70						

MALFUNCTION DATA

SYSTEM / EQUIPMENT	PART HISTORY	SCR CLS	DATE CODE	FAILURE ANALYSIS / CORRECTIVE ACTION	SYSTEM / EQUIPMENT	PART HISTORY	SCR CLS	DATE CODE	FAILURE ANALYSIS / CORRECTIVE ACTION

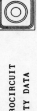
DEVICE SECTION

MANUFACTURER: CIRCUIT TECHNOLOGY INC.

TECHNOLOGY: THICK FILM

FUNCTIONAL CATEGORY: LINEAR

DEVICE FUNCTION: VOLTAGE REGULATOR

ENTRY NO.	PKG/ NO. PINS	SIZE OP TEMP	PKG SEAL	SUBSTR MTL/ BOND	SUBSTR SIZE	NO. COND LYR	SUBSTR METAL #BONDS	IC NO./ TYPE	IC CHP ATCH/ INTERCON	TRANSISTOR NO./ TYPE	TRANSISTOR CHP ATCH/ INTERCON	DIODE NO./ TYPE	DIODE CHP ATCH/ INTERCON	CAPACITOR NO./ TYPE	CAPACITOR CHP ATCH/ INTERCON	RESISTOR NO./ TYPE	RESISTOR CHP ATCH/ INTERCON	RES TOL (%)	ELMT ATCH/ INTERCON NO./ TYPE
38	Can 10	TO-5 -55/ 125C	Weld	Al$_2$O$_3$ BeO	.35D	1	AuCond N/R	0		4 N/R	Eutect AuWire	0		0		3 Cermet	Fixed AuCond	$\pm$10	

LIFE / ENVIRONMENTAL EXPERIENCE

DATA SRCE	SCR CLS	TST SRC	TEST TYP/ APP ENV	STR LVL/ EQP TYPE	TEST STD MTD/COND	NO. TSTD	TEST DUR.	PART HRS.	NO. FLD	FAILURE CLASSIFICATION IND; MODE; MECH; CAUSE (NO. FAILED / EVENT)	% DEF	TEST DATE	REMARKS
V	N	Scr/SSD	TempCyc	-65/150C 30/30 min	MS750 1051	29			0			2/71	
			ThrmShk	0/100C	MS750 1056								
			GrossLk	FC-43	MS202 112A								
			MechShk	125C 1.5KG	MS750 2010		.5 msec						
			VbVrFq	4 AXES .1/2KHZ	MS750 2016								
			CnstAcc	3 AXES 20KG X$_1$X$_2$	MS750 2006	29			0				
V		SSD Lab	StgLife	150C		44	1000 Hrs	44000	0				
V		SSD Lab	OpCnst	125C		44	1000 Hrs	44000	0				

MALFUNCTION DATA

SYSTEM / EQUIPMENT	PART HISTORY	SCR CLS	DATE CODE	FAILURE ANALYSIS / CORRECTIVE ACTION	SYSTEM / EQUIPMENT	PART HISTORY	SCR CLS	DATE CODE	FAILURE ANALYSIS / CORRECTIVE ACTION

DEVICE SECTION

MANUFACTURER: CIRCUIT TECHNOLOGY INC.   FUNCTIONAL CATEGORY: LINEAR

DEVICE FUNCTION: IF AMPLIFIER

TECHNOLOGY: THICK FILM

HYBRID MICROCIRCUIT
RELIABILITY DATA

RELIABILITY ANALYSIS CENTER

ENTRY NO.	PKG/ NO. PINS	SIZE OP TEMP	PKG MFG	PKG SEAL	SUBSTR MTL/ BOND	SUBSTR SIZE	NO. COND LYR	SUBSTR METAL #BONDS	IC NO./ TYPE	IC CHP ATCH/ INTERCON	TRANSISTOR NO./ TYPE	TRANSISTOR CHP ATCH/ INTERCON	DIODE NO./ TYPE	DIODE CHP ATCH/ INTERCON	CAPACITOR NO./ TYPE	CAPACITOR CHP ATCH/ INTERCON	RESISTOR NO./ TYPE	RESISTOR CHP ATCH/ INTERCON	RES TOL (%)	ELM ATCH/ INTERCON NO./ TYPE
39	Can 10	TO-5 -55/ 125C		Weld	Header	N/A	1	Kov/Au N/R	0		2 N/R	Eutect AuWire	2 N/R	Eutect AuWire	1 Ta	Epoxy AuCond	0			

LIFE / ENVIRONMENTAL EXPERIENCE

DATA SRCE	SCR CLS	TST SRC	TEST TYP/ APP ENV	STR LVL/ EQP TYPE	TEST STD MTD/COND	NO. TSTD	TEST DUR.	PART HRS.	NO. FLD	FAILURE CLASSIFICATION IND; MODE; MECH; CAUSE (NO. FAILED / EVENT)	% DEF	TEST DATE	REMARKS
V	N	Scr/B	VisInsp			396		18912	2	N/R	0.51	3/73	
			Bake	150C		394	48 Hrs		0				
			TempCyc	-65/150C 5/10 min			5 Cyc						
			CnstAcc	20KGY									
			FineLk	5x10^{-7} cc/sec					4				
			GrossLk	Fluoro		394							
			EM	25C		390	168 Hrs		67	N/R			
			Burn-In	125C		390							
			EM	25C									

MALFUNCTION DATA

SYSTEM / EQUIPMENT	PART HISTORY	SCR CLS	DATE CODE	FAILURE ANALYSIS / CORRECTIVE ACTION		SYSTEM / EQUIPMENT	PART HISTORY	SCR CLS	DATE CODE	FAILURE ANALYSIS / CORRECTIVE ACTION

DEVICE SECTION

MANUFACTURER: CIRCUIT TECHNOLOGY INC. **FUNCTIONAL CATEGORY:** LINEAR

DEVICE FUNCTION: 31 MHZ LIMITER

TECHNOLOGY: THICK FILM

ENTRY NO.	PKG/ NO. PINS	SIZE OP TEMP	PKG SEAL	PKG MFG	SUBSTR MTL/ BOND	SUBSTR SIZE	NO. COND LYR	SUBSTR METAL #BONDS	IC NO./TYPE	IC CHP ATCH/ INTERCON	TRANSISTOR NO./TYPE	TRANSISTOR CHP ATCH/ INTERCON	DIODE NO./TYPE	DIODE CHP ATCH/ INTERCON	CAPACITOR NO./TYPE	CAPACITOR CHP ATCH/ INTERCON	RESISTOR NO./TYPE	RESISTOR CHP ATCH/ INTERCON	RES TOL (%)	ELMT ATCH/ INTERCON
40	Can 12	TO-8 -55/ 125C	Weld			N/A	N/A	AuCond 17	0		3 N/R	Eutect AuWire	4 Ta	Solder AuWire	4 Ta	Solder AuCond	4 Cermet	Fired AuCond	±10	

LIFE / ENVIRONMENTAL EXPERIENCE

DATA SRCE	SCR CLS	TST SRC	TEST TYP/ APP ENV	STR LVL/ EQP TYPE	TEST STD MTD/COND	NO. TSTD	TEST DUR.	PART HRS.	NO. FLD	FAILURE CLASSIFICATION IND; MODE; MECH; CAUSE (NO. FAILED / EVENT)	% DEF	TEST DATE	REMARKS
V	N	Scr/SSA	VisInsp			207			43	N/R	20.8	3/73	
			Bake	150C		164	32 Hrs	5248	0				
			ThrmShk	-65/150C 5/10 min									
			CnstAcc	10KGY $_1$									
			FineLk	1×10^{-8} cc/sec		164			6	N/R	3.66		
			GrossLk	Fluoro		158			0				
			EM	25C		158			4	N/R			
			Burn-In	125C		154	240 Hrs		3	N/R			
			EM	25C		154			0				
			X-Ray			151			0				
			VisInsp			151							

MALFUNCTION DATA

SYSTEM/ EQUIPMENT	PART HISTORY	SCR CLS	DATE CODE	FAILURE ANALYSIS / CORRECTIVE ACTION

SYSTEM/ EQUIPMENT	PART HISTORY	SCR CLS	DATE CODE	FAILURE ANALYSIS / CORRECTIVE ACTION

DEVICE SECTION

MANUFACTURER: CIRCUIT TECHNOLOGY INC. FUNCTIONAL CATEGORY: LINEAR

TECHNOLOGY: THICK FILM DEVICE FUNCTION: OPERATIONAL AMPLIFIER

HYBRID MICROCIRCUIT
RELIABILITY DATA

RELIABILITY ANALYSIS CENTER

ENTRY NO.	SCR CLS	PKG/ NO. PINS	SIZE OP TEMP	PKG MFG	PKG SEAL	SUBSTR MTL/ BOND	SUBSTR SIZE	NO. COND LYR	SUBSTR METAL #BONDS	IC NO./ TYPE	IC CHP ATCH/ INTERCON	TRANSISTOR NO./ TYPE	TRANSISTOR CHP ATCH/ INTERCON	DIODE NO./ TYPE	DIODE CHP ATCH/ INTERCON	CAPACITOR NO./ TYPE	CAPACITOR CHP ATCH/ INTERCON	RESISTOR NO./ TYPE	RESISTOR CHP ATCH/ INTERCON	RES TOL (%)	ELM ATCH/ INTERCON NO./ TYPE
41		Can 12	TO-8 -55/ 125C		Weld	Header	N/A	1	Kov/Au 19	0		6 N/R	Eutect AuWire	1 N/R	Eutect AuWire	0		5 Thick	Eutect AuWire	N/R	

LIFE / ENVIRONMENTAL EXPERIENCE

DATA SRCE CLS	SCR CLS	TST SRC	TEST TYP/ APP ENV	STR LVL/ EQP TYPE	TEST STD MTD/COND	NO. TSTD	TEST DUR.	PART HRS.	NO. FLD	FAILURE CLASSIFICATION IND; MODE; MECH; CAUSE (NO. FAILED / EVENT)	% DEF	TEST DATE
V	N	Scr/SSC	VisInsp			192			5	N/R	2.60	4/73
			Bake	150C		187	60 Hrs	11220	0			
			TempCyc	-65/150C			10 Cyc					
			CnstAcc	5/10 min 20KGY								
			FineLk	5x10-8 cc/sec		187			2	N/R	1.07	
			GrossLk	Fluoro		185			6	N/R	3.24	
			Burn-In	125C		179	168 Hrs	30072	5	N/R	2.80	
			EM	25C								

FAILURE ANALYSIS / CORRECTIVE ACTION	PART HISTORY	SCR CLS	DATE CODE	SYSTEM / EQUIPMENT	PART HISTORY	SCR CLS	DATE CODE	FAILURE ANALYSIS / CORRECTIVE ACTION

MALFUNCTION DATA

SYSTEM / EQUIPMENT	PART HISTORY	SCR CLS	DATE CODE	FAILURE ANALYSIS / CORRECTIVE ACTION

DEVICE SECTION

MANUFACTURER: CIRCUIT TECHNOLOGY INC. FUNCTIONAL CATEGORY: LINEAR

DEVICE FUNCTION: MIC CURRENT AMPLIFIER

TECHNOLOGY: THICK FILM

ENTRY NO.	PKG/ NO. PINS	SIZE OP TEMP	PKG MFG	PKG SEAL	SUBSTR MTL/ BOND	SUBSTR SIZE	NO. COND LYR	SUBSTR METAL #BONDS	IC NO./ TYPE	IC CHP ATCH/ INTERCON	TRANSISTOR NO./ TYPE	TRANSISTOR CHP ATCH/ INTERCON	DIODE NO./ TYPE	DIODE CHP ATCH/ INTERCON	CAPACITOR NO./ TYPE	CAPACITOR CHP ATCH/ INTERCON	RESISTOR NO./ TYPE	RESISTOR CHP ATCH/ INTERCON	RES TOL (%)	ELMT ATCH/ INTERCON NO./ TYPE
42	FPM1 14	TO-87 -55/ 125C		Weld	Header N/A	N/A	1	AuCond N/R	0		4 N/R	Eutect AuWire	0		0		0			

LIFE / ENVIRONMENTAL EXPERIENCE

DATA SRCE	SCR CLS	TST SRC	TEST TYP/ APP ENV	STR LVL/ EQP TYPE	TEST STD MTD/COND	NO. TSTD	TEST DUR.	PART HRS.	NO. FLD	FAILURE CLASSIFICATION IND; MODE; MECH; CAUSE (NO. FAILED / EVENT)	% DEF	TEST DATE	REMARKS
V	N	Scr/B	VisInsp	150C		833	32 Hrs		5	N/R	0.60	3/73	
			Bake	-65/150C		828	10 Cyc		0				
			TempCyc	5/10 min 20KGY									
			CnstAcc	1		828			1	N/R	0.12		
			FineLk	5x10⁻⁸ cc/sec		827			7	N/R	0.85		
			GrossLk	Fluoro		820			16	N/R	1.95		
			EM	25C		804			43	N/R	5.35		
			Burn-In	125C		761	168 Hrs		0	N/R	3.15		
			EM			761			24	N/R	0.27		
			VisInsp			737			2	N/R			

MALFUNCTION DATA

SYSTEM / EQUIPMENT	PART HISTORY	SCR CLS	DATE CODE	FAILURE ANALYSIS / CORRECTIVE ACTION

SYSTEM / EQUIPMENT	PART HISTORY	SCR CLS	DATE CODE	FAILURE ANALYSIS / CORRECTIVE ACTION

DEVICE SECTION

MANUFACTURER: CIRCUIT TECHNOLOGY INC.　　**FUNCTIONAL CATEGORY:** LINEAR

TECHNOLOGY: THICK FILM　　**DEVICE FUNCTION:** 20 KHZ PREAMPLIFIER

HYBRID MICROCIRCUIT
RELIABILITY DATA

RELIABILITY ANALYSIS CENTER

ENTRY NO.	SCR CLS	PKG/ NO. PINS	SIZE OP TEMP	PKG MFG	PKG SEAL	SUBSTR MTL/ BOND	SUBSTR SIZE	NO. COND LYR	SUBSTR METAL #BONDS	IC NO./TYPE	IC CHP ATCH/ INTERCON	TRANSISTOR NO./TYPE	TRANSISTOR CHP ATCH/ INTERCON	DIODE NO./TYPE	DIODE CHP ATCH/ INTERCON	CAPACITOR NO./TYPE	CAPACITOR CHP ATCH/ INTERCON	RESISTOR NO./TYPE	RESISTOR CHP ATCH/ INTERCON	RES TOL (%)	ELMT ATCH/ INTERCON
43		FPM1 14	TO-87 -55/ 125C		Weld	Header	N/A	1	AuCond 21	0		6 N/R	Eutect AuWire	0		SiO 2 BaTi 1 1	Epoxy AuCond	10 Thick	Eutect AuCond	N/R	

LIFE / ENVIRONMENTAL EXPERIENCE

DATA SRCE	SCR CLS	TST SRC	TEST TYP/ APP ENV	STR LVL/ EQP TYPE	TEST STD MTD/COND	NO. TSTD	TEST DUR.	PART HRS.	NO. FLD	FAILURE CLASSIFICATION IND; MODE; MECH; CAUSE (NO. FAILED / EVENT)	% DEF	TEST DATE
V	N	Scr/B	VisInsp			2389			215	N/R	9.0	4/73
			Bake	125C		2174	48 Hrs	1.04E5	0			
			TempCyc	-65/150C 5/10 min			10 Cyc					
			CnstAcc	20KGY 1								
			FineLk	5x10^{-8} cc/sec		2174			63	N/R	2.89	
			GrossLk	Fluoro		2111			90	N/R	4.26	
			EM	25C		2021			101	N/R	4.99	
			Burn-In	105C		1920	250 Hrs		0			
			EM	25C		1920			33	N/R	1.72	
			VisInsp			1887			13		0.69	
V	N	Scr/SSB	VisInsp			950			19	N/R	2.00	1/72
			Bake	150C		931	24 Hrs	22344	0			
			TempCyc	-65/150C 5/10 min								
			CnstAcc	20KGY 1								
			FineLk	5x10^{-8} cc/sec		931			2	N/R	0.21	
			Gross Lk	Fluoro		929			28	N/R	3.01	

MALFUNCTION DATA

SYSTEM / EQUIPMENT	PART HISTORY	SCR CLS	DATE CODE	FAILURE ANALYSIS / CORRECTIVE ACTION	SYSTEM / EQUIPMENT	PART HISTORY	SCR CLS	DATE CODE	FAILURE ANALYSIS / CORRECTIVE ACTION

DEVICE SECTION

MANUFACTURER: CIRCUIT TECHNOLOGY INC. FUNCTIONAL CATEGORY: LINEAR

TECHNOLOGY: THICK FILM DEVICE FUNCTION: 20 KHZ PRF PREAMPLIFIER

RELIABILITY
ANALYSIS
CENTER

HYBRID MICROCIRCUIT
RELIABILITY DATA

ENTRY NO.	PKG/ NO. PINS	SIZE OP TEMP	PKG MFG	PKG SEAL	SUBSTR MTL/ BOND	SUBSTR SIZE	NO. COND LYR	SUBSTR METAL	IC NO./ TYPE	IC CHP ATCH/ INTERCON	TRANSISTOR NO./ TYPE	TRANSISTOR CHP ATCH/ INTERCON	DIODE NO./ TYPE	DIODE CHP ATCH/ INTERCON	CAPACITOR NO./ TYPE	CAPACITOR CHP ATCH/ INTERCON	RESISTOR NO./ TYPE	RESISTOR CHP ATCH/ INTERCON	RES TOL (%)	ELMT ATCH/ INTERCON NO./ TYPE
43 (Contd)																				

LIFE / ENVIRONMENTAL EXPERIENCE

DATA SRCE	SCR CLS	TST SRC	TEST TYP/ APP ENV	STR LVL/ EQP TYPE	TEST STD MTD/COND	NO. TSTD	TEST DUR.	PART HRS.	NO. FLD	FAILURE CLASSIFICATION IND; MODE; MECH; CAUSE (NO. FAILED / EVENT)	% DEF	TEST DATE	REMARKS
		EM Burn-In	25C			901	250 Hrs		28	N/R	3.11		
			105C			873			3	N/R	0.34		
		EM VisInsp	25C			870			27	N/R	3.10		
						843			1	N/R	0.12		
V	SSD	Env	TempCyc	−65/150C		11	5 Cyc		0			8/70	
			ThrmShk	0/100C			5 Cyc						
			FineLk	1x10−6			4 Hrs						
V	SSD	Env	GrossLk	60 psia Fluoro		11			0			8/70	
			CnstAcc	20KGY₁Y₂		11			0				
			MechShk	1.5KGY₁Y₂									
			VibFtg	20GX,Y₁Y₂									
				50 HZ		11			0				
			VbVrFq	.1/2KHZ X₁Y₁Z₁									
V	SSD	Env	SltAtmos	35C 40gm/m²	MS750 1041.1	26			0			8/70	
V	SSD	Env	InsRes			11			0			8/70	
V	SSD	Lab	LdFtg			11			0			8/70	
V	SSD	Lab	StgLife	150C		11	1000 Hrs	11000	0			8/70	
V	SSD	Lab	OpCnst	125C		11	1000 Hrs	11000	0			8/70	

MALFUNCTION DATA

SYSTEM / EQUIPMENT	PART HISTORY	SCR CLS	DATE CODE	FAILURE ANALYSIS / CORRECTIVE ACTION

SYSTEM / EQUIPMENT	PART HISTORY	SCR CLS	DATE CODE	FAILURE ANALYSIS / CORRECTIVE ACTION

DEVICE SECTION

MANUFACTURER: CIRCUIT TECHNOLOGY INC. FUNCTIONAL CATEGORY: LINEAR

DEVICE FUNCTION: OPERATIONAL AMPLIFIER

TECHNOLOGY: THICK FILM

ENTRY NO.	PKG/ NO. PINS	SIZE OP TEMP	PKG MFG	PKG SEAL	SUBSTR MTL/ BOND	SUBSTR SIZE	NO. COND LYR	SUBSTR METAL #BONDS	IC		TRANSISTOR		DIODE		CAPACITOR		RESISTOR		RES TOL (%)	ELMT ATCH/ INTERCON
									NO./ TYPE	CHP ATCH/ INTERCON	NO./ TYPE	CHP ATCH/ INTERCON	NO./ TYPE	CHP ATCH/ INTERCON	NO./ TYPE	CHP ATCH/ INTERCON	NO./ TYPE	CHP ATCH/ INTERCON		NO./ TYPE
44	FPM1 14	TO-87 -55/ 125C		Weld	Al₂O₃/ B₂O Eutect	N/A	1	AuCond 29	0		7 N/R	Eutect. AuWire	0		1 Ta	Epoxy AuCond	5 Cermet	Fired AuCond	±10	

LIFE / ENVIRONMENTAL EXPERIENCE

DATA SRCE NO.	SCR CLS	TST SRC	TEST TYP/ APP ENV	STR LVL/ EQP TYPE	TEST STD MTD/COND	NO. TSTD	TEST DUR.	PART HRS.	NO. FLD	FAILURE CLASSIFICATION IND; MODE; MECH; CAUSE (NO. FAILED / EVENT)	% DEF	TEST DATE
V	N	Scr/C	VisInsp			1898			23		1.21	4//73
			Temp TempCyc	150C -65/150C 5/10 min	100 Hrs 10 Cyc	1875		1.88E5	0	N/R		
			CnstAcc	20KGY₁		1875			2	N/R	0.11	
			FineLk	1x10⁻⁶ cc/sec		1873			23	N/R	1.23	
			GrossLk	Fluoro		1850			153	N/R	8.27	
			EM	25C		1697			90	N/R	5.30	
			VisInsp			1607			9	N/R	0.56	

MALFUNCTION DATA

SYSTEM / EQUIPMENT	PART HISTORY	SCR CLS	DATE CODE	FAILURE ANALYSIS / CORRECTIVE ACTION	SYSTEM / EQUIPMENT	PART HISTORY	SCR CLS	DATE CODE	FAILURE ANALYSIS / CORRECTIVE ACTION

DEVICE SECTION

MANUFACTURER: CIRCUIT TECHNOLOGY INC.
TECHNOLOGY: THICK FILM

FUNCTIONAL CATEGORY: LINEAR
DEVICE FUNCTION: TRIPLE MODULATOR

HYBRID MICROCIRCUIT RELIABILITY DATA

 RELIABILITY ANALYSIS CENTER

ENTRY NO.	PKG/NO. PINS	SIZE OP TEMP	PKG MFG	PKG SEAL	SUBSTR MTL/BOND	SUBSTR SIZE	NO. COND LYR	SUBSTR METAL #BONDS	IC NO./TYPE	IC CHP ATCH/INTERCON	TRANSISTOR NO./TYPE	TRANSISTOR CHP ATCH/INTERCON	DIODE NO./TYPE	DIODE CHP ATCH/INTERCON	CAPACITOR NO./TYPE	CAPACITOR CHP ATCH/INTERCON	RESISTOR NO./TYPE	RESISTOR CHP ATCH/INTERCON	RES TOL (%)	ELMT ATCH/INTERCON NO./TYPE
45	CM-DIP 16	TO-116 -55/125C		Weld	Al_2O_3/BeO Eutect	.20x.20	1	AuCond 71	0		15 N/R	Eutect AuWire	15 N/R	Eutect AuWire	3 Ta	Solder AuCond	18 Cermet	Fired AuCond	±10	

LIFE / ENVIRONMENTAL EXPERIENCE

DATA SRCE	SCR CLS	TST SRC	TEST TYP/APP ENV	STR LVL/EQP TYPE	TEST STD MTD/COND	NO. TSTD	TEST DUR.	PART HRS.	NO. FLD	FAILURE CLASSIFICATION IND; MODE; MECH; CAUSE (NO. FAILED / EVENT)	% DEF	TEST DATE	REMARKS
V	N	Scr / SSB	VisInsp			141			3	N/R	2.13	3/73	
			Bake	150C		138	32 Hrs		0				
			TempCyc	-55/125C 5/10 min									
			CnstAcc	5KGY1									
			FineLk	1×10^{-7} cc/sec		138			1	N/R	0.72		
			GrossLk	Fluoro		137			11	N/R	8.03		
			EM	25C		126			6	N/R	4.76		
			Burn-In	110C		120	168 Hrs		0				
			EM	25C		120			7	Spec Reject	5.83		
			VisInsp			113			0				

MALFUNCTION DATA

PART HISTORY	SCR CLS	DATE CODE	FAILURE ANALYSIS / CORRECTIVE ACTION	SYSTEM / EQUIPMENT	PART HISTORY	SCR CLS	DATE CODE	FAILURE ANALYSIS / CORRECTIVE ACTION

DEVICE SECTION

MANUFACTURER: CIRCUIT TECHNOLOGY INC.   FUNCTIONAL CATEGORY: LINEAR

TECHNOLOGY: THICK FILM   DEVICE FUNCTION: DUAL LEVEL DETECTOR

ENTRY NO.	PKG/NO. PINS	SIZE OP TEMP	PKG MFG	PKG SEAL	SUBSTR MTL/BOND	SUBSTR SIZE	NO. COND LYR	SUBSTR METAL #BONDS	IC NO./TYPE	IC CHP ATCH/INTERCON	TRANSISTOR NO./TYPE	TRANSISTOR CHP ATCH/INTERCON	DIODE NO./TYPE	DIODE CHP ATCH/INTERCON	CAPACITOR NO./TYPE	CAPACITOR CHP ATCH/INTERCON	RESISTOR NO./TYPE	RESISTOR CHP ATCH/INTERCON	RES TOL (%)	ELMT ATCH/INTERCON NO./TYPE
46	FPM1 22	TO-87 -55/125C		Weld	Al_2O_3	.63x .63	1	AuCond 31	2 N/R	Eutect AuWire	0		0		0		1 Thick	Fired AuCond	N/R	

LIFE / ENVIRONMENTAL EXPERIENCE

DATA SRCE	SCR CLS	TST SRC	TEST TYP/APP ENV	STR LVL/EQP TYPE	TEST STD MTD/COND	NO. TSTD	TEST DUR.	PART HRS.	NO. FLD	FAILURE CLASSIFICATION IND; MODE; MECH; CAUSE (NO. FAILED / EVENT)	% DEF	TEST DATE	REMARKS
V	N	Scr/B	VisInsp	150C		307	32 Hrs 10 Cyc	9696	4	N/R	1.30	3/73	
			Bake	-65/150C		303			0				
			TempCyc	5/10 min									
			CnstAcc	30KGY									
			FineLk	1×10^{-7} cc/sec									
			GrossLk	Fluoro		303			6	N/R	1.98		
			VisInsp			297			0	N/R	9.76		
			EM	25C		268	168 Hrs		29				
			Burn-In	125C		268			0	N/R	4.48		
			EM	25C		256			12	N/R	0.39		
			VisInsp						1				

MALFUNCTION DATA

SYSTEM / EQUIPMENT	PART HISTORY	SCR CLS	DATE CODE	FAILURE ANALYSIS / CORRECTIVE ACTION

SYSTEM / EQUIPMENT	PART HISTORY	SCR CLS	DATE CODE	FAILURE ANALYSIS / CORRECTIVE ACTION

DEVICE SECTION

MANUFACTURER: CIRCUIT TECHNOLOGY INC. FUNCTIONAL CATEGORY: LINEAR

TECHNOLOGY: THICK FILM DEVICE FUNCTION: RESTORING AMPLIFIER

RELIABILITY ANALYSIS CENTER

HYBRID MICROCIRCUIT
RELIABILITY DATA

ENTRY NO.	PKG/ NO. PINS	SIZE OP TEMP	PKG MFG	PKG SEAL	SUBSTR MTL/ BOND	SUBSTR SIZE	NO. COND LYR	SUBSTR METAL #BONDS	IC NO./ TYPE	IC CHP ATCH/ INTERCON	TRANSISTOR NO./ TYPE	TRANSISTOR CHP ATCH/ INTERCON	DIODE NO./ TYPE	DIODE CHP ATCH/ INTERCON	CAPACITOR NO./ TYPE	CAPACITOR CHP ATCH/ INTERCON	RESISTOR NO./ TYPE	RESISTOR CHP ATCH/ INTERCON	RES TOL (%)	ELMT ATCH/ INTERCON NO./ TYPE
47	FPM1 22	TO-87 -55/ 125C		Weld	Al_2O_3/ BeO Eutect	.35x .60	1	AuCond 48	3 N/R	Eutect AuWire	3 N/R	Eutect AuWire	0		10 Ta	Solder AuCond	17 Cermet	Fired AuCond	±10	

LIFE / ENVIRONMENTAL EXPERIENCE

DATA SRCE CLS	SCR CLS	TST SRC	TEST TYP/ APP ENV	STR LVL/ EQP TYPE	TEST STD MTD/COND	NO. TSTD	TEST DUR.	PART HRS.	NO. FLD	FAILURE CLASSIFICATION IND; MODE; MECH; CAUSE (NO. FAILED / EVENT)	% DEF	TEST DATE	REMARKS
V	N	Scr/B	VisInsp	150C		306			7	N/R		4/73	
			Bake	-55/125C		299	32 Hrs		0		2.29		
			TempCyc	5/10 min			5 Cyc						
			CnstAcc	5KGY$_1$									
			FineLk	$5x10^{-8}$ cc/sec		299			11	N/R	3.68		
			GrossLk	Fluoro		288			16	N/R			
			EM	25C		272			13	N/R	5.56		
			Burn-In	125C		259	168 Hrs		0		4.78		
			EM	25C		259			18	N/R	6.95		
			VisInsp			241			0				

MALFUNCTION DATA

SYSTEM / EQUIPMENT	PART HISTORY	SCR CLS	DATE CODE	FAILURE ANALYSIS / CORRECTIVE ACTION

SYSTEM / EQUIPMENT	PART HISTORY	SCR CLS	DATE CODE	FAILURE ANALYSIS / CORRECTIVE ACTION

RELIABILITY ANALYSIS CENTER

HYBRID MICROCIRCUIT
RELIABILITY DATA

DEVICE SECTION

MANUFACTURER: CIRCUIT TECHNOLOGY INC.   FUNCTIONAL CATEGORY: LINEAR

TECHNOLOGY: THICK FILM   DEVICE FUNCTION: BUFFER DEMODULATOR

ENTRY NO.	PKG/ NO. PINS	SIZE OP TEMP	PKG MFG	PKG SEAL	SUBSTR MTL/ BOND	SUBSTR SIZE	NO. COND LYR	SUBSTR METAL #BONDS	IC NO./ TYPE	IC CHP ATCH/ INTERCON	TRANSISTOR NO./ TYPE	TRANSISTOR CHP ATCH/ INTERCON	DIODE NO./ TYPE	DIODE CHP ATCH/ INTERCON	CAPACITOR NO./ TYPE	CAPACITOR CHP ATCH/ INTERCON	RESISTOR NO./ TYPE	RESISTOR CHP ATCH/ INTERCON	RES TOL (%)	ELMT ATCH/ INTERCON NO./ TYPE
48	FPM1 22	TO-87 -55/ 125C		Weld	Al₂O₃	.63x .63	1	AuCond. 49	4 OpAmp	Eutect AuWire	4 N/R	Eutect AuWire	0		0		26 Thick	Fired AuCond	N/R	

LIFE / ENVIRONMENTAL EXPERIENCE

DATA SRCE CLS	SCR CLS	TST SRC	TEST TYP/ APP ENV	STR LVL/ EQP TYPE	SUBSTR SIZE	NO. COND LYR	NO. TSTD	TEST DUR.	PART HRS.	NO. FLD	FAILURE CLASSIFICATION IND; MODE; MECH; CAUSE; (NO. FAILED / EVENT)	% DEF	TEST DATE	REMARKS
V	N	Scr/SSD	VisInsp BdStr Temp				60			0				
			Temp	125C			60	168 Hrs	10080	0			2/72	
V	N	Scr/B	VisIsp				369			18	N/R			
			Bake	150C			351	24 Hrs	8424	0		4.88	3/73	
			TempCyc	-65/125C				10 Cyc						
			CnstAcc	5/10 min 30KG·Y₁										
			FineLk	5x10⁻⁷ cc/sec			351			12	N/R	4.78		
			GrossLk	Fluoro			339			17	N/R	5.01		
			VisInsp				322			0				
			EM	25C			322			26	N/R	8.07		
			Burn-In	125C			296	168 Hrs		2	Mishandled	0.68		
			EM	25C			294			16	N/R	5.44		
			VisInsp				278			0				
V	N	Scr/SSB	VisInsp				222			0			2/72	
			Bake	150C			222	24 Hrs	5328	0		0.90		
			TempCyc	-65/125C										
			CnstAcc	5/10 min 30KG·Y₁			222			2	N/R			
			FineLk	5x10⁻⁷ cc/sec			220			8	N/R	3.64		

MALFUNCTION DATA

SYSTEM / EQUIPMENT	PART HISTORY	SCR CLS	DATE CODE	FAILURE ANALYSIS / CORRECTIVE ACTION

SYSTEM / EQUIPMENT	PART HISTORY	SCR CLS	DATE CODE	FAILURE ANALYSIS / CORRECTIVE ACTION

DEVICE SECTION

RELIABILITY ANALYSIS CENTER

MANUFACTURER: CIRCUIT TECHNOLOGY INC.   FUNCTIONAL CATEGORY: LINEAR

TECHNOLOGY: THICK FILM   DEVICE FUNCTION: BUFFER DEMODULATOR

HYBRID MICROCIRCUIT
RELIABILITY DATA

ENTRY NO.	PKG/ NO. PINS	SIZE OP TEMP	PKG MFG	PKG SEAL	SUBSTR MTL/ BOND	SUBSTR SIZE	NO. COND LYR	SUBSTR METAL #BONDS	IC				DIODE			TRANSISTOR			CAPACITOR			RESISTOR		RES TOL (%)	ELMT ATCH/ INTERCON
									NO./ TYPE	CHP ATCH/ INTERCON			NO./ TYPE	CHP ATCH/ INTERCON		NO./ TYPE	CHP ATCH/ INTERCON		NO./ TYPE	CHP ATCH/ INTERCON		NO./ TYPE	CHP ATCH/ INTERCON		NO./ TYPE
48 (Cntd)																										

LIFE / ENVIRONMENTAL EXPERIENCE (con't)

DATA SRCE	SCR CLS	TST SRC	TEST TYP/ APP ENV	STR LVL/ EQP TYPE	SUBSTR MTL/ BOND	SUBSTR SIZE	NO. COND LYR	TEST STD MTD/COND	NO. TSTD	TEST DUR.	PART HRS.	NO. FLD	FAILURE CLASSIFICATION IND; MODE; MECH; CAUSE (NO. FAILED / EVENT)	% DEF	TEST DATE	REMARKS
			GrossLk	Fluoro					212			4	N/R	1.89		
			VisInsp						208			0				
			EM	25C					196	168 Hrs		12	N/R	5.77		
			Burn-In	125C					196			0				
			EM	25C					190			6	N/R	3.06		
			VisInsp									1	N/R	0.53		

MALFUNCTION DATA

SYSTEM / EQUIPMENT	PART HISTORY	SCR CLS	DATE CODE	FAILURE ANALYSIS / CORRECTIVE ACTION	SYSTEM / EQUIPMENT	PART HISTORY	SCR CLS	DATE CODE	FAILURE ANALYSIS / CORRECTIVE ACTION

PAGE 74

DEVICE SECTION

MANUFACTURER: CIRCUIT TECHNOLOGY INC.   FUNCTIONAL CATEGORY: LINEAR

DEVICE FUNCTION: GAIN TRACK AND HOLD

TECHNOLOGY: THICK FILM

ENTRY NO.	PKG/ NO. PINS	SIZE OP TEMP	SUBSTR MTL/ BOND	SUBSTR SIZE	NO. COND LYR	SUBSTR METAL #BONDS	PKG SEAL	PKG MFG	IC NO./TYPE	IC CHP ATCH/INTERCON	TRANSISTOR NO./TYPE	TRANSISTOR CHP ATCH/INTERCON	DIODE NO./TYPE	DIODE CHP ATCH/INTERCON	CAPACITOR NO./TYPE	CAPACITOR CHP ATCH/INTERCON	RESISTOR NO./TYPE	RESISTOR CHP ATCH/INTERCON	RES TOL (%)	ELM ATCH/INTERCON NO./TYPE
49	FPM1 22	TO-87 -55/125C	Al_2O_3/ B_eO Eutect	.60x .60	1	AuCond 92	Weld		0		31 N/R	Eutect AuWire	2 N/R	Eutect- AuWire	2 Ta	Solder AuCond	25 Cermet	Fired AuCond	±10	

LIFE / ENVIRONMENTAL EXPERIENCE

DATA SRCE CLS	SCR CLS	TST SRC	TEST TYP/ APP ENV	STR LVL/ EQP TYPE	TEST STD MTD/COND	NO. TSTD	TEST DUR.	PART HRS.	NO. FLD	FAILURE CLASSIFICATION IND; MODE; MECH; CAUSE (NO. FAILED / EVENT)	% DEF	TEST DATE
V	N	Scr/B	VisInsp			422			25	N/R	5.92	4/73
			Bake	150C		397	32 Hrs	12704	0			
			TempCyc	-55/125C			10 Cyc					
			CnstAcc	5/10 min 5KGY 1								
			FineLk	1x10^{-7} cc/sec		397			2	N/R	0.50	
			GrossLk	Fluoro		395			12	N/R	3.04	
			EM	25C		383			27	N/R	12.1	
			Burn-In	125C		356	168 Hrs		0			
			EM	125C		356			68	N/R	19.1	
			VisInsp	25C		288			0			

			REMARKS

SYSTEM / EQUIPMENT	PART HISTORY	SCR CLS	DATE CODE	FAILURE ANALYSIS / CORRECTIVE ACTION

MALFUNCTION DATA

SYSTEM / EQUIPMENT	PART HISTORY	SCR CLS	DATE CODE	FAILURE ANALYSIS / CORRECTIVE ACTION

RELIABILITY
ANALYSIS
CENTER

DEVICE SECTION

MANUFACTURER: CIRCUIT TECHNOLOGY INC. **FUNCTIONAL CATEGORY:** LINEAR

TECHNOLOGY: THICK FILM **DEVICE FUNCTION:** VIDEO AMPLIFIER

ENTRY NO.	PKG/ NO. PINS	SIZE OP TEMP	PKG SEAL	PKG MFG	SUBSTR MTL/ BOND	SUBSTR SIZE	NO. COND LYR	SUBSTR METAL #BONDS	IC NO./ TYPE	IC CHP ATCH/ INTERCON	TRANSISTOR NO./ TYPE	TRANSISTOR CHP ATCH/ INTERCON	DIODE NO./ TYPE	DIODE CHP ATCH/ INTERCON	CAPACITOR NO./ TYPE	CAPACITOR CHP ATCH/ INTERCON	RESISTOR NO./ TYPE	RESISTOR CHP ATCH/ INTERCON	RES TOL (%)	ELMT ATCH/ INTERCON NO./ TYPE
50	FPM1 24	TO-87 -55/ 125C	Weld		Al$_2$O$_3$	.63x .63	1	AuCond 22	0		3 N/R	AgEpoxy AuCond	0		0		8 Thick	Fired AuCond	N/R	

LIFE / ENVIRONMENTAL EXPERIENCE

DATA SRCE	SCR CLS	TST SRC	TEST TYP/ APP ENV	STR LVL/ EQP TYPE	TEST STD MTD/COND	NO. TSTD	TEST DUR.	PART HRS.	FAILURE CLASSIFICATION IND; MODE; MECH; CAUSE (NO. FAILED / EVENT) NO. FLD	% DEF	TEST DATE	REMARKS
V	N	Scr/B	VisInsp			125			3			
			Bake	150C		122	48 Hrs	5856	0 N/R	2.40	6/72	
			TempCyc	-65/150C 5/10 min			10 Cyc					
			CnstAcc	20KGY1								
			FineLk	5x10^{-8} cc/sec		122			6	4.92		
			GrossLk	Fluoro		116			0 N/R			
			EM	25C		116			0			
			Burn-In	150C		116			4	3.45		
			EM	25C		112			1 N/R	0.89		
			VisInsp						N/R			

MALFUNCTION DATA

SYSTEM / EQUIPMENT	PART HISTORY	SCR CLS	DATE CODE	FAILURE ANALYSIS / CORRECTIVE ACTION	SYSTEM / EQUIPMENT	PART HISTORY	SCR CLS	DATE CODE	FAILURE ANALYSIS / CORRECTIVE ACTION

DEVICE SECTION

MANUFACTURER: CIRCUIT TECHNOLOGY INC. **FUNCTIONAL CATEGORY:** LINEAR

TECHNOLOGY: THICK FILM **DEVICE FUNCTION:** LOG IF AMPLIFIER

HYBRID MICROCIRCUIT
RELIABILITY DATA

RELIABILITY ANALYSIS CENTER

ENTRY NO.	PKG/ NO. PINS	SIZE OP TEMP	PKG MFG	PKG SEAL	SUBSTR MTL/ BOND	SUBSTR SIZE	NO. COND LYR	SUBSTR METAL #BONDS	IC NO./ TYPE	IC CHP ATCH/ INTERCON	TRANSISTOR NO./ TYPE	TRANSISTOR CHP ATCH/ INTERCON	DIODE NO./ TYPE	DIODE CHP ATCH/ INTERCON	CAPACITOR NO./ TYPE	CAPACITOR CHP ATCH/ INTERCON	RESISTOR NO./ TYPE	RESISTOR CHP ATCH/ INTERCON	RES TOL (%)	ELMT ATCH/ INTERCON NO./ TYPE
51	FPM1 24	TO-87 -55/ 125C		Weld	Al_2O_2	.37x .37	1	AuCond 18	0		1 N/R	Eutect AuWire	0		6 Ta	Solder AuCond	8 Thick	Fired AuCond		

LIFE / ENVIRONMENTAL EXPERIENCE

DATA SRCE CLS	SCR CLS	TST SRC	TEST TYP/ APP ENV	STR LVL/ EQP TYPE	TEST STD MTD/COND	NO. TSTD	TEST DUR.	PART HRS.	NO. FLD	FAILURE CLASSIFICATION IND; MODE; MECH; CAUSE (NO. FAILED / EVENT)	% DEF	TEST DATE
V	N	Scr/SSB	VisInsp	125C		925			22	N/R	2.38	3/73
			Bake	-65/150C		903	48 Hrs	4344	0			
			TempCyc	5/10 min			10 Cyc					
			CnstAcc	20KGY 1		903			2	N/R	0.22	
			FineLk	$5x10^{-8}$ cc/sec		901			24	N/R	2.67	
			GrossLk	Fluoro		877			30	N/R	3.42	
			EM	25C		847			37	N/R	4.37	
			Burn-In	105C		810	168 Hrs		0			
			EM	25C		810			31	N/R	3.83	
			VisInsp			186			1	N/R	0.54	

MALFUNCTION DATA

SYSTEM/ EQUIPMENT	PART HISTORY	SCR CLS	DATE CODE	FAILURE ANALYSIS / CORRECTIVE ACTION

RELIABILITY ANALYSIS CENTER

HYBRID MICROCIRCUIT
RELIABILITY DATA

DEVICE SECTION

MANUFACTURER: CIRCUIT TECHNOLOGY INC.   FUNCTIONAL CATEGORY: LINEAR

TECHNOLOGY: THICK FILM   DEVICE FUNCTION: DUAL POWER AMPLIFIER

ENTRY NO.	PKG/ NO. PINS	SIZE OP TEMP	PKG MFG	PKG SEAL	SUBSTR MTL/ BOND	SUBSTR SIZE	NO. COND LYR	SUBSTR METAL #BONDS	IC		TRANSISTOR			DIODE			CAPACITOR			RESISTOR			RES TOL (%)	ELMT ATCH/ INTERCON
									NO./ TYPE	CHP ATCH/ INTERCON	NO./ TYPE	CHP ATCH/ INTERCON		NO./ TYPE	CHP ATCH/ INTERCON		NO./ TYPE	CHP ATCH/ INTERCON		NO./ TYPE	CHP ATCH/ INTERCON		NO./ TYPE	
52	P-InLn 20	1.00x 1.00 0/70C		Epoxy	Al_2O_3 Be O	1.00x 1.00	1	AuCond 46	0		10 N/R	Eutect AuWire		2 N/R	Eutect AuWire		0			28 Cermet	Fired AuCond	±10	

LIFE / ENVIRONMENTAL EXPERIENCE

DATA SRCE	SCR CLS	TST SRC	TEST TYP/ APP ENV	STR LVL/ EQP TYPE	TEST STD MTD/COND	NO. TSTD	TEST DUR.	PART HRS.	NO. FLD	FAILURE CLASSIFICATION IND; MODE; MECH; CAUSE (NO. FAILED / EVENT)	% DEF	TEST DATE	REMARKS
V	N	Scr/SSB	VisInsp		MS883 2010	109			2	N/R	1.82	2/72	
			ThrmShk	−55/125C	MS883 1011	107			0				
			CnstAcc	5KGY$_1$	MS883 2001								
			GrossLk	Fluoro	MS883 1014C								
			FineLk	$5x10^{-7}$ cc/sec	MS883 1014B	107			1	N/R	0.93		
			Burn-In	125C	MS883 1015	106			0				
			EM	25C		106	120 Hrs		1	N/R	0.94		

MALFUNCTION DATA

SYSTEM / EQUIPMENT	PART HISTORY	SCR CLS	DATE CODE	FAILURE ANALYSIS / CORRECTIVE ACTION		SYSTEM / EQUIPMENT	PART HISTORY	SCR CLS	DATE CODE	FAILURE ANALYSIS / CORRECTIVE ACTION

PAGE 78

HYBRID MICROCIRCUIT
RELIABILITY DATA

DEVICE SECTION

MANUFACTURER: CIRCUIT TECHNOLOGY INC.   FUNCTIONAL CATEGORY: LINEAR

DEVICE FUNCTION: BUFFER AMPLIFIER

TECHNOLOGY: THICK FILM

ENTRY NO.	PKG/ NO. PINS	SIZE OP TEMP	PKG MFG	PKG SEAL	SUBSTR MTL/ BOND	SUBSTR SIZE	NO. COND LYR	SUBSTR METAL #BONDS	IC NO./ TYPE	IC CHP ATCH/ INTERCON	TRANSISTOR NO./ TYPE	TRANSISTOR CHP ATCH/ INTERCON	DIODE NO./ TYPE	DIODE CHP ATCH/ INTERCON	CAPACITOR NO./ TYPE	CAPACITOR CHP ATCH/ INTERCON	RESISTOR NO./ TYPE	RESISTOR CHP ATCH/ INTERCON	RES TOL (%)	ELMT ATCH/ INTERCON NO./ TYPE
53	FPM1 22	TO-87 -55/ 125C		Weld	Al$_2$O$_3$/ BeO Eutect	N/A	1	AuCond 17	0	0	0		0		2 Ta	Solder AuCond	8 Cermet	Fired AuCond	±10	

LIFE / ENVIRONMENTAL EXPERIENCE

DATA SRCE	SCR CLS	TST SRC	TEST TYP/ APP ENV	STR LVL/ EQP TYPE	TEST STD MTD/COND	NO. TSTD	TEST DUR.	PART HRS.	NO. FLD	FAILURE CLASSIFICATION IND; MODE; MECH; CAUSE (NO. FAILED / EVENT)	% DEF	TEST DATE
V	N	Scy/C	VisInsp	150C		518			5	N/R	0.97	4/73
			Bake	-65/150C		513	32 Hrs 10 Cyc	16416	0			
			TempCyc	5/10 min								
			CnstAcc	20KGY$_1$								
			FineLk	1x10^{-6} cc/sec		513			18	N/R	3.51	
			GrossLk	Fluoro		495			8	N/R	1.62	
			EM	25C		487			22	N/R	4.52	
			VisInsp			465			2	N/R	0.43	

MALFUNCTION DATA

SYSTEM / EQUIPMENT	PART HISTORY	SCR CLS	DATE CODE	FAILURE ANALYSIS / CORRECTIVE ACTION	SYSTEM / EQUIPMENT	PART HISTORY	SCR CLS	DATE CODE	FAILURE ANALYSIS / CORRECTIVE ACTION

DEVICE SECTION

MANUFACTURER: CIRCUIT TECHNOLOGY INC   FUNCTIONAL CATEGORY: LINEAR

TECHNOLOGY: THICK FILM   DEVICE FUNCTION: PULSE TIME MULTIPLIER

RELIABILITY ANALYSIS CENTER

HYBRID MICROCIRCUIT
RELIABILITY DATA

ENTRY NO.	PKG/ NO. PINS	SIZE OP TEMP	PKG MFG	PKG SEAL	SUBSTR MTL/ BOND	SUBSTR SIZE	NO. COND LYR	SUBSTR METAL #BONDS	IC NO./ TYPE	IC CHP ATCH/ INTERCON	TRANSISTOR NO./ TYPE	TRANSISTOR CHP ATCH/ INTERCON	DIODE NO./ TYPE	DIODE CHP ATCH/ INTERCON	CAPACITOR NO./ TYPE	CAPACITOR CHP ATCH/ INTERCON	RESISTOR NO./ TYPE	RESISTOR CHP ATCH/ INTERCON	RES TOL (%)	ELMT ATCH/ INTERCON NO./ TYPE
54	FPM1 22	TO-87 -55/ 125C		Weld	Header	N/A	1	AuCond 40	2 N/R	Eutect AuWire	6 N/R	Eutect AuWire	0		3 Ta	N/R AuWire	10 Thick	Eutect AuWire	N/R	

LIFE / ENVIRONMENTAL EXPERIENCE

DATA SRCE SRG	SCR CLS	TST SRC	TEST TYP/ APP ENV	STR LVL/ EQP TYPE	TEST STD MTD/COND	NO. TSTD	TEST DUR.	PART HRS.	NO. FLD	FAILURE CLASSIFICATION IND; MODE; MECH; CAUSE (NO. FAILED / EVENT)	% DEF	TEST DATE
V	N	Scr/B	VisInsp	150C		2718		85216	55	N/R	2.02	3/73
			Bake	-55/150C		2663	32 Hrs		0			
			TempCyc	5/10 min			10 Cyc					
				30XGY								
			CnstAcc	5x10⁻⁷		2663			3	N/R	0.11	
			FineLk	cc/sec		2660			30	N/R	1.13	
			GrossLk	Fluoro		2630			51	N/R	1.94	
			EM	25C		2579			61	N/R	2.36	
			Burn-In	125C		2518			0			
			EM	25C		2518	168 Hrs		109	N/R	4.33	
			VisInsp			2409			2	N/R	0.83	

MALFUNCTION DATA

SYSTEM / EQUIPMENT	PART HISTORY	SCR CLS	DATE CODE	FAILURE ANALYSIS / CORRECTIVE ACTION				SYSTEM / EQUIPMENT	PART HISTORY	SCR CLS	DATE CODE	FAILURE ANALYSIS / CORRECTIVE ACTION	

REMARKS

PAGE 80

RELIABILITY ANALYSIS CENTER

DEVICE SECTION

MANUFACTURER: CIRCUIT TECHNOLOGY INC **FUNCTIONAL CATEGORY:** LINEAR

TECHNOLOGY: THICK FILM **DEVICE FUNCTION:** QUAD HEAD SELECTOR

ENTRY NO.	PKG/ NO. PINS	SIZE OP TEMP	PKG SEAL	SUBSTR MTL/ BOND	SUBSTR SIZE	NO. COND LYR	SUBSTR METAL #BONDS	IC NO./ TYPE	IC CHP ATCH/ INTERCON	TRANSISTOR NO./ TYPE	TRANSISTOR CHP ATCH/ INTERCON	DIODE NO./ TYPE	DIODE CHP ATCH/ INTERCON	CAPACITOR NO./ TYPE	CAPACITOR CHP ATCH/ INTERCON	RESISTOR NO./ TYPE	RESISTOR CHP ATCH/ INTERCON	RES TOL (%)	ELMT ATCH/ INTERCON NO./ TYPE
55	FPP1 22	.63x .63x .09 0/70C	Epoxy	Al₂O₃/ Be Eutect	.63x .63	1	AuCond 53	1 N/R	Eutect AuWire	8 N/R	Eutect AuWire	0		0		12 Cermet	Fired AuCond	±10	

LIFE / ENVIRONMENTAL EXPERIENCE

DATA SRCE	SCR CLS	TST SRC	TEST TYP/ APP ENV	STR LVL/ EQP TYPE	TEST STD MTD/COND	NO. TSTD	TEST DUR.	PART HRS.	NO. FLD	FAILURE CLASSIFICATION IND; MODE; MECH; CAUSE (NO. FAILED / EVENT)	% DEF	TEST DATE
V	N	Scr/B	VisInsp			1535			13	N/R	0.85	4/73
			Bake	150C		1522	32 Hrs	45664	0			
			TempCyc	-55/125C 5/10 min			5 Cyc					
			CnstAcc	30KGY₁		1522			2	N/R	0.13	
			FineLk	5x10⁻⁷ cc/sec		1520			14	N/R	0.92	
			GrossLk	Fluoro		1506			15	N/R	0.99	
			EM	25C		1491			59	N/R	3.96	
			Burn-In	125C		1432	168 Hrs		0	N/R	4.39	
			EM	25C		1432			63	N/R	0.37	
			VisInsp			1369			5	N/R		

MALFUNCTION DATA

SYSTEM/ EQUIPMENT	PART HISTORY	SCR CLS	DATE CODE	FAILURE ANALYSIS / CORRECTIVE ACTION

SYSTEM/ EQUIPMENT	PART HISTORY	SCR CLS	DATE CODE	FAILURE ANALYSIS / CORRECTIVE ACTION

HYBRID MICROCIRCUIT
RELIABILITY DATA

RELIABILITY
ANALYSIS
CENTER

DEVICE SECTION

MANUFACTURER: CIRCUIT TECHNOLOGY INC.   FUNCTIONAL CATEGORY: LINEAR

TECHNOLOGY: THICK FILM   DEVICE FUNCTION: RESTORING AMPLIFIER

ENTRY NO.	PKG/ NO. PINS	SIZE OP TEMP	PKG MFG	PKG SEAL	SUBSTR MTL/ BOND	SUBSTR SIZE	NO. COND LYR	SUBSTR METAL/ #BONDS	IC NO./ TYPE	IC CHP ATCH/ INTERCON	TRANSISTOR NO./ TYPE	TRANSISTOR CHP ATCH/ INTERCON	DIODE NO./ TYPE	DIODE CHP ATCH/ INTERCON	CAPACITOR NO./ TYPE	CAPACITOR CHP ATCH/ INTERCON	RESISTOR NO./ TYPE	RESISTOR CHP ATCH/ INTERCON	RES TOL (%)	ELM ATCH/ INTERCON NO./ TYPE
56	FPP1 22	.38x .63x .09 0/70C		Epoxy	Al_2O_3/ BeO Eutect	.38x .63	1	AuCond 48	3 N/R	Eutect AuWire	3 N/R	Eutect AuWire	0		10 Ta	Solder AuCond	17 Cermet	Fired AuCond	±10	

LIFE / ENVIRONMENTAL EXPERIENCE

DATA SRCE	SCR CLS	TST SRC	TEST TYP/ APP ENV	STR LVL/ EQP TYPE	TEST STD MTD/COND	NO. TSTD	TEST DUR.	PART HRS.	NO. FLD	FAILURE CLASSIFICATION IND; MODE; MECH: CAUSE (NO. FAILED / EVENT)	% DEF	TEST DATE
V	N	Scr/SSB	VisInsp			32			0			2/73
			Bake	150C			32 Hrs	1024				
			TempCyc	-55/125C 5/10 min			5 Cyc					
			CnstAcc	5KGY1								
			FineLk	5x10^{-8} cc/sec								
			GrossLk	Fluoro		32			1	N/R	6.25	
			EM	25C		31			1	N/R	3.23	
			Burn-In	125C		30	168 Hrs					
			EM	25C		30						
			VisInsp			30						

REMARKS

MALFUNCTION DATA

SYSTEM / EQUIPMENT	PART HISTORY	SCR CLS	DATE CODE	FAILURE ANALYSIS / CORRECTIVE ACTION

SYSTEM / EQUIPMENT	PART HISTORY	SCR CLS	DATE CODE	FAILURE ANALYSIS / CORRECTIVE ACTION

DEVICE SECTION

MANUFACTURER: CIRCUIT TECHNOLOGY INC **FUNCTIONAL CATEGORY:** LINEAR

TECHNOLOGY: THICK FILM **DEVICE FUNCTION:** PREAMPLIFIER AND DC RESTORER

ENTRY NO.	PKG/ NO. PINS	SIZE OP TEMP	PKG MFG	PKG SEAL	SUBSTR MTL/ BOND	SUBSTR SIZE	NO. COND LYR	SUBSTR METAL #BONDS	IC NO./ TYPE	IC CHP ATCH/ INTERCON	TRANSISTOR NO./ TYPE	TRANSISTOR CHP ATCH/ INTERCON	DIODE NO./ TYPE	DIODE CHP ATCH/ INTERCON	CAPACITOR NO./ TYPE	CAPACITOR CHP ATCH/ INTERCON	RESISTOR NO./ TYPE	RESISTOR CHP ATCH/ INTERCON	RES TOL (%)	ELMT ATCH/ INTERCON NO./ TYPE
57	FPM1 30	TO-87 -55/ 125C		Weld	Al_2O_3	1.00x 1.00	1	AuCond N/R ≈ 58	1 N/R	Eutect AuWire	10 N/R	Eutect AuWire	4 N/R	Eutect AuWire	3 Ta	Solder AuCond	23 Thick	Eutect AuCond	N/R	

LIFE / ENVIRONMENTAL EXPERIENCE

DATA SRCE	SCR CLS	TST SRC	TEST TYP/ APP ENV	STR LVL/ EQP TYPE	TEST STD MTD/COND	NO. TSTD	TEST DUR.	PART HRS.	NO. FLD	FAILURE CLASSIFICATION IND; MODE; MECH: CAUSE (NO. FAILED / EVENT)	% DEF	TEST DATE	REMARKS
V	N	Scr/SSB	VisInsp			1127			32	N/R	2.84	2/73	
			Bake	150C		1095	32 Hrs		0				
			TempCyc	-65/150C 5/10 min			10 Cyc						
			CnstAcc	5 KGY 1									
			FineLk	5×10^{-7} cc/sec		1095			5	N/R	0.46		
			GrossLk	Fluoro		1090			42	N/R	3.85		
			EM	25C		1048			9	N/R	0.86		
			Burn-In	85C		1039	168 Hrs		0				
			EM	25C		1039			71	N/R	6.83		
			VisInsp			968			3	N/R	0.31		

MALFUNCTION DATA

SYSTEM / EQUIPMENT	PART HISTORY	SCR CLS	DATE CODE	FAILURE ANALYSIS / CORRECTIVE ACTION	SYSTEM / EQUIPMENT	PART HISTORY	SCR CLS	DATE CODE	FAILURE ANALYSIS / CORRECTIVE ACTION

RELIABILITY ANALYSIS CENTER

HYBRID MICROCIRCUIT
RELIABILITY DATA

DEVICE SECTION

MANUFACTURER: CIRCUIT TECHNOLOGY INC   FUNCTIONAL CATEGORY: LINEAR

TECHNOLOGY: THICK FILM   DEVICE FUNCTION: SERVO-AMPLIFIER

ENTRY NO.	PKG/ NO. PINS	SIZE OP TEMP	PKG MFG	PKG SEAL	SUBSTR MTL/ BOND	SUBSTR SIZE	NO. COND LYR	SUBSTR METAL #BONDS	IC NO./TYPE	IC CHP ATCH/ INTERCON	TRANSISTOR NO./TYPE	TRANSISTOR CHP ATCH/ INTERCON	DIODE NO./TYPE	DIODE CHP ATCH/ INTERCON	CAPACITOR NO./TYPE	CAPACITOR CHP ATCH/ INTERCON	RESISTOR NO./TYPE	RESISTOR CHP ATCH/ INTERCON	RES TOL (%)	ELMT ATCH/ INTERCON NO./TYPE
58	FPM1 30	1.00x 1.00 -55/ 125C		Weld	Al_2O_3	1.00x 1.00	1	AuCond 56	1 N/R	Eutect AuWire	7 N/R	Eutect AuWire	5 N/R	AgEpoxy AuWire	2 N/R	N/R AuCond	26 Thick	Fired AuCond	N/R	

LIFE / ENVIRONMENTAL EXPERIENCE

DATA SRCE	SCR CLS	TST SRC	TEST TYP/ APP ENV	STR LVL/ EQP TYPE	TEST STD MTD/COND	NO. TSTD	TEST DUR.	PART HRS.	NO. FLD	FAILURE CLASSIFICATION IND; MODE; MECH; CAUSE (NO. FAILED / EVENT)	% DEF	TEST DATE
V	N	Scr/B	VisInsp			438		13888	4	N/R	0.91	3/73
			Bake	150C		434	32 Hrs		0			
			TempCyc	-55/ 125C 5/10 min			10 Cyc					
			CnstAcc	$10KGY_1$		434			1	N/R	0.23	
			FineLk	$1x10^{-6}$ cc/sec		433			9	N/R	2.08	
			GrossLk	Fluoro		424			31	N/R	7.31	
			EM T	25C		393			11	N/R	2.79	
			Burn-In	125C		382	168 Hrs		0			
			EM	25C		361			21	N/R	5.49	
			VisInsp						0			

SYSTEM / EQUIPMENT	PART HISTORY	SCR CLS	DATE CODE	FAILURE ANALYSIS / CORRECTIVE ACTION	CORRECTIVE ACTION

MALFUNCTION DATA

SYSTEM / EQUIPMENT	PART HISTORY	SCR CLS	DATE CODE	FAILURE ANALYSIS / CORRECTIVE ACTION	CORRECTIVE ACTION

DEVICE SECTION

MANUFACTURER: CIRCUIT TECHNOLOGY INC   **FUNCTIONAL CATEGORY:** LINEAR

TECHNOLOGY: THICK FILM   **DEVICE FUNCTION:** SAMPLE & HOLD

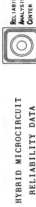

HYBRID MICROCIRCUIT
RELIABILITY DATA

ENTRY NO.	PKG/ NO. PINS	SIZE OP TEMP	PKG MFG	PKG SEAL	SUBSTR MTL/ BOND	SUBSTR SIZE	NO. COND LYR	SUBSTR METAL #BONDS	IC NO./ TYPE	IC CHP ATCH/ INTERCON	TRANSISTOR NO./ TYPE	TRANSISTOR CHP ATCH/ INTERCON	DIODE NO./ TYPE	DIODE CHP ATCH/ INTERCON	CAPACITOR NO./ TYPE	CAPACITOR CHP ATCH/ INTERCON	RESISTOR NO./ TYPE	RESISTOR CHP ATCH/ INTERCON	RES TOL (%)	ELMT ATCH/ INTERCON NO./ TYPE
59	FPM1 30	TO-87 -55/ 125C		Weld	Al_2O_3	1.00x 1.00	1	AuCond 64	2 N/R	Eutect AuWire	6 N/R	Eutect AuWire	4 N/R	Eutect AuWire	3 Ta	N/R AuCond	32 Thick	Fired AuCond	N/R	

LIFE / ENVIRONMENTAL EXPERIENCE

DATA SRCE	SCR CLS	TST SRC	TEST TYP/ APP ENV	STR LVL/ EQP TYPE	TEST STD MTD/COND	NO. TSTD	TEST DUR.	PART HRS.	NO. FLD	FAILURE CLASSIFICATION IND; MODE; MECH; CAUSE (NO. FAILED / EVENT)	% DEF	TEST DATE	REMARKS
V	N	Scr/B	VisInsp			12			1	N/R	8.33	1/73	
			Temp	150C		11			0				
			TempCyc	-65/150C 5/15 min			100 Cyc						
			CnstAcc	5KGY 1									
			FineLk	5x10⁻⁷ cc/sec									
			GrossLk	Fluoro		11			0				
			EM	25C		11			0				
			Burn-In	125C		11	168 Hrs		0				
			EM	25C		11			0				
			VisInsp										

MALFUNCTION DATA

SYSTEM/ EQUIPMENT	PART HISTORY	SCR CLS	DATE CODE	FAILURE ANALYSIS / CORRECTIVE ACTION	SYSTEM/ EQUIPMENT	PART HISTORY	SCR CLS	DATE CODE	FAILURE ANALYSIS / CORRECTIVE ACTION

RELIABILITY ANALYSIS CENTER

HYBRID MICROCIRCUIT
RELIABILITY DATA

DEVICE SECTION

MANUFACTURER: CIRCUIT TECHNOLOGY INC   FUNCTIONAL CATEGORY: LINEAR

TECHNOLOGY: THICK FILM   DEVICE FUNCTION: SAMPLE & HOLD

ENTRY NO.	PKG/ NO. PINS	SIZE OP TEMP	PKG MFG	PKG SEAL	SUBSTR MTL/ BOND	SUBSTR SIZE	NO. COND LYR	SUBSTR METAL #BONDS	IC NO./ TYPE	IC CHP ATCH/ INTERCON	TRANSISTOR NO./ TYPE	TRANSISTOR CHP ATCH/ INTERCON	DIODE NO./ TYPE	DIODE CHP ATCH/ INTERCON	CAPACITOR NO./ TYPE	CAPACITOR CHP ATCH/ INTERCON	RESISTOR NO./ TYPE	RESISTOR CHP ATCH/ INTERCON	RES TOL (%)	ELMT ATCH/ INTERCON NO./ TYPE
60	FPM1 30	TO-87 -55/ 125C		Weld	Al₂O₃	N/A	1	AuCond 62	2 N/R	Eutect AuWire	13 N/R	Eutect AuWire	0		3 N/R	N/R AuCond	32 Thick	Fired AuCond		

LIFE / ENVIRONMENTAL EXPERIENCE

DATA SRCE	SCR CLS	TST SRC	TEST TYP/ APP ENV	STR LVL/ EQP TYPE	TEST STD MTD/COND	SUBSTR MTL/ BOND	NO. TSTD	TEST DUR.	PART HRS.	NO. FLD	FAILURE CLASSIFICATION IND; MODE; MECH; CAUSE (NO. FAILED / EVENT)	% DEF	TEST DATE	REMARKS
V	N	Scr/C	VisInsp Temp TempCyc	150C -65/150C 5/15 min			322 313	32 Hrs	21824	9 0	N/R	2.79	3/73	
			CnstAcc	10KGY 1			313			3	N/R	0.96		
			FineLk	5x10⁻⁷ cc/sec			310			1	N/R	0.32		
			GrossLk EM VisInsp	Fluoro 25C			309 296 252			13 34 0	N/R N/R	4.21 11.9		

MALFUNCTION DATA

SYSTEM / EQUIPMENT	PART HISTORY	SCR CLS	DATE CODE	FAILURE ANALYSIS / CORRECTIVE ACTION

SYSTEM / EQUIPMENT	PART HISTORY	SCR CLS	DATE CODE	FAILURE ANALYSIS / CORRECTIVE ACTION

FUNCTIONAL CATEGORY: LINEAR

DEVICE FUNCTION: DUAL DIFFERENTIAL THRESHOLD

HYBRID MICROCIRCUIT
RELIABILITY DATA

DEVICE SECTION

MANUFACTURER: CIRCUIT TECHNOLOGY INC

TECHNOLOGY: THICK FILM

ENTRY NO.	PKG/ NO. PINS	SIZE OP TEMP	PKG MFG	PKG SEAL	SUBSTR MTL/ BOND	SUBSTR SIZE	NO. COND LYR	SUBSTR METAL #BONDS	IC NO./TYPE	IC CHP ATCH/ INTERCON	TRANSISTOR NO./TYPE	TRANSISTOR CHP ATCH/ INTERCON	DIODE NO./TYPE	DIODE CHP ATCH/ INTERCON	CAPACITOR NO./TYPE	CAPACITOR CHP ATCH/ INTERCON	RESISTOR NO./TYPE	RESISTOR CHP ATCH/ INTERCON	RES TOL (%)	ELMT ATCH/ INTERCON NO./TYPE
61	FPM1 30	TO-87 -55/ 125C		Weld	Al_2O_3	1.00x 1.00	1	AuCond 57	5 N/R	Eutect AuWire	0		0		5 Ta	N/R AuCond	18 Thick	Fired AuCond	N/R	

LIFE / ENVIRONMENTAL EXPERIENCE

DATA SRCE	SCR CLS	TST SRC	TEST TYP/ APP ENV	STR LVL/ EQP TYPE	TEST STD MTD/COND	NO. TSTD	TEST DUR.	PART HRS.	NO. FLD	FAILURE CLASSIFICATION IND; MODE; MECH; CAUSE (NO. FAILED / EVENT)	% DEF	TEST DATE	REMARKS
V	N	Scr/B	VisInsp	150C		189	32 Hrs	5952	3	N/R	1.59	11/72	
			Bake	-55/125C		186	10 Cyc		0				
			TempCyc	5/10 min									
			ThrmShk	-55/125C 1/1 min			5 Cyc						
			MechShk	500G		186			1	N/R	0.54		
			CnstAcc	$7.5KGY_1$		185			15	N/R	8.11		
			FineLk	$5x10^{-7}$ cc/sec		170			17	N/R	10.0		
			GrossLk	Fluoro		153			9	N/R	5.88		
			EM	25C		144			0	N/R			
			Burn-In	125C	168 Hrs	144			5	N/R	3.47		
			EM	25C		139			5	N/R	3.59		
			VisInsp										

MALFUNCTION DATA

SYSTEM / EQUIPMENT	PART HISTORY	SCR CLS	DATE CODE	FAILURE ANALYSIS / CORRECTIVE ACTION	SYSTEM / EQUIPMENT	PART HISTORY	SCR CLS	DATE CODE	FAILURE ANALYSIS / CORRECTIVE ACTION

DEVICE SECTION

MANUFACTURER: CIRCUIT TECHNOLOGY INC. FUNCTIONAL CATEGORY: LINEAR

TECHNOLOGY: THICK FILM DEVICE FUNCTION: VOICE FILTER

ENTRY NO.	PKG/ NO. PINS	SIZE/ OP TEMP	PKG MFG	PKG SEAL	SUBSTR MTL/ BOND	SUBSTR SIZE	NO. COND LYR	SUBSTR METAL #BONDS	IC NO./ TYPE	IC CHP ATCH/ INTERCON	TRANSISTOR NO./ TYPE	TRANSISTOR CHP ATCH/ INTERCON	DIODE NO./ TYPE	DIODE CHP ATCH/ INTERCON	CAPACITOR NO./ TYPE	CAPACITOR CHP ATCH/ INTERCON	RESISTOR NO./ TYPE	RESISTOR CHP ATCH/ INTERCON	RES TOL (%)	ELMT ATCH/ INTERCON NO./ TYPE
62	FPM1 44	TO-87 -55/ 125C		Weld	Al_2O_3 Be_2O_3 Eutect	1.0x 1.0	1	AuCond N/R	2*	Eutect AuWire	0		0		15 Ta	Solder AuCond	23 Cermet	Fired AuCond	±10	

* PACKAGED DEVICES

LIFE / ENVIRONMENTAL EXPERIENCE

DATA SRCE	SCR CLS	TST SRC	TEST TYP/ APP ENV	STR LVL/ EQP TYPE	TEST STD MTD/COND	NO. TSTD	TEST DUR.	PART HRS.	NO. FLD	FAILURE CLASSIFICATION IND; MODE; MECH; CAUSE (NO. FAILED / EVENT)	% DEF	TEST DATE	REMARKS
V	N	Scr/B	VisInsp			268			5	N/R	1.87	4/73	
			BndStr	150C		30			0				
			Temp	-10/125C									
			TempCyc	5/10 min		263	32 Hrs 10 Cyc						
			CnstAcc	5KGY1		263			1	N/R	0.38		
			FineLk	$5x10^{-7}$ cc/sec		262			11	N/R	4.20		
			GrossLk	Fluoro		251			10	N/R	3.98		
			EM	25C		241			18	N/R	7.47		
			Burn-In	70C		223	168 Hrs		0	N/R			
			EM	25C		223			7	N/R	3.14		
			VisInsp			216			1	N/R	0.46		

MALFUNCTION DATA

SYSTEM / EQUIPMENT	PART HISTORY	SCR CLS	DATE CODE	FAILURE ANALYSIS / CORRECTIVE ACTION

SYSTEM / EQUIPMENT	PART HISTORY	SCR CLS	DATE CODE	FAILURE ANALYSIS / CORRECTIVE ACTION

DEVICE SECTION

MANUFACTURER: COLLINS RADIO CO
TECHNOLOGY: THIN FILM

FUNCTIONAL CATEGORY: DIGITAL
DEVICE FUNCTION: FLIP FLOP

HYBRID MICROCIRCUIT
RELIABILITY DATA

ENTRY NO.	PKG/ NO. PINS	SIZE OP TEMP	PKG MFG	PKG SEAL	SUBSTR MTL/ BOND	SUBSTR SIZE	NO. COND LYR	SUBSTR METAL #BONDS	IC NO./ TYPE	IC CHP ATCH/ INTERCON	TRANSISTOR NO./ TYPE	TRANSISTOR CHP ATCH/ INTERCON	DIODE NO./ TYPE	DIODE CHP ATCH/ INTERCON	CAPACITOR NO./ TYPE	CAPACITOR CHP ATCH/ INTERCON	RESISTOR NO./ TYPE	RESISTOR CHP ATCH/ INTERCON	RES TOL (%)	ELMT ATCH/ INTERCON NO./ TYPE
63	FPCm 30	TO-87 -55/ 125C		Weld	Al_2O_3 Epoxy	.75x .75	1	AlCond ≈30	1 2JKFLFL	Eutect AuWire	6 SiNPN	Eutect AuWire	9 SiGP	Eutect AuWire	7 MetO	Dep AlCond	N/R Ta	Fired AlCond	±10	

LIFE / ENVIRONMENTAL EXPERIENCE

DATA SRCE	SCR CLS	TST SRC	TEST TYP/ APP ENV	STR LVL/ EQP TYPE	TEST STD MTD/COND	NO. TSTD	TEST DUR.	PART HRS.	NO. FLD	FAILURE CLASSIFICATION IND; MODE; MECH; CAUSE (NO. FAILED / EVENT)	% DEF	TEST DATE	REMARKS
U	C	Chk	N/R	30C 90/11J%	MS781A	12	1600 Hrs	9200	0			10/70	
U	C	Rel	N/R	70C 2.2G 20/60HZ 90/100%	MS781A	12	1715 Hrs	20580	0				

MALFUNCTION DATA

SYSTEM / EQUIPMENT	PART HISTORY	SCR CLS	DATE CODE	FAILURE ANALYSIS / CORRECTIVE ACTION	SYSTEM / EQUIPMENT	PART HISTORY	SCR CLS	DATE CODE	FAILURE ANALYSIS / CORRECTIVE ACTION
TSC-50	Bench Test	C	N/R	Fault & Initiate Lights on at Remote T_x Control; Open Al Ultrasonic Bond to Pad/1					

RELIABILITY ANALYSIS CENTER

HYBRID MICROCIRCUIT
RELIABILITY DATA

DEVICE SECTION

MANUFACTURER: COLLINS RADIO CO
TECHNOLOGY: SEMICONDUCTOR

FUNCTIONAL CATEGORY: DIGITAL
DEVICE FUNCTION: SHIFT REGISTER

ENTRY NO.	PKG/ NO. PINS	SIZE OP TEMP	PKG SEAL	PKG MFG	SUBSTR MTL/ BOND	SUBSTR SIZE	NO. COND LYR	SUBSTR METAL #BONDS	IC NO./ TYPE	IC CHP ATCH/ INTERCON	TRANSISTOR NO./ TYPE	TRANSISTOR CHP ATCH/ INTERCON	DIODE NO./ TYPE	DIODE CHP ATCH/ INTERCON	CAPACITOR NO./ TYPE	CAPACITOR CHP ATCH/ INTERCON	RESISTOR NO./ TYPE	RESISTOR CHP ATCH/ INTERCON	RES TOL (%)	ELMT ATCH/ INTERCON NO./ TYPE	ELMT ATCH/ INTERCON
64	FPCm 30	TO-87 -55/ 125C	Weld		Al$_2$O$_3$ Epoxy	.75x .75	1	AlCond $\approx$56	8 RSFlFl (4) 8 Driver (1) 8 Gate (3)	Eutect AuWire	0		0		0		0				

LIFE / ENVIRONMENTAL EXPERIENCE

DATA SRCE SCR CLS	TST SRC	TEST TYP/ APP ENV	STR LVL/ EQP TYPE	TEST STD MTD/COND	NO. TSTD	TEST DUR.	PART HRS.	NO. FLD	FAILURE CLASSIFICATION IND; MODE; MECH; CAUSE (NO. FAILED / EVENT)	% DEF	TEST DATE	REMARKS
U C	Chk	N/R	30C 90/110%	MS781A	6	1600 Hrs	9600	0			10/70	
U C	Rel	N/R	70C 2.2G 20/60HZ 90/110%	MS781A	6	1715 Hrs	10290	0				

MALFUNCTION DATA

SYSTEM / EQUIPMENT	PART HISTORY	SCR CLS	DATE CODE	FAILURE ANALYSIS / CORRECTIVE ACTION	SYSTEM / EQUIPMENT	PART HISTORY	SCR CLS	DATE CODE	FAILURE ANALYSIS / CORRECTIVE ACTION
TSC-60	Bench Test	C	N/R	R$_x$ 1 Would not Tune; Open Circuit From IC Chip; Random Failure of Collins made T.C. Ball Bond to IC Chip/1 Pin 4 Output Signal Bad; Lid was Removed & Contam- ination of 22 of Pins; Pin 4 Contamination was under Ball Bond which was Loose/1					

RELIABILITY ANALYSIS CENTER

HYBRID MICROCIRCUIT
RELIABILITY DATA

DEVICE SECTION

MANUFACTURER: COLLINS RADIO CO
TECHNOLOGY: SEMICONDUCTOR

FUNCTIONAL CATEGORY: DIGITAL
DEVICE FUNCTION: OUTPUT CONTROL

ENTRY NO.	PKG/ NO. PINS	SIZE OP TEMP	PKG MFG	PKG SEAL	SUBSTR MTL/ BOND	SUBSTR SIZE	NO. COND LYR	SUBSTR METAL #BONDS	IC NO./ TYPE	IC CHP ATCH/ INTERCON	TRANSISTOR NO./ TYPE	TRANSISTOR CHP ATCH/ INTERCON	DIODE NO./ TYPE	DIODE CHP ATCH/ INTERCON	CAPACITOR NO./ TYPE	CAPACITOR CHP ATCH/ INTERCON	RESISTOR NO./ TYPE	RESISTOR CHP ATCH/ INTERCON	RES TOL (%)	ELMT ATCH/ INTERCON NO./ TYPE
65	FPCm 30	TO-87 -55/ 125C		Weld	Al$_2$O$_3$ Epoxy	.75x .75	1	AlCond ≈84	14 JKF1F1 (5) 8 Gate (9)	Eutect AuWire	0		0		0		0			

LIFE / ENVIRONMENTAL EXPERIENCE

DATA SRCE	SCR CLS	TST SRC	TEST TYP/ APP ENV	STR LVL/ EQP TYPE	TEST STD MTD/COND	NO. TSTD	TEST DUR.	PART HRS.	NO. FLD	FAILURE CLASSIFICATION IND; MODE; MECH; CAUSE (NO. FAILED / EVENT)	% DEF	TEST DATE	REMARKS
U	C	Chk	N/R	3OC 90/110%	MS781A	3	1600 Hrs	4800	0				
U	C	Rel	N/R	70C 2.2G 20/60HZ 90/110%	MS781A	3	1715 Hrs	5145	0			10/70	

MALFUNCTION DATA

SYSTEM/ EQUIPMENT	PART HISTORY	SCR CLS	DATE CODE	FAILURE ANALYSIS / CORRECTIVE ACTION	SYSTEM / EQUIPMENT	PART HISTORY	SCR CLS	DATE CODE	FAILURE ANALYSIS / CORRECTIVE ACTION

DEVICE SECTION

MANUFACTURER: COLLINS RADIO CO
TECHNOLOGY: SEMICONDUCTOR

FUNCTIONAL CATEGORY: DIGITAL
DEVICE FUNCTION: TIME BASE

HYBRID MICROCIRCUIT
RELIABILITY DATA

 RELIABILITY ANALYSIS CENTER

ENTRY NO.	PKG/ NO. PINS	SIZE OP TEMP	PKG MFG	PKG SEAL	SUBSTR MTL/ BOND	SUBSTR SIZE	NO. COND LYR	SUBSTR METAL #BONDS	IC NO./TYPE	IC CHP ATCH/INTERCON	TRANSISTOR NO./TYPE	TRANSISTOR CHP ATCH/INTERCON	DIODE NO./TYPE	DIODE CHP ATCH/INTERCON	CAPACITOR NO./TYPE	CAPACITOR CHP ATCH/INTERCON	RESISTOR NO./TYPE	RESISTOR CHP ATCH/INTERCON	RES TOL (%)	ELMT ATCH/INTERCON NO./TYPE
66	FPCm 30	TO-87 -55/ 125C		Weld	Al₂O₃ Epoxy	.75x .75	1	AlCond ≈56	15 JKFlFl (6) 8 Gate (8) 8' Driver	Eutect AuWire	0		0		0		0			

LIFE / ENVIRONMENTAL EXPERIENCE

DATA SRCE	SCR CLS	TST SRC	TEST TYP/ APP ENV	STR LVL/ EQP TYPE	TEST STD MTD/COND	NO. TSTD	TEST DUR.	PART HRS.	NO. FLD	FAILURE CLASSIFICATION IND; MODE; MECH; CAUSE (NO. FAILED / EVENT)	% DEF	TEST DATE	REMARKS
U	C	Chk	N/R	30C 90/110%	MS781A	12	1600 Hrs	19200	0			10/70	
U	C	Rel	N/R	70C 2.2G 20/6GHZ 90/110%	MS781A	12	1715	20580	0				

MALFUNCTION DATA

SYSTEM / EQUIPMENT	PART HISTORY	SCR CLS	DATE CODE	FAILURE ANALYSIS / CORRECTIVE ACTION	SYSTEM / EQUIPMENT	PART HISTORY	SCR CLS	DATE CODE	FAILURE ANALYSIS / CORRECTIVE ACTION

DEVICE SECTION

MANUFACTURER: COLLINS RADIO CO.

TECHNOLOGY: THIN FILM

FUNCTIONAL CATEGORY: LINEAR

DEVICE FUNCTION: SQUELCH AMPLIFIER

HYBRID MICROCIRCUIT
RELIABILITY DATA

RELIABILITY
ANALYSIS
CENTER

DEVICE SECTION

ENTRY NO.	PKG/ NO. PINS	SIZE OP TEMP	PKG MFG	PKG SEAL	SUBSTR MTL/ BOND	SUBSTR SIZE	NO. COND LYR	SUBSTR METAL #BONDS	IC NO./ TYPE	IC CHP ATCH/ INTERCON	TRANSISTOR NO./ TYPE	TRANSISTOR CHP ATCH/ INTERCON	DIODE NO./ TYPE	DIODE CHP ATCH/ INTERCON	CAPACITOR NO./ TYPE	CAPACITOR CHP ATCH/ INTERCON	RESISTOR NO./ TYPE	RESISTOR CHP ATCH/ INTERCON	RES TOL (%)	ELMT ATCH/ INTERCON NO./ TYPE
67	FPCm 15	TO-87 -55/ 125C		Weld	Al_2O_3 Epoxy	.46x .46	1	AlCond ≈12	0		3 N/R	Eutect AuWire	2 N/R	Eutect AuWire	7 N/R	N/R AlCond	N/R Ta	Fired AlCond	±10	

LIFE / ENVIRONMENTAL EXPERIENCE

DATA SRCE	SCR CLS	TST SRC	TEST TYP/ APP ENV	STR LVL/ EQP TYPE	TEST STD MTD/COND	NO. TSTD	TEST DUR.	PART HRS.	NO. FLD	FAILURE CLASSIFICATION IND; MODE; MECH; CAUSE (NO. FAILED / EVENT)	% DEF	TEST DATE	REMARKS
U	C	Chk	N/R	30C 90/110%	MS781A	3	1600 Hrs	4800	0			10/70	
U	C	Rel	N/R	70C 2.2G 20/60HZ 90/110%	MS781A	3	1715 Hrs	5145	0				

MALFUNCTION DATA

SYSTEM / EQUIPMENT	PART HISTORY	SCR CLS	DATE CODE	FAILURE ANALYSIS / CORRECTIVE ACTION	SYSTEM / EQUIPMENT	PART HISTORY	SCR CLS	DATE CODE	FAILURE ANALYSIS / CORRECTIVE ACTION

RELIABILITY ANALYSIS CENTER

DEVICE SECTION

MANUFACTURER: COLLINS RADIO CO
TECHNOLOGY: THIN FILM

FUNCTIONAL CATEGORY: LINEAR
DEVICE FUNCTION: AMPLIFIER

HYBRID MICROCIRCUIT RELIABILITY DATA

ENTRY NO.	PKG/ NO. PINS	SIZE OP TEMP	PKG SEAL	PKG MFG	SUBSTR MTL/ BOND	SUBSTR SIZE	NO. COND LYR	SUBSTR METAL #BONDS	IC NO./ TYPE	IC CHP ATCH/ INTERCON	TRANSISTOR NO./ TYPE	TRANSISTOR CHP ATCH/ INTERCON	DIODE NO./ TYPE	DIODE CHP ATCH/ INTERCON	CAPACITOR NO./ TYPE	CAPACITOR CHP ATCH/ INTERCON	RESISTOR NO./ TYPE	RESISTOR CHP ATCH/ INTERCON	RES TOL (%)	ELMT ATCH/ INTERCON NO./ TYPE
68	FPCm 30	TO-87 -55/ 125C	Weld		Al_2O_3 Epoxy	.75x .75	1	AlCond $\approx$24	0		12 SiNPN (8) SiPNP (4)	Eutect AuWire	0		0		N/R Ta	Fired AlCond	±10	

LIFE / ENVIRONMENTAL EXPERIENCE

DATA SRCE NO.	SCR CLS	TST SRC	TEST TYP/ APP ENV	STR LVL/ EQP TYPE	TEST STD MTD/COND	NO. TSTD	TEST DUR.	PART HRS.	NO. FLD	FAILURE CLASSIFICATION IND; MODE; MECH; CAUSE (NO. FAILED / EVENT)	% DEF	TEST DATE	REMARKS
U	C	Chk	N/R	30C 90/110%	MS781A	3	1600 Hrs	4800	0			10/70	
U	C	Rel	N/R	70C 2.2G 20/60HZ 90/110%	MS781A	3	1715 Hrs	5145	0				

MALFUNCTION DATA

SYSTEM / EQUIPMENT	PART HISTORY	SCR CLS	DATE CODE	FAILURE ANALYSIS / CORRECTIVE ACTION			SYSTEM / EQUIPMENT	PART HISTORY	SCR CLS	DATE CODE	FAILURE ANALYSIS / CORRECTIVE ACTION

DEVICE SECTION

MANUFACTURER: COLLINS RADIO CO

TECHNOLOGY: THIN FILM

FUNCTIONAL CATEGORY: LINEAR

DEVICE FUNCTION: MODULATOR

HYBRID MICROCIRCUIT
RELIABILITY DATA

RELIABILITY ANALYSIS CENTER

ENTRY NO.	PKG/ NO. PINS	SIZE OP TEMP	PKG MFG	PKG SEAL	SUBSTR MTL/ BOND	SUBSTR SIZE	NO. COND LYR	SUBSTR METAL #BONDS	IC NO./ TYPE	IC CHP ATCH/ INTERCON	TRANSISTOR NO./ TYPE	TRANSISTOR CHP ATCH/ INTERCON	DIODE NO./ TYPE	DIODE CHP ATCH/ INTERCON	CAPACITOR NO./ TYPE	CAPACITOR CHP ATCH/ INTERCON	RESISTOR NO./ TYPE	RESISTOR CHP ATCH/ INTERCON	RES TOL (%)	ELMT ATCH/ INTERCON NO./ TYPE
69	FPCm 30	TO-87 -55/ 125C		Weld	Al$_2$O$_3$ Epoxy	.75x .75	1	AlCond ≈ 22	1 OpAmp	Eutect AuWire	10 SiPNP (4) SiNPN (6)	Eutect AuWire	1 HiV	Eutect AuWire	5 MetO (4) Ceramic (1)	Dept Solder AlCond	N/R Ta	Fired AlCond	-10	

LIFE / ENVIRONMENTAL EXPERIENCE

DATA SRCE	SCR CLS	TST SRC	TEST TYP/ APP ENV	STR LVL/ EQP TYPE	TEST STD MTD/COND	NO. TSTD	TEST DUR.	PART HRS.	NO. FLD	FAILURE CLASSIFICATION IND; MODE; MECH; CAUSE (NO. FAILED / EVENT)	% DEF	TEST DATE	REMARKS
U	C	Chk	N/R	30C 90/110%	MS781A	3	1600 Hrs	4800	0			10/70	
U	C	Rel	N/R	70C 2.2G 20/60HZ 90/110%	MS781A	3	1715 Hrs	5145	0				

MALFUNCTION DATA

SYSTEM / EQUIPMENT	PART HISTORY	SCR CLS	DATE CODE	FAILURE ANALYSIS / CORRECTIVE ACTION	SYSTEM / EQUIPMENT	PART HISTORY	SCR CLS	DATE CODE	FAILURE ANALYSIS / CORRECTIVE ACTION

PAGE 95

RELIABILITY ANALYSIS CENTER

FUNCTIONAL CATEGORY: LINEAR

DEVICE FUNCTION: DEMODULATOR BUFFER

HYBRID MICROCIRCUIT
RELIABILITY DATA

DEVICE SECTION

MANUFACTURER: COLLINS RADIO CO

TECHNOLOGY: THIN FILM

ENTRY NO.	PKG/ NO. PINS	SIZE OP TEMP	PKG MFG	PKG SEAL	SUBSTR MTL/ BOND	SUBSTR SIZE	NO. COND LYR	SUBSTR METAL #BONDS	IC NO./ TYPE	IC CHP ATCH/ INTERCON	TRANSISTOR NO./ TYPE	TRANSISTOR CHP ATCH/ INTERCON	DIODE NO./ TYPE	DIODE CHP ATCH/ INTERCON	CAPACITOR NO./ TYPE	CAPACITOR CHP ATCH/ INTERCON	RESISTOR NO./ TYPE	RESISTOR CHP ATCH/ INTERCON	RES TOL (%)	ELMT ATCH/ INTERCON NO./ TYPE
7Q	FPCm 30	TO-87 -55/ 125C		Weld	Al$_2$O$_3$ Epoxy	.75x .75	1	AlCond ≈ 42	4 Volt Comp	Eutect AuWire	7 SiNPN (3) SiPNP (4)	Eutect AuWire	0		4 MetO	Dep AlCond	N/R Ta	Fired AlCond	±10	

LIFE / ENVIRONMENTAL EXPERIENCE

DATA SRCE	SCR CLS	TST SRC	TEST TYP/ APP ENV	STR LVL/ EQP TYPE	TEST STD MTD/COND	NO. TSTD	TEST DUR.	PART HRS.	NO. FLD	FAILURE CLASSIFICATION IND; MODE; MECH; CAUSE (NO. FAILED / EVENT)	% DEF	TEST DATE	REMARKS
U	C	Chk	N/R	30C 90/100%	MS781A	3	1600 Hrs	4800	0			10/70	
U	C	Rel	N/R	70C 2.2g 20/60HZ 90/100%	MS781A	3	1715 Hrs	5145	0				

MALFUNCTION DATA

SYSTEM / EQUIPMENT	PART HISTORY	SCR CLS	DATE CODE	FAILURE ANALYSIS / CORRECTIVE ACTION	SYSTEM / EQUIPMENT	PART HISTORY	SCR CLS	DATE CODE	FAILURE ANALYSIS / CORRECTIVE ACTION

DEVICE SECTION

MANUFACTURER: COLLINS RADIO CO.

TECHNOLOGY: THIN FILM

FUNCTIONAL CATEGORY: LINEAR

DEVICE FUNCTION: DATA DETECTOR

HYBRID MICROCIRCUIT

RELIABILITY DATA

ENTRY NO.	PKG/ NO. PINS	SIZE OP TEMP	PKG MFG	PKG SEAL	SUBSTR MTL/ BOND	SUBSTR SIZE	NO. COND LYR	SUBSTR METAL #BONDS	IC NO./ TYPE	IC CHP ATCH/ INTERCON	TRANSISTOR NO./ TYPE	TRANSISTOR CHP ATCH/ INTERCON	DIODE NO./ TYPE	DIODE CHP ATCH/ INTERCON	CAPACITOR NO./ TYPE	CAPACITOR CHP ATCH/ INTERCON	RESISTOR NO./ TYPE	RESISTOR CHP ATCH/ INTERCON	RES TOL (%)	ELMT ATCH/ INTERCON NO./ TYPE
71	FPCm 30	TO-87 -55/ 125C		Weld	Al$_2$O$_3$ Epoxy	.75x .75	1	AlCond ≈80	10 8 Gate (6) 6 Driver (1) OpAmp (1) Compar (1) 9 Gate (1)	Eutect AuWire	8 SiNPN (4) SiPNP (4)	Eutect AuWire	3 SiSig (2) ZeAv (1)	Eutect AuWire	7 N/R	N/R AlCond	N/R Ta (1) Chip (Ta)	Fired AlCond Solder AlCond	±10	

LIFE / ENVIRONMENTAL EXPERIENCE

DATA SRCE	SCR CLS	PART HISTORY	TEST TYP/ APP ENV	DATE CODE	TST SRC	STR LVL/ EQP TYPE	TEST STD MTD/COND	NO. TSTD	TEST DUR.	PART HRS.	NO. FLD	FAILURE CLASSIFICATION IND; MODE; MECH; CAUSE (NO. FAILED / EVENT)	% DEF	TEST DATE
U	C		N/R		Chk	30C 90/110%	MS781A	3	1600 Hrs	4800	0			10/70
U	C		N/R		Rel	70C 2.2G 20/60HZ 90/110%	MS781A	3	1715 Hrs	5145	0			

REMARKS

MALFUNCTION DATA

SYSTEM / EQUIPMENT	PART HISTORY	SCR CLS	DATE CODE	FAILURE ANALYSIS / CORRECTIVE ACTION

SYSTEM / EQUIPMENT	PART HISTORY	SCR CLS	DATE CODE	FAILURE ANALYSIS / CORRECTIVE ACTION

PAGE 97

RELIABILITY ANALYSIS CENTER

DEVICE SECTION

MANUFACTURER: COLLINS RADIO Co.
TECHNOLOGY: SEMICONDUCTOR

FUNCTIONAL CATEGORY: LINEAR
DEVICE FUNCTION: SQUELCH CONTROL

HYBRID MICROCIRCUIT
RELIABILITY DATA

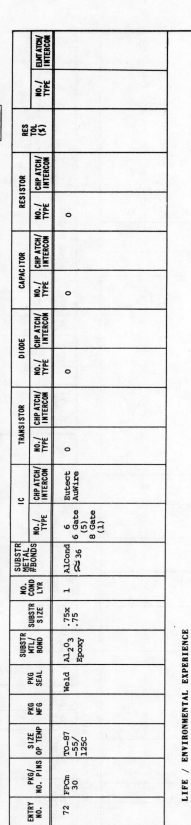

RELIABILITY ANALYSIS CENTER

ENTRY NO.	PKG/ NO. PINS	SIZE OP TEMP	PKG MFG	PKG SEAL	SUBSTR MTL/ BOND	SUBSTR SIZE	NO. COND LYR	SUBSTR METAL #BONDS	IC NO./ TYPE	IC CHP ATCH/ INTERCON	TRANSISTOR NO./ TYPE	TRANSISTOR CHP ATCH/ INTERCON	DIODE NO./ TYPE	DIODE CHP ATCH/ INTERCON	CAPACITOR NO./ TYPE	CAPACITOR CHP ATCH/ INTERCON	RESISTOR NO./ TYPE	RESISTOR CHP ATCH/ INTERCON	RES TOL (%)	ELMT ATCH/ INTERCOM NO./ TYPE
72	FPCm 30	TO-87 -55/ 125C		Weld	Al₂O₃ Epoxy	.75x .75	1	AlCond ≈ 36	6 6 Gate (5) 8 Gate (1)	Eutect AuWire	0		0		0		0			

LIFE / ENVIRONMENTAL EXPERIENCE

DATA SRCE	SCR CLS	PART HISTORY	SCR CLS	DATE CODE	FAILURE ANALYSIS / CORRECTIVE ACTION	TST SRC	TEST TYP/ APP ENV	STR LVL/ EQP TYPE	TEST STD MTD/COND	NO. TSTD	TEST DUR.	PART HRS.	NO. FLD	FAILURE CLASSIFICATION IND; MODE; MECH; CAUSE (NO. FAILED / EVENT)	% DEF	TEST DATE	REMARKS
U	C					Chk	N/R	3CC 90/110%	MS781A	3	1600 Hrs	4800	0				
U	C					Rel	N/R	70C 2.2G 20/60HZ 90/110%	MS781A	3	1715 Hrs	5145	0			10/70	

MALFUNCTION DATA

SYSTEM / EQUIPMENT	PART HISTORY	SCR CLS	DATE CODE	FAILURE ANALYSIS / CORRECTIVE ACTION	SYSTEM / EQUIPMENT	PART HISTORY	SCR CLS	DATE CODE	FAILURE ANALYSIS / CORRECTIVE ACTION

DEVICE SECTION

MANUFACTURER: CRYSTALONICS
TECHNOLOGY: THIN FILM

FUNCTIONAL CATEGORY: DIGITAL
DEVICE FUNCTION: LADDER SWITCH

HYBRID MICROCIRCUIT RELIABILITY DATA

RELIABILITY ANALYSIS CENTER

ENTRY NO.	PKG/ NO. PINS	SIZE/ OP TEMP	PKG MFG	PKG SEAL	SUBSTR MTL/ BOND	SUBSTR SIZE	NO. COND LYR	SUBSTR METAL #BONDS	IC NO./ TYPE	IC CHP ATCH/ INTERCON	TRANSISTOR NO./ TYPE	TRANSISTOR CHP ATCH/ INTERCON	DIODE NO./ TYPE	DIODE CHP ATCH/ INTERCON	CAPACITOR NO./ TYPE	CAPACITOR CHP ATCH/ INTERCON	RESISTOR NO./ TYPE	RESISTOR CHP ATCH/ INTERCON	RES TOL (%)	ELM ATCH/ INTERCON
73	Can 10	TO-100 -55/ 125C		Weld	Al$_2$O$_3$/ Epoxy	.30D	1	Cr-Ni- Au N/R	0		2 SiNPN SiPNP	AgEpoxy AuWire	1 ZenAv	AgEpoxy AuWire	2 MetO	AgEpoxy AuCond	4 N/R	Fired AuCond	N/R	

LIFE / ENVIRONMENTAL EXPERIENCE

DATA SRCE	SCR CLS	TST SRC	TEST TYP/ APP ENV	STR LVL/ EQP TYPE	TEST STD MTD/COND	NO. TSTD	TEST DUR.	PART HRS.	NO. FLD	FAILURE CLASSIFICATION IND; MODE; MECH; CAUSE (NO. FAILED / EVENT)	% DEF	TEST DATE	REMARKS
V	S&D	Env	CnstAcc	20KG	MS750 2006	38			0			11/68	
			MechShk	4 AXES 1.5KG	MS750 2016		0.5 msec						
			VibFtg		MS750 2046								
			VibVrFrq	.1/2KHZ	MS750 2058	38							
			TempCyc	-65/150C	MS750 1052		10 Cyc		0				
			ThmShk	0/100C	MS750 1056	38	5 Cyc		0				
			Solder		MS750 2026	22			0				
			Moistr	-10/65C	MS750 1021	22			0				
			TrmStr	98%RH	MS750 2036E	18			1	N/R	5.56		
			SltAtm		MS750 1041	11			0				
V	SSD	Lab	StgLif	150C	MS750 1031	38	1000 Hr	38000	0				
V	SSD	Lab	OpCnst	125C 100%	MS750 1026	38	1000 Hr	38000	0				

MALFUNCTION DATA

SYSTEM/ EQUIPMENT	PART HISTORY	SCR CLS	DATE CODE	FAILURE ANALYSIS / CORRECTIVE ACTION

SYSTEM/ EQUIPMENT	PART HISTORY	SCR CLS	DATE CODE	FAILURE ANALYSIS / CORRECTIVE ACTION

HYBRID MICROCIRCUIT
RELIABILITY DATA

RELIABILITY ANALYSIS CENTER

FUNCTIONAL CATEGORY: DIGITAL
DEVICE FUNCTION: DUAL FET ANALOG GATE

DEVICE SECTION

MANUFACTURER: CRYSTALONICS
TECHNOLOGY: THIN FILM

ENTRY NO.	PKG/ NO. PINS	SIZE OP TEMP	PKG MFG	PKG SEAL	SUBSTR MTL/ BOND	SUBSTR SIZE	NO. COND LYR	SUBSTR METAL #BONDS	IC NO./ TYPE	IC CHP ATCH/ INTERCON	TRANSISTOR NO./ TYPE	TRANSISTOR CHP ATCH/ INTERCON	DIODE NO./ TYPE	DIODE CHP ATCH/ INTERCON	CAPACITOR NO./ TYPE	CAPACITOR CHP ATCH/ INTERCON	RESISTOR NO./ TYPE	RESISTOR CHP ATCH/ INTERCON	RES TOL (%)	ELMT ATCH/ INTERCON
74	Can 10	TO-100 -55/ 125C		Weld	Al₂O₃ Epoxy	.30D	1	Cr-Ni- Au N/R	0		6 FET (2) SiNPN (2) SiPNP (2)	AgEpoxy AuWire	2 Varact	AgEpoxy AuWire	0		4 N/R	Fired AuCond	N/R	

LIFE / ENVIRONMENTAL EXPERIENCE

DATA SRCE	SCR CLS	TST SRC	TEST TYP/ APP ENV	STR LVL/ EQP TYPE	TEST STD MTD/COND	NO. TSTD	TEST DUR.	PART HRS.	NO. FLD	FAILURE CLASSIFICATION IND; MODE; MECH; CAUSE (NO. FAILED / EVENT)	% DEF	TEST DATE	REMARKS
V	N/R	Env	EM	75C	MS750	152			0			2/70- 4/70	
			VisInsp		2071	25			0				
			Solder		2026	38							
			FineLk	Radioiso	202/112								
			GrossLk	Min Oil	202/112								
			ThermShk	125C									
			ThrmShk	0/100C	1056		15/15 sec						
			Moistr	-10/65C 98% RH	1021								
	N/R	Env	EM	25C		38			0				
			MechShk	1.5KG	2016	38							
			VibFtg	60HZ 20G 3 AXES	2046								
			CnstAcc	20KG 6 AXES	2006								
			FineLk	Radioiso	202/112								
			GrossLk	Min Oil 125C	202/112								
	N/R	Env	EM	25C		38			0				
			TrmStr		2036	38							
			FineLk	Radioiso	202/112								
			GrossLk	Min Oil 125C	202/112								
			EM	25C		38			0				

MALFUNCTION DATA

SYSTEM / EQUIPMENT	PART HISTORY	SCR CLS	DATE CODE	FAILURE ANALYSIS / CORRECTIVE ACTION	SYSTEM / EQUIPMENT	PART HISTORY	SCR CLS	DATE CODE	FAILURE ANALYSIS / CORRECTIVE ACTION
N/R	Bench Test Ambient	B	N/R	Intermittent Output, Short-Circuit Transistor/1					

DEVICE SECTION

HYBRID MICROCIRCUIT
RELIABILITY DATA

MANUFACTURER: CRYSTALONICS
FUNCTIONAL CATEGORY: DIGITAL
DEVICE FUNCTION: DUAL FET ANALOG GATE
TECHNOLOGY: THIN FILM

ENTRY NO.	PKG/ NO. PINS	SIZE OP TEMP	PKG MFG	PKG SEAL	SUBSTR MTL/ BOND	SUBSTR SIZE	NO. COND LYR	SUBSTR METAL	IC NO./TYPE	IC CHP ATCH/ INTERCON	TRANSISTOR NO./TYPE	TRANSISTOR CHP ATCH/ INTERCON	DIODE NO./TYPE	DIODE CHP ATCH/ INTERCON	CAPACITOR NO./TYPE	CAPACITOR CHP ATCH/ INTERCON	RESISTOR NO./TYPE	RESISTOR CHP ATCH/ INTERCON	RES TOL (%)	ELMT ATCH/ INTERCON NO./TYPE
74 (contd)																				

LIFE / ENVIRONMENTAL EXPERIENCE (con't)

DATA SRCE	SCR CLS	TST SRC	TEST TYP/ APP ENV	STR LVL/ EQP TYPE	TEST STD MTD/COND	NO. TSTD	TEST DUR.	PART HRS.	NO. FLD	FAILURE CLASSIFICATION IND; MODE; MECH; CAUSE (NO. FAILED / EVENT)	% DEF	TEST DATE	REMARKS
N/R		Lab	StgLif	150C	MS750 1031	38	1000 Hrs	38000	0				
N/R		Lab	OpCnst	125C	1026	38	1000 Hrs	38000	0				

MALFUNCTION DATA

SYSTEM / EQUIPMENT	PART HISTORY	SCR CLS	DATE CODE	FAILURE ANALYSIS / CORRECTIVE ACTION

SYSTEM / EQUIPMENT	PART HISTORY	SCR CLS	DATE CODE	FAILURE ANALYSIS / CORRECTIVE ACTION

DEVICE SECTION

MANUFACTURER: CTS MICROELECTRONICS

TECHNOLOGY: THICK FILM

FUNCTIONAL CATEGORY: DIGITAL

DEVICE FUNCTION: DUAL FLIP FLOP

HYBRID MICROCIRCUIT
RELIABILITY DATA

 RELIABILITY ANALYSIS CENTER

ENTRY NO.	PKG/ NO. PINS	SIZE OP TEMP	PKG MFG	PKG SEAL	SUBSTR MTL/ BOND	SUBSTR SIZE	NO. COND LYR	SUBSTR METAL #BONDS	IC NO./ TYPE	IC CHP ATCH/ INTERCON	TRANSISTOR NO./ TYPE	TRANSISTOR CHP ATCH/ INTERCON	DIODE NO./ TYPE	DIODE CHP ATCH/ INTERCON	CAPACITOR NO./ TYPE	CAPACITOR CHP ATCH/ INTERCON	RESISTOR NO./ TYPE	RESISTOR CHP ATCH/ INTERCON	RES TOL (%)	ELMT ATCH/ INTERCON NO./ TYPE
75	Can 10	TO-100 -55/ 125C		Weld	Al$_2$O$_3$ Eutect	.30D	1	AuCond 24	0		4 SiNPN	Eutect AuWire	4 SiSig	Eutect AuWire	0		10 Cermet	Fired AuCond	±5	

LIFE / ENVIRONMENTAL EXPERIENCE

DATA SRCE CLS	TST SRC	TEST TYP/ APP ENV	STR LVL/ EQP TYPE	TEST STD MTD/COND	NO. TSTD	TEST DUR.	PART HRS.	NO. FLD	FAILURE CLASSIFICATION IND; MODE; MECH; CAUSE (NO. FAILED / EVENT)	% DEF	TEST DATE	REMARKS
V N	Lab	StgLif	25C				2.274E6	0			9/69	
V N	Lab	OpCnst	105C				6.04E5	1	Thermal Comp. Bond 13000 Hrs			

MALFUNCTION DATA

SYSTEM / EQUIPMENT	PART HISTORY	SCR CLS	DATE CODE	FAILURE ANALYSIS / CORRECTIVE ACTION		SYSTEM / EQUIPMENT	PART HISTORY	SCR CLS	DATE CODE	FAILURE ANALYSIS / CORRECTIVE ACTION	

DEVICE SECTION

MANUFACTURER: CTS MICROELECTRONICS

TECHNOLOGY: THICK FILM

FUNCTIONAL CATEGORY: DIGITAL

DEVICE FUNCTION: FLIP FLOP

HYBRID MICROCIRCUIT
RELIABILITY DATA

RELIABILITY ANALYSIS CENTER

ENTRY NO.	PKG/ NO. PINS	SIZE OP TEMP	PKG MFG	PKG SEAL	SUBSTR MTL/ BOND	SUBSTR SIZE	NO. COND LYR	SUBSTR METAL #BONDS	IC NO./ TYPE	IC CHP ATCH/ INTERCON	TRANSISTOR NO./ TYPE	TRANSISTOR CHP ATCH/ INTERCON	DIODE NO./ TYPE	DIODE CHP ATCH/ INTERCON	CAPACITOR NO./ TYPE	CAPACITOR CHP ATCH/ INTERCON	RESISTOR NO./ TYPE	RESISTOR CHP ATCH/ INTERCON	RES TOL (%)	ELM ATCH/ INTERCON NO./ TYPE
76	FPPI 18	N/R 15/55C		Epoxy	Al_2O_3 N/R	N/A	1	AuCond N/R	0		6 SiNPN	AgEpoxy AuWire	2 SiGP	AgEpoxy AuWire	0		17 Cermet	Fired AuCond	±5	

LIFE / ENVIRONMENTAL EXPERIENCE

DATA SRCE	SCR CLS	TST SRC	TEST TYP/ APP ENV	STR LVL/ EQP TYPE	TEST STD MTD/COND	NO. TSTD	TEST DUR.	PART HRS.	NO. FLD	FAILURE CLASSIFICATION IND; MODE; MECH; CAUSE (NO. FAILED / EVENT)	% DEF	TEST DATE	REMARKS
V	N	Lab	OpCnst	105C		130	3000 Hrs	3.92E5	3	Thermal Comp Bond; Contamination 2,291 Hrs 7,244 Hrs 2,668 Hrs		9/69	

MALFUNCTION DATA

SYSTEM/ EQUIPMENT	PART HISTORY	SCR CLS	DATE CODE	FAILURE ANALYSIS / CORRECTIVE ACTION

SYSTEM/ EQUIPMENT	PART HISTORY	SCR CLS	DATE CODE	FAILURE ANALYSIS / CORRECTIVE ACTION

DEVICE SECTION

MANUFACTURER: CTS MICROELECTRONICS FUNCTIONAL CATEGORY: LINEAR

TECHNOLOGY: THICK FILM DEVICE FUNCTION: VIDEO AMPLIFIER

 RELIABILITY ANALYSIS CENTER

HYBRID MICROCIRCUIT
RELIABILITY DATA

ENTRY NO.	PKG/ NO. PINS	SIZE OP TEMP	PKG MFG	PKG SEAL	SUBSTR MTL/ BOND	SUBSTR SIZE	NO. COND LYR	SUBSTR METAL #BONDS	IC NO./ TYPE	IC CHP ATCH/ INTERCON	TRANSISTOR NO./ TYPE	TRANSISTOR CHP ATCH/ INTERCON	DIODE NO./ TYPE	DIODE CHP ATCH/ INTERCON	CAPACITOR NO./ TYPE	CAPACITOR CHP ATCH/ INTERCON	RESISTOR NO./ TYPE	RESISTOR CHP ATCH/ INTERCON	RES TOL (%)	ELMT ATCH/ INTERCON NO./ TYPE
77	Can 10	TO-100 -55/ 125C		Weld	Al_2O_3 Eutect	.30D	2	AuCond 8	0		2	Eutect AuWire	0		0		7 Cermet	Fired AuCond	±5	

LIFE / ENVIRONMENTAL EXPERIENCE

DATA SRCE	SCR CLS	TST SRC	TEST TYP/ APP ENV	STR LVL/ EQP TYPE	TEST STD MTD/COND	NO. TSTD	TEST DUR.	PART HRS.	NO. FLD	FAILURE CLASSIFICATION IND; MODE; MECH; CAUSE (NO. FAILED / EVENT)	% DEF	TEST DATE
V	N/R	Lab	StgLif	25C	N/R	N/R	N/R	1.69E6	0			9/69
V	N/R	Lab	OpCnst	105C				3.50E5	0			

REMARKS

MALFUNCTION DATA

SYSTEM / EQUIPMENT	PART HISTORY	SCR CLS	DATE CODE	FAILURE ANALYSIS / CORRECTIVE ACTION	SYSTEM / EQUIPMENT	PART HISTORY	SCR CLS	DATE CODE	FAILURE ANALYSIS / CORRECTIVE ACTION

PAGE 104

DEVICE SECTION

MANUFACTURER: CTS MICROELECTRONICS

FUNCTIONAL CATEGORY: N/A

DEVICE FUNCTION: RESISTOR ARRAY

TECHNOLOGY: THICK FILM

HYBRID MICROCIRCUIT
RELIABILITY DATA

RELIABILITY ANALYSIS CENTER

ENTRY NO.	PKG/ NO. PINS	SIZE OP TEMP	PKG MFG	PKG SEAL	SUBSTR MTL/ BOND	SUBSTR SIZE	NO. COND LYR	SUBSTR METAL #BONDS	IC NO./ TYPE	IC CHP ATCH/ INTERCON	TRANSISTOR NO./ TYPE	TRANSISTOR CHP ATCH/ INTERCON	DIODE NO./ TYPE	DIODE CHP ATCH/ INTERCON	CAPACITOR NO./ TYPE	CAPACITOR CHP ATCH/ INTERCON	RESISTOR NO./ TYPE	RESISTOR CHP ATCH/ INTERCON	RES TOL (%)	ELMT ATCH/ INTERCON NO./ TYPE
78	S-DIP 14	.95x .30 15/55C		Silic	Al$_2$O$_3$ N/A	.85x .25	1	AuCond (Pd) N/R	0		0		0		0		8 Cermet	Fired AuCond	±5	

LIFE / ENVIRONMENTAL EXPERIENCE

DATA SRCE	SCR CLS	TST SRC	TEST TYP/ APP ENV	STR LVL/ EQP TYPE	TEST STD MTD/COND	NO. TSTD	TEST DUR.	PART HRS.	NO. FLD	FAILURE CLASSIFICATION IND; MODE; MECH; CAUSE (NO. FAILED / EVENT)	% DEF	TEST DATE
I	SSD	Scr	Temp Brn VisInsp	TempCyc -35/85C 70C N/R	N/R	14820	10/10 min 168 Hrs	0	0 0			10/73- 4/74

MALFUNCTION DATA

SYSTEM / EQUIPMENT	PART HISTORY	SCR CLS	DATE CODE	FAILURE ANALYSIS / CORRECTIVE ACTION

SYSTEM / EQUIPMENT	PART HISTORY	SCR CLS	DATE CODE	FAILURE ANALYSIS / CORRECTIVE ACTION

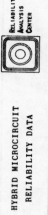
DEVICE SECTION

MANUFACTURER: DALE ELECTRONICS INC

TECHNOLOGY: THICK FILM

FUNCTIONAL CATEGORY: N/A

DEVICE FUNCTION: RESISTOR ARRAY

ENTRY NO.	PKG/ NO. PINS	SIZE/ OP TEMP	PKG MFG	PKG SEAL	SUBSTR MTL/ BOND	SUBSTR SIZE	NO. COND LYR	SUBSTR METAL #/BONDS	IC NO./TYPE	IC CHP ATCH/ INTERCON	TRANSISTOR NO./TYPE	TRANSISTOR CHP ATCH/ INTERCON	DIODE NO./TYPE	DIODE CHP ATCH/ INTERCON	CAPACITOR NO./TYPE	CAPACITOR CHP ATCH/ INTERCON	RESISTOR NO./TYPE	RESISTOR CHP ATCH/ INTERCON	RES TOL (%)	ELMT ATCH/ INTERCON NO./TYPE
79	E-InLn 4	1.00x .375x .025 0/70C	Dale	Epoxy	Al₂O₃ N/A	1.00x .375x .025	1	Cu/Sn N/R	0		0		0		0		4 N/A	Fired Cu/Sn		

LIFE / ENVIRONMENTAL EXPERIENCE

DATA SRCE	SCR CLS	TST SRC	TEST TYP/ APP ENV	STR LVL/ EQP TYPE	TEST STD MTD/COND	NO. TSTD	TEST DUR.	PART HRS.	NO. FLD	FAILURE CLASSIFICATION IND; MODE; MECH; CAUSE (NO. FAILED / EVENT)	% DEF	TEST DATE
V	SSD	Env	Solder TempCyc	-25/125C 100%		8			0	TC > Spec		7/10
V	SSD	Env	Moistr	-10/65C 98%RH		8			1	Deviation > Spec	1.25	
V	SSD	Env	OpCnst	70C 100%		8	2000 Hr	16000	1	Res Δ > Spec	1.25	
V	SSD	Env	TrmStr	2Lb 5 sec		8			0		1.25	

MALFUNCTION DATA

SYSTEM / EQUIPMENT	PART HISTORY	SCR CLS	DATE CODE	FAILURE ANALYSIS / CORRECTIVE ACTION	SYSTEM / EQUIPMENT	PART HISTORY	SCR CLS	DATE CODE	FAILURE ANALYSIS / CORRECTIVE ACTION

DEVICE SECTION

FUNCTIONAL CATEGORY: N/A
MANUFACTURER: DALE ELECTRONICS
DEVICE FUNCTION: RESISTOR NETWORK
TECHNOLOGY: THICK FILM

ENTRY NO.	PKG/ NO. PINS	SIZE OP TEMP	PKG MFG	PKG SEAL	SUBSTR MTL/ BOND	SUBSTR SIZE	NO. COND LYR	SUBSTR METAL #BONDS	IC NO./ TYPE	IC CHP ATCH/ INTERCON	TRANSISTOR NO./ TYPE	TRANSISTOR CHP ATCH/ INTERCON	DIODE NO./ TYPE	DIODE CHP ATCH/ INTERCON	CAPACITOR NO./ TYPE	CAPACITOR CHP ATCH/ INTERCON	RESISTOR NO./ TYPE	RESISTOR CHP ATCH/ INTERCON	RES TOL (%)	ELMT ATCH/ INTERCON NO./ TYPE
80	N/A	N/R 0/70C		N/A	Al_2O_3		1	N/R	0		0		0		0		4 Ta	Fired Sldr Tabs	±5	

LIFE / ENVIRONMENTAL EXPERIENCE

DATA SRCE	SCR CLS	PART HISTORY	SCR CLS	DATE CODE	TST SRC	TEST TYP/ APP ENV	STR LVL/ EQP TYPE	TEST STD MTD/COND	NO. TSTD	TEST DUR.	PART HRS.	NO. FLD	FAILURE CLASSIFICATION IND; MODE; MECH; CAUSE (NO. FAILED / EVENT)	% DEF	TEST DATE	REMARKS
V	SSD				Lab	OpCnst	45C	N/R	40	1000 Hrs	40000	0		0	12/71	

MALFUNCTION DATA

SYSTEM / EQUIPMENT	PART HISTORY	SCR CLS	DATE CODE	FAILURE ANALYSIS / CORRECTIVE ACTION	SYSTEM / EQUIPMENT	PART HISTORY	SCR CLS	DATE CODE	FAILURE ANALYSIS / CORRECTIVE ACTION

DEVICE SECTION

MANUFACTURER: DALE ELECTRONICS
TECHNOLOGY: THICK FILM

FUNCTIONAL CATEGORY: N/A
DEVICE FUNCTION: RESISTOR ARRAY

HYBRID MICROCIRCUIT RELIABILITY DATA

RELIABILITY ANALYSIS CENTER

ENTRY NO.	PKG/ NO. PINS	SIZE OP TEMP	PKG MFG	PKG SEAL	SUBSTR MTL/ BOND	SUBSTR SIZE	NO. COND LYR	SUBSTR METAL #BONDS	IC NO./ TYPE	IC CHP ATCH/ INTERCON	TRANSISTOR NO./ TYPE	TRANSISTOR CHP ATCH/ INTERCON	DIODE NO./ TYPE	DIODE CHP ATCH/ INTERCON	CAPACITOR NO./ TYPE	CAPACITOR CHP ATCH/ INTERCON	RESISTOR NO./ TYPE	RESISTOR CHP ATCH/ INTERCON	RES TOL (%)	ELM ATCH/ INTERCON NO./ TYPE
82	N/R	N/R 0/70C	N/R	N/R	Al_2O_3	N/R	1	AuCond N/A	0		0		0		0		10 NiCr	Fired AuWire	±1	

LIFE / ENVIRONMENTAL EXPERIENCE

DATA SRCE	SCR CLS	TST SRC	TEST TYP/ APP ENV	STR LVL/ EQP TYPE	TEST STD MTD/COND	NO. TSTD	TEST DUR.	PART HRS.	NO. FLD	FAILURE CLASSIFICATION IND; MODE; MECH; CAUSE (NO. FAILED / EVENT)	% DEF	TEST DATE	REMARKS
V	SSD	Env	TempChar	-55/125C		10			0			12/70	
			TempCyc	-55/150C		20	5/5 sec						
			InsRes	5/10W		20							
V	SSD	Env	TempCyc	N/R		10			0				
V	SSD	Env	Moistr	-10/65C 98%RH 5/1W		10			0				
V	SSD	Lab	OpCnst	5/0W 125C 100% 125C 125% 125C 140%		10	1000	10000	0				
						10	1000	10000	0				

MALFUNCTION DATA

SYSTEM / EQUIPMENT	PART HISTORY	SCR CLS	DATE CODE	FAILURE ANALYSIS / CORRECTIVE ACTION	SYSTEM / EQUIPMENT	PART HISTORY	SCR CLS	DATE CODE	FAILURE ANALYSIS / CORRECTIVE ACTION

RELIABILITY
ANALYSIS
CENTER

DEVICE SECTION

FUNCTIONAL CATEGORY: N/A

MANUFACTURER: DALE ELECTRONICS

DEVICE FUNCTION: RESISTOR ARRAY

TECHNOLOGY: THICK FILM

ENTRY NO.	PKG/ NO. PINS	SIZE OP TEMP	PKG MFG	PKG SEAL	SUBSTR ·MTL· BOND	SUBSTR SIZE	NO. COND LYR	SUBSTR METAL #BONDS	IC NO./ TYPE	IC CHP ATCH/ INTERCON	TRANSISTOR NO./ TYPE	TRANSISTOR CHP ATCH/ INTERCON	DIODE NO./ TYPE	DIODE CHP ATCH/ INTERCON	CAPACITOR NO./ TYPE	CAPACITOR CHP ATCH/ INTERCON	RESISTOR NO./ TYPE	RESISTOR CHP ATCH/ INTERCON	RES TOL (%)	ELMT ATCH/ INTERCON NO./ TYPE
82	N/A	N/R 0/70C	N/R	N/A	Al$_2$O$_3$ N/A	N/R	1	AuCond N/A	0		0		0		0		9 Cermet	Fired N/R	±1	

LIFE / ENVIRONMENTAL EXPERIENCE

DATA SRCE	SCR CLS	TST SRC	TEST TYP/ APP ENV	STR LVL/ EQP TYPE	TEST STD MTD/COND	NO. TSTD	TEST DUR.	PART HRS.	NO. FLD	FAILURE CLASSIFICATION IND; MODE; MECH; CAUSE (NO. FAILED / EVENT)	% DEF	TEST DATE
V	SSD	Env	StatChar									4/70
V	SSD	Env	Solder									
V	SSD	Env	MechShk Vib									
V	SSD	Lab	OpCnst	85C		2	10000 Hrs	2000	0			

MALFUNCTION DATA

SYSTEM / EQUIPMENT	PART HISTORY	SCR CLS	DATE CODE	FAILURE ANALYSIS / CORRECTIVE ACTION	SYSTEM / EQUIPMENT	PART HISTORY	SCR CLS	DATE CODE	FAILURE ANALYSIS / CORRECTIVE ACTION

HYBRID MICROCIRCUIT
RELIABILITY DATA

FUNCTIONAL CATEGORY: N/A

DEVICE FUNCTION: RESISTOR ARRAY

DEVICE SECTION

MANUFACTURER: DALE ELECTRONICS

TECHNOLOGY: THICK FILM

ENTRY NO.	PKG/ NO. PINS	SIZE OP TEMP	PKG MFG	PKG SEAL	SUBSTR MTL/ BOND	SUBSTR SIZE	NO. COND LYR	SUBSTR METAL #BONDS	IC NO./ TYPE	IC CHP ATCH/ INTERCON	TRANSISTOR NO./ TYPE	TRANSISTOR CHP ATCH/ INTERCON	DIODE NO./ TYPE	DIODE CHP ATCH/ INTERCON	CAPACITOR NO./ TYPE	CAPACITOR CHP ATCH/ INTERCON	RESISTOR NO./ TYPE	RESISTOR CHP ATCH/ INTERCON	RES TOL (%)	ELMT ATCH/ INTERCON NO./ TYPE
83	S-DIP 14	.72x .30x .20 0/70C		Silic	Al_2O_3 N/A	.72x .30x .20	1	AuCond N/R	0		0		0		0		6 NiCr	Fired AuCond	±1	

LIFE / ENVIRONMENTAL EXPERIENCE

DATA SRCE NO.	SCR CLS	TST SRC	TEST TYP/ APP ENV	STR LVL/ EQP TYPE	TEST STD MTD/COND	NO. TSTD	TEST DUR.	PART HRS.	NO. FLD	FAILURE CLASSIFICATION IND; MODE; MECH; CAUSE (NO. FAILED / EVENT)	% DEF	TEST DATE	REMARKS
V	N	Lab	OpCnst	70C		10	1000 Hrs	10000	0			5/71	

MALFUNCTION DATA

SYSTEM / EQUIPMENT	PART HISTORY	SCR CLS	DATE CODE	FAILURE ANALYSIS / CORRECTIVE ACTION

SYSTEM / EQUIPMENT	PART HISTORY	SCR CLS	DATE CODE	FAILURE ANALYSIS / CORRECTIVE ACTION

DEVICE SECTION

MANUFACTURER: DALE ELECTRONICS

TECHNOLOGY: THIN FILM

FUNCTIONAL CATEGORY: N/A

DEVICE FUNCTION: RESISTOR ARRAY

HYBRID MICROCIRCUIT
RELIABILITY DATA

ENTRY NO.	PKG/ NO. PINS	SIZE OP TEMP	PKG MFG	PKG SEAL	SUBSTR MTL/ BOND	SUBSTR SIZE	NO. COND LYR	SUBSTR METAL #BONDS	IC NO./ TYPE	IC CHP ATCH/ INTERCON	TRANSISTOR NO./ TYPE	TRANSISTOR CHP ATCH/ INTERCON	DIODE NO./ TYPE	DIODE CHP ATCH/ INTERCON	CAPACITOR NO./ TYPE	CAPACITOR CHP ATCH/ INTERCON	RESISTOR NO./ TYPE	RESISTOR CHP ATCH/ INTERCON	RES TOL (%)	ELMT ATCH/ INTERCON NO./ TYPE
84	N/A	N/R 0/70C	N/R	N/A	Al$_2$O$_3$ N/A	N/R	1	AuCond N/R	0		0		0		0		20 NiCr	Fired AuCond	±1	

LIFE / ENVIRONMENTAL EXPERIENCE

DATA SRCE	SCR CLS	PART HISTORY	TST SRC	TEST TYP/ APP ENV	STR LVL/ EQP TYPE	TEST STD MTD/COND	NO. TSTD	TEST DUR.	PART HRS.	NO. FLD.	FAILURE CLASSIFICATION IND; MODE; MECH; CAUSE (NO. FAILED / EVENT)	% DEF	TEST DATE	REMARKS
V	N		Lab	OpCnst	70C		8	1000 Hrs	8000	0			4/71	

MALFUNCTION DATA

SYSTEM / EQUIPMENT	PART HISTORY	SCR CLS	DATE CODE	FAILURE ANALYSIS / CORRECTIVE ACTION	SYSTEM / EQUIPMENT	PART HISTORY	SCR CLS	DATE CODE	FAILURE ANALYSIS / CORRECTIVE ACTION

HYBRID MICROCIRCUIT
RELIABILITY DATA

RELIABILITY ANALYSIS CENTER

DEVICE SECTION

MANUFACTURER: DUPONT ELECTRIC PRODS   FUNCTIONAL CATEGORY: N/A

TECHNOLOGY: THICK FILM   DEVICE FUNCTION: RESISTOR NETWORK

ENTRY NO.	PKG/NO. PINS	SIZE OP TEMP	PKG MFG	PKG SEAL	SUBSTR MTL/BOND	SUBSTR SIZE	NO. COND LYR	SUBSTR METAL #BONDS	IC NO./TYPE	IC CHP ATCH/INTERCON	TRANSISTOR NO./TYPE	TRANSISTOR CHP ATCH/INTERCON	DIODE NO./TYPE	DIODE CHP ATCH/INTERCON	CAPACITOR NO./TYPE	CAPACITOR CHP ATCH/INTERCON	RESISTOR NO./TYPE	RESISTOR CHP ATCH/INTERCON	RES TOL (%)	ELMT ATCH/INTERCON NO./TYPE
85	None 5	1.00x 1.00 0/70°C	N/R	N/A	Al_2O_3	1.00x 1.00	1	AuCond N/A	0		0		0		0		5 Carbon	Fired AuCond	3@ ±5 2@ ±1	

LIFE / ENVIRONMENTAL EXPERIENCE

DATA SRCE	SCR CLS	TST SRC	TEST TYP/APP ENV	STR LVL/EQP TYPE	TEST STD MTD/COND	NO. TSTD	TEST DUR.	PART HRS.	NO. FLD	FAILURE CLASSIFICATION IND; MODE; MECH; CAUSE (NO. FAILED / EVENT)	% DEF	TEST DATE	REMARKS
V	N	Lab	StgLif	70C		20	10000 Hrs	100000	0			12/72	
V	N	Lab	OpLif	70C		25	10000 Hrs	100000	0				
V	N	Lab	OpLif	70C		20	10000 Hrs	150000	0				
V	N	Lab	OpLif	70C		15	10000 Hrs	50000	0				
V	N	Lab	StgLif	70C		25	10000 Hrs	150000	0				

MALFUNCTION DATA

SYSTEM / EQUIPMENT	PART HISTORY	SCR CLS	DATE CODE	FAILURE ANALYSIS / CORRECTIVE ACTION

DEVICE SECTION

MANUFACTURER: DUPONT ELECTRIC PRODS   FUNCTIONAL CATEGORY: N/A

TECHNOLOGY: THICK FILM   DEVICE FUNCTION: RESISTOR NETWORK

HYBRID MICROCIRCUIT
RELIABILITY DATA

RELIABILITY ANALYSIS CENTER

ENTRY NO.	PKG/NO. PINS	SIZE/OP TEMP	PKG MFG	PKG SEAL	SUBSTR MTL/BOND	SUBSTR SIZE	NO. COND LYR	SUBSTR METAL #BONDS	IC NO./TYPE	IC CHP ATCH/INTERCON	TRANSISTOR NO./TYPE	TRANSISTOR CHP ATCH/INTERCON	DIODE NO./TYPE	DIODE CHP ATCH/INTERCON	CAPACITOR NO./TYPE	CAPACITOR CHP ATCH/INTERCON	RESISTOR NO./TYPE	RESISTOR CHP ATCH/INTERCON	RES TOL (%)	ELMT ATCH/INTERCON NO./TYPE
86	None 5	1.00x 1.00 0/70C	N/R	N/A	Al_2O_3	1.00x 1.00	1	PdAu N/A	0		0		0		0		5 Carbon	Fired PdAu	3@ ±5 2@ ±1	

LIFE / ENVIRONMENTAL EXPERIENCE

DATA SRCE	SCR CLS	TST SRC	TEST TYP/APP ENV	STR LVL/EQP TYPE	TEST STD MTD/COND	NO. TSTD	TEST DUR.	PART HRS.	NO. FLD	FAILURE CLASSIFICATION IND; MODE; MECH; CAUSE (NO. FAILED / EVENT)	% DEF	TEST DATE	REMARKS
V	N	Lab	OpLif	70C		20	10000 Hrs	2.05E5	0			12/72	
V	N	Lab	StgLif	70C		20	10000 Hrs	50000	0				

MALFUNCTION DATA

SYSTEM/EQUIPMENT	PART HISTORY	SCR CLS	DATE CODE	FAILURE ANALYSIS / CORRECTIVE ACTION	SYSTEM/EQUIPMENT	PART HISTORY	SCR CLS	DATE CODE	FAILURE ANALYSIS / CORRECTIVE ACTION

DEVICE SECTION

MANUFACTURER: DUPONT ELECTRIC PRODS   **FUNCTIONAL CATEGORY:** N/A

TECHNOLOGY: THICK FILM   **DEVICE FUNCTION:** RESISTOR NETWORK

HYBRID MICROCIRCUIT
RELIABILITY DATA

RELIABILITY ANALYSIS CENTER

ENTRY NO.	PKG/ NO. PINS	SIZE OP TEMP	PKG MFG	PKG SEAL	SUBSTR MTL/ BOND	SUBSTR SIZE	NO. COND LYR	SUBSTR METAL/ #BONDS	IC NO./ TYPE	IC CHP ATCH/ INTERCON	TRANSISTOR NO./ TYPE	TRANSISTOR CHP ATCH/ INTERCON	DIODE NO./ TYPE	DIODE CHP ATCH/ INTERCON	CAPACITOR NO./ TYPE	CAPACITOR CHP ATCH/ INTERCON	RESISTOR NO./ TYPE	RESISTOR CHP ATCH/ INTERCON	RES TOL (%)	NO./ TYPE	ELMT ATCH/ INTERCON
87	None 5	1.00x 1.00 0/70C	N/R	N/A	Al$_2$O$_3$ N/A	1.00x 1.00	1	PdAg N/A	0		0		0		0		5 Carbon	Fired PdAg	3@ ±5 2@ ±1		

LIFE / ENVIRONMENTAL EXPERIENCE

DATA SRCE	SCR CLS	TST SRC	TEST TYP/ APP ENV	STR LVL/ EQP TYPE	TEST STD MTD/COND	NO. TSTD	TEST DUR.	PART HRS.	NO. FLD	FAILURE CLASSIFICATION IND; MODE; MECH; CAUSE (NO. FAILED / EVENT)	% DEF	TEST DATE	REMARKS
V	N	Lab	OpLif	70C		5	10000 Hrs	50000	0			12/72	
V	N	Lab	StgLif	70C		5	10000 Hrs	50000	0				

MALFUNCTION DATA

SYSTEM/ EQUIPMENT	PART HISTORY	SCR CLS	DATE CODE	FAILURE ANALYSIS / CORRECTIVE ACTION	SYSTEM/ EQUIPMENT	PART HISTORY	SCR CLS	DATE CODE	FAILURE ANALYSIS / CORRECTIVE ACTION

DEVICE SECTION

MANUFACTURER: ELECTRO-MATERIALS CORP. **FUNCTIONAL CATEGORY:** N/A

DEVICE FUNCTION: RESISTOR NETWORK

TECHNOLOGY: THICK FILM

ENTRY NO.	PKG/NO. PINS	SIZE OP TEMP	PKG MFG	PKG SEAL	SUBSTR MTL/BOND	SUBSTR SIZE	NO. COND LYR	SUBSTR METAL #BONDS	IC NO./TYPE	IC CHP ATCH/INTERCON	TRANSISTOR NO./TYPE	TRANSISTOR CHP ATCH/INTERCON	DIODE NO./TYPE	DIODE CHP ATCH/INTERCON	CAPACITOR NO./TYPE	CAPACITOR CHP ATCH/INTERCON	RESISTOR NO./TYPE	RESISTOR CHP ATCH/INTERCON	RES TOL (%)	ELMT ATCH/INTERCON NO./TYPE
88	None 5	1.00x 1.00	N/R	N/A	Al_2O_3 N/A	1.00x 1.00	1	PtAu N/A	0		0		0		0		5 Carbon	Fired PtAu	3@ ±5 2@ ±1	

LIFE / ENVIRONMENTAL EXPERIENCE

DATA SRCE	SCR CLS	TST SRC	TEST TYP/APP ENV	STR LVL/EQP TYPE	TEST STD MTD/COND	NO. TSTD	TEST DUR.	PART HRS.	NO. FLD	FAILURE CLASSIFICATION IND; MODE; MECH; CAUSE (NO. FAILED / EVENT)	% DEF	TEST DATE	REMARKS
U	N	Lab	StgLif	70C		5	10000 Hrs	50000	0			12/72	
U	N	Lab	OpCnst	70C		5	10000 Hrs	50000					

MALFUNCTION DATA

SYSTEM/EQUIPMENT	PART HISTORY	SCR CLS	DATE CODE	FAILURE ANALYSIS / CORRECTIVE ACTION	SYSTEM/EQUIPMENT	PART HISTORY	SCR CLS	DATE CODE	FAILURE ANALYSIS / CORRECTIVE ACTION

DEVICE SECTION

MANUFACTURER: ELECTRONIC COMMUNICATIONS INC.
TECHNOLOGY: THIN FILM
FUNCTIONAL CATEGORY: LINEAR
DEVICE FUNCTION: FREQUENCY DIVIDE BY TWO

RELIABILITY ANALYSIS CENTER

HYBRID MICROCIRCUIT
RELIABILITY DATA

ENTRY NO.	PKG/ NO. PINS	SIZE OP TEMP	SUBSTR MTL/ BOND	SUBSTR SIZE	PKG SEAL	PKG MFG	NO. COND LYR	SUBSTR METAL #BONDS	IC NO./TYPE	IC CHP ATCH/ INTERCON	TRANSISTOR NO./TYPE	TRANSISTOR CHP ATCH/ INTERCON	DIODE NO./TYPE	DIODE CHP ATCH/ INTERCON	CAPACITOR NO./TYPE	CAPACITOR CHP ATCH/ INTERCON	RESISTOR NO./TYPE	RESISTOR CHP ATCH/ INTERCON	RES TOL (%)	LID NO./TYPE	LID ELMT ATCH/ INTERCON
89	FPM1 10	.83x .69x -125 -55/ 125C	Al₂O₃ Eutect	.80x .65	Weld	N/R	1	AlCond 40	0		4 SiPNP (1) SiNPN (3)	Eutect AuWire	0		6 Ceramic	Epoxy AlCond	16 Cermet	Fired AlCond	N/R	4 Ceramic	AgEpoxy AlCond

LIFE / ENVIRONMENTAL EXPERIENCE

DATA SRCE	SCR CLS	TST SRC	TEST TYP/ APP ENV	STR LVL/ EQP TYPE	TEST STD MTD/COND	NO. TSTD	TEST DUR.	PART HRS.	NO. FLD	FAILURE CLASSIFICATION IND; MODE; MECH; CAUSE (NO. FAILED / EVENT)	% DEF	TEST DATE	REMARKS
U	B	Rel	AirInhab	54/71C Cnctns 0/100% Pd	MS781A	13	1400 Hrs	18200	0			6/72	
U	B	Fld	AirInhab	Cnctns/ Operate		13	148 Hrs	1924	0			6/73	

MALFUNCTION DATA

SYSTEM / EQUIPMENT	PART HISTORY	SCR CLS	DATE CODE	FAILURE ANALYSIS / CORRECTIVE ACTION	SYSTEM / EQUIPMENT	PART HISTORY	SCR CLS	DATE CODE	FAILURE ANALYSIS / CORRECTIVE ACTION

DEVICE SECTION

MANUFACTURER: ELECTRONIC COMMUNICATIONS INC.

TECHNOLOGY: THIN FILM

FUNCTIONAL CATEGORY: LINEAR

DEVICE FUNCTION: DUAL AMPLIFIER

ENTRY NO.	PKG/ NO. PINS	SIZE OP TEMP	PKG MFG	PKG SEAL	SUBSTR MTL/ BOND	SUBSTR SIZE	NO. COND LYR	SUBSTR METAL #BONDS	IC NO./TYPE	IC CHP ATCH/ INTERCON	TRANSISTOR NO./TYPE	TRANSISTOR CHP ATCH/ INTERCON	DIODE NO./TYPE	DIODE CHP ATCH/ INTERCON	CAPACITOR NO./TYPE	CAPACITOR CHP ATCH/ INTERCON	RESISTOR NO./TYPE	RESISTOR CHP ATCH/ INTERCON	RES TOL (%)	INDUCTOR NO./TYPE	INDUCTOR ELMT ATCH/ INTERCON
90	FPM1 14	.94x 1.08x .13 -55 125C	N/R	Weld	Al₂O₃ Eutect	.90x 1.00	1	AlCond 64	0		8 SiNPN	Eutect AlCond	0		24 CeramAg	Epoxy AuWire	24 Cermet	Fired AlCond	N/R	4 Thin	Dep AlCond

LIFE / ENVIRONMENTAL EXPERIENCE

DATA SRCE	SCR CLS	TST SRC	TEST TYP/ APP ENV	STR LVL/ EQP TYPE	TEST STD MTD/COND	NO. TSTD	TEST DUR.	PART HRS.	NO. FLD	FAILURE CLASSIFICATION IND; MODE; MECH; CAUSE (NO. FAILED / EVENT)	% DEF	TEST DATE	REMARKS
U	B	Rel	AirInhab	-54/71C Cnnctns 0/100% Pd	MS781A	52	1400 Hrs	72800	0			6/72	
U	B	Fld	AirInhab	Cnnctns/ Operate		52	148 Hrs	7696	0			6/73	

MALFUNCTION DATA

SYSTEM / EQUIPMENT	PART HISTORY	SCR CLS	DATE CODE	FAILURE ANALYSIS / CORRECTIVE ACTION	SYSTEM / EQUIPMENT	PART HISTORY	SCR CLS	DATE CODE	FAILURE ANALYSIS / CORRECTIVE ACTION

DEVICE SECTION

RELIABILITY ANALYSIS CENTER

MANUFACTURER: ELECTRONIC COMMUNICATIONS INC. FUNCTIONAL CATEGORY: LINEAR

TECHNOLOGY: THIN FILM DEVICE FUNCTION: FREQUENCY DIVIDE; BY FIVE

HYBRID MICROCIRCUIT
RELIABILITY DATA

ENTRY NO.	PKG/ NO. PINS	SIZE/ OP TEMP	PKG MFG	PKG SEAL	SUBSTR MTL/ BOND	SUBSTR SIZE	NO. COND LYR	SUBSTR METAL #BONDS	IC NO./ TYPE	IC CHP ATCH/ INTERCON	TRANSISTOR NO./ TYPE	TRANSISTOR CHP ATCH/ INTERCON	DIODE NO./ TYPE	DIODE CHP ATCH/ INTERCON	CAPACITOR NO./ TYPE	CAPACITOR CHP ATCH/ INTERCON	RESISTOR NO./ TYPE	RESISTOR CHP ATCH/ INTERCON	RES TOL (%)	LID NO./ TYPE	LID ELMT ATCH/ INTERCON
91	FPM1 14	.94x 1.08x -.125 -55/ 125C	N/R	Weld	Al₂O₃ Eutect	.90x 1.00	1	AlCond N/R	0		10 SiNPN	Eutect AuWire	5 ZenAv	Eutect AuWire	1 Ceramic	Epoxy AlCond	33 Cermet	Fired AlCond	N/R	I5 Ceramic	AgEpoxy AlCond

LIFE / ENVIRONMENTAL EXPERIENCE

DATA SRCE	SCR CLS	TST SRC	TEST TYP/ APP ENV	STR LVL/ EQP TYPE	TEST STD MTD/COND	NO. TSTD	TEST DUR.	PART HRS.	NO. FLD	FAILURE CLASSIFICATION IND; MODE; MECH; CAUSE (NO. FAILED / EVENT)	% DEF	TEST DATE	REMARKS
U	B	Rel	Airlnhab	-54/71C Cmctns 0/100% Pd-	MS781A	13	1400 Hrs	18200	0			6/72	
U	B	Fld	Airlnhab	Cmctns/ Operate		13	148 Hrs	1924	0			6/73	

MALFUNCTION DATA

SYSTEM / EQUIPMENT	PART HISTORY	SCR CLS	DATE CODE	FAILURE ANALYSIS / CORRECTIVE ACTION	SYSTEM / EQUIPMENT	PART HISTORY	SCR CLS	DATE CODE	FAILURE ANALYSIS / CORRECTIVE ACTION

DEVICE SECTION

MANUFACTURER: ELECTRONIC COMMUNICATIONS INC. FUNCTIONAL CATEGORY: LINEAR

TECHNOLOGY: THIN FILM DEVICE FUNCTION: OSCILLATOR

ENTRY NO.	PKG/ NO. PINS	SIZE OP TEMP	PKG MFG	PKG SEAL	SUBSTR MTL/ BOND	SUBSTR SIZE	NO. COND LYR	SUBSTR METAL/#BONDS	IC NO./TYPE	IC CHP ATCH/INTERCON	TRANSISTOR NO./TYPE	TRANSISTOR CHP ATCH/INTERCON	DIODE NO./TYPE	DIODE CHP ATCH/INTERCON	CAPACITOR NO./TYPE	CAPACITOR CHP ATCH/INTERCON	RESISTOR NO./TYPE	RESISTOR CHP ATCH/INTERCON	RES TOL (%)	TOROID NO./TYPE	TOROID ELM ATCH/INTERCON
92	FPM1 20	1.94x 1.08x .156 -55/ 125C	N/R	Weld	Al₂O₃ Eutect	1.90x 1.00	1	AlCond 28	0		1 SiNPN (LID)	Eutect AuWire	4 Ceram (3) Varac (1) (LID)	Eutect AlCond	8 Cermet	Epoxy AlCond	7 Cermet	Fired AlCond	N/R	1 RF	Epoxy AlCond

LIFE / ENVIRONMENTAL EXPERIENCE

DATA SRCE	SCR CLS	TST SRC	TEST TYP/ APP ENV	STR LVL/ EQP TYPE	TEST STD MTD/COND	NO. TSTD	TEST DUR.	PART HRS.	NO. FLD	FAILURE CLASSIFICATION IND; MODE; MECH; CAUSE (NO. FAILED / EVENT)	% DEF	TEST DATE	REMARKS
U	B	Rel	AirInhab	-54/71C Cmctns 0/100% Pd	MS781A	13	1400 Hrs	18200	0			6/72	
U	B	Fld	AirInhab	Cmctns/ Operate		13	148 Hrs	1924	0			6/73	

MALFUNCTION DATA

SYSTEM / EQUIPMENT	PART HISTORY	SCR CLS	DATE CODE	FAILURE ANALYSIS / CORRECTIVE ACTION

SYSTEM / EQUIPMENT	PART HISTORY	SCR CLS	DATE CODE	FAILURE ANALYSIS / CORRECTIVE ACTION

DEVICE SECTION

MANUFACTURER: ELECTRONIC COMMUNICATIONS INC.
FUNCTIONAL CATEGORY: LINEAR

TECHNOLOGY: THIN FILM
DEVICE FUNCTION: DUAL OSCILLATOR

HYBRID MICROCIRCUIT
RELIABILITY DATA

ENTRY NO.	PKG/ NO. PINS	SIZE/ OP TEMP	PKG MFG	PKG SEAL	SUBSTR MTL/ BOND	SUBSTR SIZE	NO. COND LYR	SUBSTR METAL #/BONDS	IC NO./TYPE	IC CHP ATCH/INTERCON	TRANSISTOR NO./TYPE	TRANSISTOR CHP ATCH/INTERCON	DIODE NO./TYPE	DIODE CHP ATCH/INTERCON	CAPACITOR NO./TYPE	CAPACITOR CHP ATCH/INTERCON	RESISTOR NO./TYPE	RESISTOR CHP ATCH/INTERCON	RES TOL (%)	TOROID NO./TYPE	TOROID ELMT ATCH/INTERCON
93	FPMI 20	1.94x 1.08x .156 -55/ 125C	N/R	Weld	Al₂O₃ Eutect	1.90x 1.00	1	AlCond 32	0		4 SiNPN (LID)	Eutect AuWire	16 SiGen 12 Varac 4 (LID)	Eutect AuWire	32 Ceramic	Epoxy AlCond	28 Cermet	Fired AlCond	N/R	4 RF	Epoxy AlCond

LIFE / ENVIRONMENTAL EXPERIENCE

DATA SRCE	SCR CLS	TST SRC	PART HISTORY	SCR CLS	DATE CODE	TEST TYP/ APP ENV	STR LVL/ EQP TYPE	TEST STD MTD/COND	NO. TSTD	TEST DUR.	PART HRS.	NO. FLD	FAILURE CLASSIFICATION IND; MODE; MECH; CAUSE (NO. FAILED / EVENT)	% DEF	TEST DATE	REMARKS
U	B	Rel				AirInhab	-54/71C Cmctns 0/100% Pd	MS781A	26	1400 Hrs	36400	0			6/72	
U	B	Fld				AirInhab	Cmctns/ Operate		26	148 Hrs	3848	0			6/73	

MALFUNCTION DATA

SYSTEM / EQUIPMENT	PART HISTORY	SCR CLS	DATE CODE	FAILURE ANALYSIS / CORRECTIVE ACTION	SYSTEM / EQUIPMENT	PART HISTORY	SCR CLS	DATE CODE	FAILURE ANALYSIS / CORRECTIVE ACTION

HYBRID MICROCIRCUIT
RELIABILITY DATA

DEVICE SECTION

MANUFACTURER: ELECTRONIC COMMUNICATIONS INC.
TECHNOLOGY: THIN FILM

FUNCTIONAL CATEGORY: LINEAR
DEVICE FUNCTION: DRIVER SWITCH

ENTRY NO.	PKG/ NO. PINS	SIZE OP TEMP	PKG MFG	PKG SEAL	SUBSTR MTL/ BOND	SUBSTR SIZE	NO. COND LYR	SUBSTR METAL #BONDS	IC NO./ TYPE	IC CHP ATCH/ INTERCON	TRANSISTOR NO./ TYPE	TRANSISTOR CHP ATCH/ INTERCON	DIODE NO./ TYPE	DIODE CHP ATCH/ INTERCON	CAPACITOR NO./ TYPE	CAPACITOR CHP ATCH/ INTERCON	RESISTOR NO./ TYPE	RESISTOR CHP ATCH/ INTERCON	RES TOL (%)	LID NO./ TYPE	ELMT ATCH/ INTERCON
94	FPM1 30	.98x 1.05x -34 -55/ 125C	N/R	Weld	.95x 1.00 Eutect	N/R	1	AlCond N/R	0		5 SiNPN	Eutect AuWire	0		0		30 Cermet	Fired AlCond	N/R	5 Ceramic	AgEpoxy AlCond

LIFE / ENVIRONMENTAL EXPERIENCE

DATA SRCE	SCR CLS	TST SRC	TEST TYP/ APP ENV	STR LVL/ EQP TYPE	TEST STD MTD/COND	NO. TSTD	TEST DUR.	PART HRS.	NO. FLD	FAILURE CLASSIFICATION IND; MODE; MECH; CAUSE (NO. FAILED / EVENT)	% DEF	TEST DATE	REMARKS
U	B	Rel	AirInhab	-54/71C Cmctns 0/100% Pd	MS781A	13	1400 Hrs	18200	0			6/72	
U	B	Fld	AirInhab	Cmctns/ Operate		13	148 Hrs	1924	0			6/73	

MALFUNCTION DATA

SYSTEM/ EQUIPMENT	PART HISTORY	SCR CLS	DATE CODE	FAILURE ANALYSIS / CORRECTIVE ACTION	SYSTEM/ EQUIPMENT	PART HISTORY	SCR CLS	DATE CODE	FAILURE ANALYSIS / CORRECTIVE ACTION

H.M.R.D.—E

DEVICE SECTION

MANUFACTURER: FAIRCHILD SEMICONDUCTOR FUNCTIONAL CATEGORY: DIGITAL

TECHNOLOGY: THIN FILM DEVICE FUNCTION: HIGH VOLTAGE, HIGH CURRENT DRIVER

HYBRID MICROCIRCUIT
RELIABILITY DATA

RELIABILITY ANALYSIS CENTER

ENTRY NO.	PKG/ NO. PINS	SIZE OP TEMP	PKG MFG	PKG SEAL	SUBSTR MTL/ BOND	SUBSTR SIZE	NO. COND LYR	SUBSTR METAL #BONDS	IC NO./ TYPE	IC CHP ATCH/ INTERCON	TRANSISTOR NO./ TYPE	TRANSISTOR CHP ATCH/ INTERCON	DIODE NO./ TYPE	DIODE CHP ATCH/ INTERCON	CAPACITOR NO./ TYPE	CAPACITOR CHP ATCH/ INTERCON	RESISTOR NO./ TYPE	RESISTOR CHP ATCH/ INTERCON	RES TOL (%)	ELMT ATCH/ INTERCON NO./ TYPE
95	FPCm 10	TO-91 -55/ 125C	N/R	Glass Header	N/A	1	AuCotd N/R	2 8 Gate	Eutect AuWire	1 SiNPN	Eutect AuWire	0		0		1 Cermet	Epoxy AuWire	N/R	

LIFE / ENVIRONMENTAL EXPERIENCE

DATA SRCE	SCR CLS	TST SRC	TEST TYP/ APP ENV	STR LVL/ EQP TYPE	TEST STD MTD/COND	NO. TSTD	TEST DUR.	PART HRS.	NO. FLD	FAILURE CLASSIFICATION IND; MODE; MECH; CAUSE (NO. FAILED / EVENT)	% DEF	TEST DATE	REMARKS
V	N	Scr	Burn-In	125C	N/R	215	168 Hrs	36120	0			11/70	

MALFUNCTION DATA

SYSTEM / EQUIPMENT	PART HISTORY	SCR CLS	DATE CODE	FAILURE ANALYSIS / CORRECTIVE ACTION

SYSTEM / EQUIPMENT	PART HISTORY	SCR CLS	DATE CODE	FAILURE ANALYSIS / CORRECTIVE ACTION

DEVICE SECTION

MANUFACTURER: FAIRCHILD SEMICONDUCTOR **FUNCTIONAL CATEGORY:** DIGITAL

TECHNOLOGY: THIN FILM **DEVICE FUNCTION:** QUAD DRIVER

ENTRY NO.	PKG/ NO. PINS	SIZE OP TEMP	PKG MFG	PKG SEAL	SUBSTR MTL/ BOND	SUBSTR SIZE	NO. COND LYR	SUBSTR METAL #BONDS	IC NO./ TYPE	IC CHP ATCH/ INTERCON	TRANSISTOR NO./ TYPE	TRANSISTOR CHP ATCH/ INTERCON	DIODE NO./ TYPE	DIODE CHP ATCH/ INTERCON	CAPACITOR NO./ TYPE	CAPACITOR CHP ATCH/ INTERCON	RESISTOR NO./ TYPE	RESISTOR CHP ATCH/ INTERCON	RES TOL (%)	ELMT ATCH/ INTERCON NO./ TYPE
96	FPCm 14	TO-86 -55 125C	N/R	Glass Header N/A	0.25x 0.25	1	Kov/Au 8	0		4 SiNPN	Eutect AuWire	0		0		0			

LIFE / ENVIRONMENTAL EXPERIENCE

DATA SRCE	SCR CLS	TST SRC	TEST TYP/ APP ENV	STR LVL/ EQP TYPE	TEST STD MTD/COND	NO. TSTD	TEST DUR.	PART HRS.	NO. FLD	FAILURE CLASSIFICATION IND; MODE; MECH; CAUSE (NO. FAILED / EVENT)	% DEF	TEST DATE	REMARKS
U	A	Fld	St1Orbt	Combine/ Operate		8	41375 Hrs	3.31E5	0			4/70- 1/75	

MALFUNCTION DATA

SYSTEM / EQUIPMENT	PART HISTORY	SCR CLS	DATE CODE	FAILURE ANALYSIS / CORRECTIVE ACTION

SYSTEM / EQUIPMENT	PART HISTORY	SCR CLS	DATE CODE	FAILURE ANALYSIS / CORRECTIVE ACTION

RELIABILITY ANALYSIS CENTER

DEVICE SECTION

MANUFACTURER: FAIRCHILD SEMICONDUCTOR

TECHNOLOGY: THIN FILM

FUNCTIONAL CATEGORY: LINEAR

DEVICE FUNCTION: ADJUSTABLE POSITIVE DC VOLTAGE REGULATOR

HYBRID MICROCIRCUIT
RELIABILITY DATA

ENTRY NO.	PKG/ NO. PINS	SIZE OP TEMP	PKG MFG	PKG SEAL	SUBSTR MTL/ BOND	SUBSTR SIZE	NO. COND LYR	SUBSTR METAL #BONDS	IC NO./ TYPE	IC CHP ATCH/ INTERCON	TRANSISTOR NO./ TYPE	TRANSISTOR CHP ATCH/ INTERCON	DIODE NO./ TYPE	DIODE CHP ATCH/ INTERCON	CAPACITOR NO./ TYPE	CAPACITOR CHP ATCH/ INTERCON	RESISTOR NO./ TYPE	RESISTOR CHP ATCH/ INTERCON	RES TOL (%)	ELMT ATCH/ INTERCON NO./ TYPE
97	Can 8	TO-99 -55/ 125C	N/R	Weld	Header N/A	0.38D	1	Kov/Au 11	0		5 SiPNP (4) Unij (1)	Eutect AuWire	1 ZenAv	Eutect AuWire	0		3 Cermet	Epoxy AuWire	N/R	

LIFE / ENVIRONMENTAL EXPERIENCE

DATA SRCE	SCR CLS	TST SRC	TEST TYP/ APP ENV	STR LVL/ EQP TYPE	TEST STD MTD/COND	NO. TSTD	TEST DUR.	PART HRS.	NO. FLD	FAILURE CLASSIFICATION IND; MODE; MECH; CAUSE (NO. FAILED / EVENT)	% DEF	TEST DATE
U	B	Env	VisInsp		MS883	25			0			9/69
U	SSD	Brn	X-Ray		1008B	25			0			
U	SSD	Env	Temp TempCyc	125C -55/125C 10/10 min	1010B	23 23	72 Hrs	1656	0			
			CnstAcc	10KG 6 AXES	2001B	23			0			
V	SSD	Lab	OpCnst	125C 100% 5stp 2.5 KG inct.		15	500 Hrs	7500	0			
V	SSD	Stp	MechShk	500G/stp 3 Blo	2002	3			1	Wire Bond Failure	33.3	
V	SSD	Env	ThrmShk LeadFtg Moistr	-55/125C -10/65C 98%RH	1011B 1004B	4 4			0 0			
V	SSD	Env	Solder MechShk	1.5KG 6 AXES	1014A 2002B	4 4	5/5 min		0 1	Failed to Meet E.M.	25.0	
V	SSD		VbVrFrq	.02/2KHZ 2OG	2007A	4			0			
U	A	Fld	StlOrbit	Combin/ Operate		14	35700	5.00E5	0			4/70
U	A	Fld	StlOrbit	Combin/ Operate		1	35700	35700	0			5/74

REMARKS

MALFUNCTION DATA

SYSTEM / EQUIPMENT	PART HISTORY	SCR CLS	DATE CODE	FAILURE ANALYSIS / CORRECTIVE ACTION
	Bench Test Ambient	B	N/R	Failed Electrical Broken Substrate Header Bond/1

SYSTEM / EQUIPMENT	PART HISTORY	SCR CLS	DATE CODE	FAILURE ANALYSIS / CORRECTIVE ACTION

RELIABILITY
ANALYSIS
CENTER

HYBRID MICROCIRCUIT
RELIABILITY DATA

DEVICE SECTION

MANUFACTURER: FAIRCHILD SEMICONDUCTOR FUNCTIONAL CATEGORY: N/A

TECHNOLOGY: THIN FILM DEVICE FUNCTION: RESISTOR NETWORK

ENTRY NO.	PKG/ NO. PINS	SIZE OP TEMP	PKG MFG	PKG SEAL	SUBSTR MTL/ BOND	SUBSTR SIZE	NO. COND LYR	SUBSTR METAL #BONDS	IC NO./TYPE	IC CHP ATCH/ INTERCON	TRANSISTOR NO./TYPE	TRANSISTOR CHP ATCH/ INTERCON	DIODE NO./TYPE	DIODE CHP ATCH/ INTERCON	CAPACITOR NO./TYPE	CAPACITOR CHP ATCH/ INTERCON	RESISTOR NO./TYPE	RESISTOR CHP ATCH/ INTERCON	RES TOL (%)	ELMT ATCH/ INTERCON NO./TYPE
98	Can 3	TO-5 -55/ 125C	N/R	Weld	PsG Eutect	.30D	1	AuCond 4	0		0		0		0		2 SiCr	Fired AuCond	+5	

LIFE / ENVIRONMENTAL EXPERIENCE

DATA SRCE	SCR CLS	TST SRC	TEST TYP/ APP ENV	STR LVL/ EQP TYPE	TEST STD MTD/COND	NO. TSTD	TEST DUR.	PART HRS.	NO. FLD	FAILURE CLASSIFICATION IND; MODE; MECH; CAUSE (NO. FAILED / EVENT)	% DEF	TEST DATE	REMARKS
V	N/R	Env	Humidity	-25C 100% 495C/15 min		20	1162	148	18	Opens; Al Corrosion	90.0	12/72	
V	N/R	Env	TempCyc Humidity	-25/25C 100%RH		96		1.12B5	0			12/72	

MALFUNCTION DATA

SYSTEM / EQUIPMENT	PART HISTORY	SCR CLS	DATE CODE	FAILURE ANALYSIS / CORRECTIVE ACTION	SYSTEM / EQUIPMENT	PART HISTORY	SCR CLS	DATE CODE	FAILURE ANALYSIS / CORRECTIVE ACTION

DEVICE SECTION

RELIABILITY ANALYSIS CENTER

MANUFACTURER: FAIRCHILD SEMICONDUCTOR   **FUNCTIONAL CATEGORY:** N/A

TECHNOLOGY: THIN FILM   **DEVICE FUNCTION:** RESISTOR NETWORK

HYBRID MICROCIRCUIT
RELIABILITY DATA

ENTRY NO.	PKG/ NO. PINS	SIZE OP TEMP	PKG MFG	PKG SEAL	SUBSTR MTL/ BOND	SUBSTR SIZE	NO. COND LYR	SUBSTR METAL #BONDS	IC NO./ TYPE	IC CHP ATCH/ INTERCON	TRANSISTOR NO./ TYPE	TRANSISTOR CHP ATCH/ INTERCON	DIODE NO./ TYPE	DIODE CHP ATCH/ INTERCON	CAPACITOR NO./ TYPE	CAPACITOR CHP ATCH/ INTERCON	RESISTOR NO./ TYPE	RESISTOR CHP ATCH/ INTERCON	RES TOL (%)	ELMT ATCH/ INTERCON NO./ TYPE
99	Can 8	TO-5 -55/ 125C	Weld	PsG Eutect	.30D	1	AuCond 10	0	0	0	0	0	0	0	6 SiCr	Fired AuWire	±5		

LIFE / ENVIRONMENTAL EXPERIENCE

DATA SRCE	SCR CLS	TST SRC	TEST TYP/ APP ENV	STR LVL/ EQP TYPE	TEST STD MTD/COND	NO. TSTD	TEST DUR.	PART HRS.	NO. FLD	FAILURE CLASSIFICATION IND; MODE; MECH; CAUSE (NO. FAILED / EVENT)	% DEF	TEST DATE	REMARKS
V	N/R	Env	Temp			28	24 Hrs	654	0			12/72	Cans Punctured prior to 495C Bake
V	N/R	Env	Temp			29	23 Hrs	654	0				Cans Punctured Piror to 495C Bake
V	N/R	Env	Temp			28	24 Hrs	654	27	Open; Corrosion	96.0		Cans not Punctured prior to 495C Bake

MALFUNCTION DATA

SYSTEM / EQUIPMENT	PART HISTORY	SCR CLS	DATE CODE	FAILURE ANALYSIS / CORRECTIVE ACTION	SYSTEM / EQUIPMENT	PART HISTORY	SCR CLS	DATE CODE	FAILURE ANALYSIS / CORRECTIVE ACTION

DEVICE SECTION

MANUFACTURER: FAIRCHILD SEMICONDUCTOR   FUNCTIONAL CATEGORY: N/A

TECHNOLOGY: THIN FILM   DEVICE FUNCTION: RESISTOR NETWORK

ENTRY NO.	PKG/ NO. PINS	SIZE OP TEMP	PKG MFG	PKG SEAL	SUBSTR MTL/ BOND	SUBSTR SIZE	NO. COND LYR	SUBSTR METAL #BONDS	IC NO./TYPE	IC CHP ATCH/ INTERCON	TRANSISTOR NO./TYPE	TRANSISTOR CHP ATCH/ INTERCON	DIODE NO./TYPE	DIODE CHP ATCH/ INTERCON	CAPACITOR NO./TYPE	CAPACITOR CHP ATCH/ INTERCON	RESISTOR NO./TYPE	RESISTOR CHP ATCH/ INTERCON	RES TOL (%)	ELMT ATCH/ INTERCON NO./TYPE
100	FPCm 14	TO-86 -55/ 125C		Glass	PsG Eutect	.20x .20	1	AuCond 16	0	0	0		0		0		8 SiCr	Fired AuWire	±5	

LIFE / ENVIRONMENTAL EXPERIENCE

DATA SRCE	SCR CLS	TST SRC	TEST TYP/ APP ENV	STR LVL/ EQP TYPE	TEST STD MTD/COND	NO. TSTD	TEST DUR.	PART HRS.	NO. FLD	FAILURE CLASSIFICATION IND; MODE; MECH; CAUSE (NO. FAILED / EVENT)	% DEF	TEST DATE	REMARKS
V	N/R Lab		StgLif	150C		232	1000 Hrs	232000	0			12/72	
V	N/R Lab		StgLif	150C		83	1000 Hrs	83000	0				

MALFUNCTION DATA

SYSTEM / EQUIPMENT	PART HISTORY	SCR CLS	DATE CODE	FAILURE ANALYSIS / CORRECTIVE ACTION

SYSTEM / EQUIPMENT	PART HISTORY	SCR CLS	DATE CODE	FAILURE ANALYSIS / CORRECTIVE ACTION

RELIABILITY ANALYSIS CENTER

HYBRID MICROCIRCUIT
RELIABILITY DATA

DEVICE SECTION

FUNCTIONAL CATEGORY: N/A

MANUFACTURER: FAIRCHILD

DEVICE FUNCTION: RESISTOR ARRAY

TECHNOLOGY: THIN FILM

ENTRY NO.	PKG/ NO. PINS	SIZE OP TEMP	PKG MFG	PKG SEAL	SUBSTR MTL/ BOND	SUBSTR SIZE	NO. COND LYR	SUBSTR METAL #BONDS	IC NO./ TYPE	IC CHP ATCH/ INTERCON	TRANSISTOR NO./ TYPE	TRANSISTOR CHP ATCH/ INTERCON	DIODE NO./ TYPE	DIODE CHP ATCH/ INTERCON	CAPACITOR NO./ TYPE	CAPACITOR CHP ATCH/ INTERCON	RESISTOR NO./ TYPE	RESISTOR CHP ATCH/ INTERCON	RES TOL (%)	ELMT ATCH/ INTERCON NO./ TYPE
101	C-DIP 14	TO-116 -55/		Glass	PsG Eutect	.20x .20	1	AuCond 16	0	0	0	0	0	0	0	0	7 SiO$_2$ Chip	Fired AlWire	±5	

LIFE / ENVIRONMENTAL EXPERIENCE

DATA SRCE	SCR CLS	TST SRC	TEST TYP/ APP ENV	STR LVL/ EQP TYPE	TEST STD MTD/COND	NO. TSTD	TEST DUR.	PART HRS.	NO. FLD	FAILURE CLASSIFICATION IND; MODE; MECH; CAUSE (NO. FAILED / EVENT)	% DEF	TEST DATE	REMARKS
V	N/R	Lab	StgLif	150C		70	1000 Hrs	70000	0			12/72	
V	N/R	Lab	StgLif	150C		104	1000 Hrs	1.04E5	0				

MALFUNCTION DATA

SYSTEM / EQUIPMENT	PART HISTORY	SCR CLS	DATE CODE	FAILURE ANALYSIS / CORRECTIVE ACTION	SYSTEM / EQUIPMENT	PART HISTORY	SCR CLS	DATE CODE	FAILURE ANALYSIS / CORRECTIVE ACTION

PAGE 128

DEVICE SECTION

MANUFACTURER: GENERAL INSTRUMENTS

FUNCTIONAL CATEGORY: LINEAR

DEVICE FUNCTION: PREAMPLIFIER

TECHNOLOGY: THICK FILM

ENTRY NO.	PKG/ NO. PINS	SIZE OP TEMP	PKG MFG	PKG SEAL	SUBSTR MTL/ BOND	SUBSTR SIZE	NO. COND LYR	SUBSTR METAL #BONDS	IC NO./ TYPE	IC CHP ATCH/ INTERCON	TRANSISTOR NO./ TYPE	TRANSISTOR CHP ATCH/ INTERCON	DIODE NO./ TYPE	DIODE CHP ATCH/ INTERCON	CAPACITOR NO./ TYPE	CAPACITOR CHP ATCH/ INTERCON	RESISTOR NO./ TYPE	RESISTOR CHP ATCH/ INTERCON	RES TOL (%)	ELMT ATCH/ INTERCON NO./ TYPE
102	Can 10	TO-5 -55/ 125C	N/R	Weld	Al$_2$O$_3$ Eutect	.30D	1	PdAu ≈6	0		3 N/R	Eutect AuWire	0		0		N/R		N/R	

LIFE / ENVIRONMENTAL EXPERIENCE

DATA SRCE	SCR CLS	TST SRC	TEST TYP/ APP ENV	STR LVL/ EQP TYPE	TEST STD MTD/COND	NO. TSTD	TEST DUR.	PART HRS.	NO. FLD	FAILURE CLASSIFICATION IND; MODE; MECH; CAUSE (NO. FAILED / EVENT)	% DEF	TEST DATE	REMARKS
U	SSDEnv		Hrmtc	Fluoro 125C	MS883 1014C	10			0			8/69	
U	SSD	Env	MechShk	.8KG 1 msec	2002	10			0				
U	SSD	Env	ThrmShk VisInsp	-65/157C	1011 2008	10 2	500 cyc		0 0				

MALFUNCTION DATA

SYSTEM / EQUIPMENT	PART HISTORY	SCR CLS	DATE CODE	FAILURE ANALYSIS / CORRECTIVE ACTION	SYSTEM / EQUIPMENT	PART HISTORY	SCR CLS	DATE CODE	FAILURE ANALYSIS / CORRECTIVE ACTION

RELIABILITY
ANALYSIS
CENTER

DEVICE SECTION

FUNCTIONAL CATEGORY: LINEAR

MANUFACTURER: GENERAL INSTRUMENTS

DEVICE FUNCTION: DEMODULATOR

TECHNOLOGY: THICK FILM

ENTRY NO.	PKG/ NO. PINS	SIZE OP TEMP	PKG MFG	PKG SEAL	SUBSTR MTL/ BOND	SUBSTR SIZE	NO. COND LYR	SUBSTR METAL #BONDS	IC NO./ TYPE	IC CHP ATCH/ INTERCON	TRANSISTOR NO./ TYPE	TRANSISTOR CHP ATCH/ INTERCON	DIODE NO./ TYPE	DIODE CHP ATCH/ INTERCON	CAPACITOR NO./ TYPE	CAPACITOR CHP ATCH/ INTERCON	RESISTOR NO./ TYPE	RESISTOR CHP ATCH/ INTERCON	RES TOL (%)	ELMT ATCH/ INTERCON NO./ TYPE
103	Can 10	TO-5 -55/ 125C		Weld	Al₂O₃ Eutect	.30D	1	PdAu 8	0		4 N/R	Eutect AuWire	0		0		N/R		N/R	

LIFE / ENVIRONMENTAL EXPERIENCE

DATA SRCE	SCR CLS	TST SRC	TEST TYP/ APP ENV	STR LVL/ EQP TYPE	TEST STD MTD/COND	NO. TSTD	TEST DUR.	PART HRS.	NO. FLD	FAILURE CLASSIFICATION IND; MODE; MECH; CAUSE (NO. FAILED / EVENT)	% DEF	TEST DATE	REMARKS
U	SSD	Env	Hrmtc	Fluoro 125C	MS883 1014C	10			0			8/69	
U	SSD	Env	MechShk	.8KG 1 msec	2002	10			0				
U	SSD	Env	ThrmShk VisInsp	065/175C	1011 2008	10 2	500 cyc		0 0				

MALFUNCTION DATA

SYSTEM / EQUIPMENT	PART HISTORY	SCR CLS	DATE CODE	FAILURE ANALYSIS / CORRECTIVE ACTION

SYSTEM / EQUIPMENT	PART HISTORY	SCR CLS	DATE CODE	FAILURE ANALYSIS / CORRECTIVE ACTION

DEVICE SECTION

MANUFACTURER: GENERAL INSTRUMENTS

TECHNOLOGY: THICK FILM

FUNCTIONAL CATEGORY: LINEAR

DEVICE FUNCTION: ANALOG SWITCH

HYBRID MICROCIRCUIT
RELIABILITY DATA

ENTRY NO.	PKG/ NO. PINS	SIZE OP TEMP	PKG MFG	PKG SEAL	SUBSTR MTL/ BOND	SUBSTR SIZE	NO. COND LYR	SUBSTR METAL #BONDS	IC NO./ TYPE	IC CHP ATCH/ INTERCON	TRANSISTOR NO./ TYPE	TRANSISTOR CHP ATCH/ INTERCON	DIODE NO./ TYPE	DIODE CHP ATCH/ INTERCON	CAPACITOR NO./ TYPE	CAPACITOR CHP ATCH/ INTERCON	RESISTOR NO./ TYPE	RESISTOR CHP ATCH/ INTERCON	RES TOL (%)	ELMT ATCH/ INTERCON NO./ TYPE
104	FPM1 14	TO-87 -55/ 125C		Glass	Al_2O_3 Eutect	.20x .20	1	PdAu N/R	0		5 SiNPN	Eutect AuWire	1 SiGP	Eutect AuWire	2 Ceramic	Epoxy PdAu	5 N/R	Fired PdAu	N/R	

LIFE / ENVIRONMENTAL EXPERIENCE

DATA SRCE CLS	SCR CLS	PART HISTORY	TST SRC	TEST TYP/ APP ENV	DATE CODE	STR LVL/ EQP TYPE	TEST STD MTD/COND	NO. TSTD	TEST DUR.	PART HRS.	NO. FLD	FAILURE CLASSIFICATION IND; MODE; MECH; CAUSE (NO. FAILED / EVENT)	% DEF	TEST DATE	REMARKS
U	SSD Brn			RevBias		125°C		16	240	3840	3	N/R	18.8	8/73	

MALFUNCTION DATA

SYSTEM/ EQUIPMENT	PART HISTORY	SCR CLS	DATE CODE	FAILURE ANALYSIS / CORRECTIVE ACTION	SYSTEM/ EQUIPMENT	PART HISTORY	SCR CLS	DATE CODE	FAILURE ANALYSIS / CORRECTIVE ACTION
	EM(30°C)	B		Excessive Current in Input and Output Circuit; Improper connection of Power to Units/5					

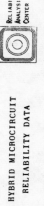

RELIABILITY ANALYSIS CENTER

HYBRID MICROCIRCUIT
RELIABILITY DATA

DEVICE SECTION

MANUFACTURER: GENERAL INSTRUMENTS
TECHNOLOGY: THICK FILM
FUNCTIONAL CATEGORY: LINEAR
DEVICE FUNCTION: OPERATIONAL AMPLIFIER

ENTRY NO.	PKG/ NO. PINS	SIZE OP TEMP	PKG MFG	PKG SEAL	SUBSTR MTL/ BOND	SUBSTR SIZE	NO. COND LYR	SUBSTR METAL #BONDS	IC NO./ TYPE	IC CHP ATCH/ INTERCON	TRANSISTOR NO./ TYPE	TRANSISTOR CHP ATCH/ INTERCON	DICE NO./ TYPE	DICE CHP ATCH/ INTERCON	CAPACITOR NO./ TYPE	CAPACITOR CHP ATCH/ INTERCON	RESISTOR NO./ TYPE	RESISTOR CHP ATCH/ INTERCON	RES TOL (%)	ELMT ATCH/ INTERCON NO./ TYPE
105	FPCm 14	TO-87 -55/ 125C		Glass	Al$_2$O$_3$ Eutect	.20x .20	1	PdAu N/R	0		6 SiNPN	Eutect AuWire	1 SiGP	Eutect AuWire	0		5 N/R	Fired PdAu	N/R	

LIFE / ENVIRONMENTAL EXPERIENCE

DATA SRCE SCR CLS	TST SRC	PART HISTORY	SCR CLS	DATE CODE	TEST TYP/ APP ENV	STR LVL/ EQP TYPE	TEST STD MTD/COND	NO. TSTD	TEST DUR.	PART HRS.	NO. FLD	FAILURE CLASSIFICATION IND; MODE; MECH; CAUSE (NO. FAILED / EVENT)	% DEF	TEST DATE	REMARKS

MALFUNCTION DATA

SYSTEM / EQUIPMENT	PART HISTORY	SCR CLS	DATE CODE	FAILURE ANALYSIS / CORRECTIVE ACTION	SYSTEM / EQUIPMENT	PART HISTORY	SCR CLS	DATE CODE	FAILURE ANALYSIS / CORRECTIVE ACTION
N/R	Bench Test Ambient (1/72)	N/R		Package, Gross Leaks, Damaged Glass Seal/2					

PAGE 132

RELIABILITY ANALYSIS CENTER

DEVICE SECTION

MANUFACTURER: GENERAL INSTRUMENTS

TECHNOLOGY: THICK FILM

FUNCTIONAL CATEGORY: LINEAR

DEVICE FUNCTION: SIGNAL PROCESSOR

ENTRY NO.	PKG/ NO. PINS	SIZE OP TEMP	PKG MFG	PKG SEAL	SUBSTR MTL/ BOND	SUBSTR SIZE	NO. COND LYR	SUBSTR METAL #BONDS	IC NO./ TYPE	IC CHP ATCH/ INTERCON	TRANSISTOR NO./ TYPE	TRANSISTOR CHP ATCH/ INTERCON	DIODE NO./ TYPE	DIODE CHP ATCH/ INTERCON	CAPACITOR NO./ TYPE	CAPACITOR CHP ATCH/ INTERCON	RESISTOR NO./ TYPE	RESISTOR CHP ATCH/ INTERCON	RES TOL (%)	ELMT ATCH/ INTERCON NO./ TYPE
106	Can 16	.265x .550D -55/ 125C	N/R	Weld	Al$_2$O$_3$ Eutect	1	2	AuPst 48	3 OpAmp	Eutect AuWire	1 SiNPN	Eutect AuWire	6 SiGP	Eutect AuWire	0		5 Cermet	Fired AuPst	N/R	

LIFE / ENVIRONMENTAL EXPERIENCE

DATA SRCE	SCR CLS	TST SRC	TEST TYP/ APP ENV	STR LVL/ EQP TYPE	TEST STD MTD/COND	NO. TSTD	TEST DUR.	PART HRS.	NO. FLD	FAILURE CLASSIFICATION IND; MODE; MECH; CAUSE (NO. FAILED / EVENT)	% DEF	TEST DATE	REMARKS
U	C	Fld	AirInhab	Navgtn/ Operate 30C		10	25400 Hrs	2.54E5	1	Malfunction	10.	3/72	
U	C	Fld	AirInhab	Navgtn/ Operate 30C		10	14100 Hrs	1.41E6	7	Malfunction/1 N/R/6	70,	5/73	

MALFUNCTION DATA

SYSTEM/ EQUIPMENT	PART HISTORY	SCR CLS	DATE CODE	FAILURE ANALYSIS / CORRECTIVE ACTION

SYSTEM/ EQUIPMENT	PART HISTORY	SCR CLS	DATE CODE	FAILURE ANALYSIS / CORRECTIVE ACTION

DEVICE SECTION

MANUFACTURER: GTE SYLVANIA
TECHNOLOGY: SEMICONDUCTOR

FUNCTIONAL CATEGORY: DIGITAL
DEVICE FUNCTION: 4 BIT DUAL RANK SHIFT REGISTOR

HYBRID MICROCIRCUIT
RELIABILITY DATA

 RELIABILITY ANALYSIS CENTER

ENTRY NO.	PKG/ NO. PINS	SIZE OP TEMP	PKG MFG	PKG SEAL	SUBSTR MTL/ BOND	SUBSTR SIZE	NO. COND LYR	SUBSTR METAL #BONDS	IC NO./ TYPE	IC CHP ATCH/ INTERCON	TRANSISTOR NO./ TYPE	TRANSISTOR CHP ATCH/ INTERCON	DIODE NO./ TYPE	DIODE CHP ATCH/ INTERCON	CAPACITOR NO./ TYPE	CAPACITOR CHP ATCH/ INTERCON	RESISTOR NO./ TYPE	RESISTOR CHP ATCH/ INTERCON	RES TOL (%)	ELMT ATCH/ INTERCON NO./ TYPE
107	FPCm 28	2.00x 2.00 -55/ 125C		Weld	Al$_2$O$_3$ Eutect	2.00x 2.00	1	AuCond AuTabs N/R	12 FLFL (4) 8 Gate (8)	BmLd AuCond AuTabs	0		0		0		N/R			

LIFE / ENVIRONMENTAL EXPERIENCE

DATA SRCE	SCR CLS	TST SRC	TEST TYP/ APP ENV	STR LVL/ EQP TYPE	TEST STD MTD/COND	NO. TSTD	TEST DUR.	PART HRS.	NO. FLD	FAILURE CLASSIFICATION IND; MODE; MECH; CAUSE (NO. FAILED / EVENT)	% DEF	TEST DATE
U	SSD	Env	TempCyc		MS750	11			0	N/R		8/71
			ThrmShk		1051F	11			3	Degr. Moisture Penetration	27.0	
			Moistr		1056B	11			5		45.0	
			Solder	28 Leads	1021/1	11			1	Open Int. Elect. Path, Solderability	9.0	
			CnstAcc	20KG	2006	11			0	Ext. Broken Lead Test Fixture	9.0	
			VbVrFrq	20G	2046	11			0			
			VibFtg		2056	11			0			
			MechShk	1.5KG X$_1$Y$_1$Z$_1$ 5 Blos	2016	11			0			
U	SSD	Lab	StgLif	200C		11	1000 Hrs	11000	0			
			OpDyn	25C		27	1000 Hrs	27000	0			
U	N	Scr/SSD	Immrsn		1011C&A	25			0			
			Moistr		1021/1							
			SltSpy		1046A							
			TempCyc		1051F							
			ThrmShk		1051B							
			InsRes	Each Lead to Sub- strate	1016A							
U	SSD	Env	Solder		2026	25			0			
			TrmStr		2036E	15			5	N/R	33.3	
			Hrmtc		1014	15			1	N/R	66.7	

MALFUNCTION DATA

SYSTEM/ EQUIPMENT	PART HISTORY	SCR CLS	DATE CODE	FAILURE ANALYSIS / CORRECTIVE ACTION	SYSTEM/ EQUIPMENT	PART HISTORY	SCR CLS	DATE CODE	FAILURE ANALYSIS / CORRECTIVE ACTION

RELIABILITY ANALYSIS CENTER

HYBRID MICROCIRCUIT
RELIABILITY DATA

DEVICE SECTION

MANUFACTURER: HALEX

TECHNOLOGY: THIN FILM

FUNCTIONAL CATEGORY: LINEAR

DEVICE FUNCTION: AMPLIFIER

ENTRY NO.	PKG/ NO. PINS	SIZE OP TEMP	PKG MFG	PKG SEAL	SUBSTR MTL/ BOND	SUBSTR SIZE	NO. COND LYR	SUBSTR METAL #BONDS	IC NO./ TYPE	IC CHP ATCH/ INTERCON	TRANSISTOR NO./ TYPE	TRANSISTOR CHP ATCH/ INTERCON	DIODE NO./ TYPE	DIODE CHP ATCH/ INTERCON	CAPACITOR NO./ TYPE	CAPACITOR CHP ATCH/ INTERCON	RESISTOR NO./ TYPE	RESISTOR CHP ATCH/ INTERCON	RES TOL (%)	ELMT ATCH/ INTERCON NO./ TYPE
108	Can 12	TO-101 -55/ 125C		Weld	Al$_2$O$_3$ Eutect	.30D	1	AuPst 12	0		1 SiNPN	Eutect AuWire	N/R		1 N/R	N/R	1 N/R	Fired AuWire	N/R	

LIFE / ENVIRONMENTAL EXPERIENCE

DATA SRCE	SCR CLS	TST SRC	TEST TYP/ APP ENV	STR LVL/ EQP TYPE	TEST STD MTD/COND	NO. TSTD	TEST DUR.	PART HRS.	NO. FLD	FAILURE CLASSIFICATION IND; MODE; MECH; CAUSE (NO. FAILED / EVENT)	% DEF	TEST DATE
U	SSD	Env	VisIns LeadFtg	2lbs Axial	MS883 2008	4			0			3/71
U	SSD	Env	TempCyc	-55/125C 10/10min	1010A	4			0			
U	SSD	Env	MechShk	.5KG 1 msec 3 AXES	2002A	4			0			
U	SSD	Env	VbVrFq	.02/2KHZ 20G	2007A	4			0			
U	SSD	Brn	RevBias	125C 100%	1005A	4	168 Hrs	672	0			

MALFUNCTION DATA

SYSTEM / EQUIPMENT	PART HISTORY	SCR CLS	DATE CODE	FAILURE ANALYSIS / CORRECTIVE ACTION	SYSTEM / EQUIPMENT	PART HISTORY	SCR CLS	DATE CODE	FAILURE ANALYSIS / CORRECTIVE ACTION

PAGE 1.35

DEVICE SECTION

FUNCTIONAL CATEGORY: DIGITAL/LINEAR
DEVICE FUNCTION: INITIATE MONITOR LOGIC

HYBRID MICROCIRCUIT
RELIABILITY DATA

RELIABILITY
ANALYSIS
CENTER

MANUFACTURER: HALEX
TECHNOLOGY: THIN FILM

ENTRY NO.	PKG/ NO. PINS	SIZE OP TEMP	PKG MFG	PKG SEAL	SUBSTR MTL/ BOND	SUBSTR SIZE	NO. COND LYR	SUBSTR METAL #BONDS	IC NO./ TYPE	IC CHP ATCH/ INTERCON	TRANSISTOR NO./ TYPE	TRANSISTOR CHP ATCH/ INTERCON	DIODE NO./ TYPE	DIODE CHP ATCH/ INTERCON	CAPACITOR NO./ TYPE	CAPACITOR CHP ATCH/ INTERCON	RESISTOR NO./ TYPE	RESISTOR CHP ATCH/ INTERCON	RES TOL (%)	ELMT ATCH/ INTERCON NO./ TYPE
109	FPM1 22	.75x .75x .16 -55/ 125C		Weld	Header N/A	.75x .75	1	N/R ≈ 228	13 8 Gate (5) 6 Invert (2) 9 Gate (1) OpAmp (4) VoltReg (1)	Eutect AuWire	4 SiNPN	Eutect AuWire	6 ZeAv (2) SiSig (4)	Eutect AuWire	9 BaTi₃/ K.1200 (8) SiO₂ (1)	Epoxy AuWire	35 TaO₂/ NiCr	Fired N/R	N/R	

LIFE / ENVIRONMENTAL EXPERIENCE

DATA SRCE	SCR CLS	PART HISTORY	SCR CLS	DATE CODE	TST SRC	TEST TYP/ APP ENV	STR LVL/ EQP TYPE	TEST STD MTD/COND	NO. TSTD	TEST DUR.	PART HRS.	NO. FLD	FAILURE CLASSIFICATION IND; MODE; MECH: CAUSE (NO. FAILED / EVENT)	% DEF	TEST DATE	REMARKS

MALFUNCTION DATA

SYSTEM / EQUIPMENT	PART HISTORY	SCR CLS	DATE CODE	FAILURE ANALYSIS / CORRECTIVE ACTION	SYSTEM / EQUIPMENT	PART HISTORY	SCR CLS	DATE CODE	FAILURE ANALYSIS / CORRECTIVE ACTION
	Bench Test Ambient/ Vibration	B		Capacitor Shook Loose During Vibration; Epoxy Bonding Material Failed to Adhere Due to the Lack of Proper Cleaning of Substrate/1					

DEVICE SECTION

MANUFACTURER: HEWLETT PACKARD

TECHNOLOGY: THIN FILM

FUNCTIONAL CATEGORY: DIGITAL

DEVICE FUNCTION: LED INDICATOR

ENTRY NO.	PKG/ NO. PINS	SIZE OP TEMP	PKG SEAL	PKG MFG	SUBSTR MTL/ BOND	SUBSTR SIZE	NO. COND LYR	SUBSTR METAL #BONDS	IC NO./ TYPE	IC CHP ATCH/ INTERCON	TRANSISTOR NO./ TYPE	TRANSISTOR CHP ATCH/ INTERCON	DIODE NO./ TYPE	DIODE CHP ATCH/ INTERCON	CAPACITOR NO./ TYPE	CAPACITOR CHP ATCH/ INTERCON	RESISTOR NO./ TYPE	RESISTOR CHP ATCH/ INTERCON	RES TOL (%)	ELMT ATCH/ INTERCON NO./ TYPE
110	$\overline{MC}$–DIP 24	1.3Bx 1.05x .06 −55/ 125C	Weld		Al$_2$O$_3$ Eutect	N/R	1	N/R N/R	3 N/R	Eutect AuWire	0		81 N/R	Eutect AuWire	0		0			

LIFE / ENVIRONMENTAL EXPERIENCE

DATA SRCE	SCR CLS	TST SRC	TEST TYP/ APP ENV	STR LVL/ EQP TYPE	TEST STD MTD/COND	NO. TSTD	TEST DUR.	PART HRS.	NO. FLD	FAILURE CLASSIFICATION IND; MODE; MECH; CAUSE (NO. FAILED / EVENT)	% DEF	TEST DATE	REMARKS
U	C	Scr	Burn–In	70C		1793	168 Hrs	3.01E5	12	N/R	0.67	8/72– 5/74	

MALFUNCTION DATA

SYSTEM / EQUIPMENT	PART HISTORY	SCR CLS	DATE CODE	FAILURE ANALYSIS / CORRECTIVE ACTION

SYSTEM / EQUIPMENT	PART HISTORY	SCR CLS	DATE CODE	FAILURE ANALYSIS / CORRECTIVE ACTION

RELIABILITY ANALYSIS CENTER

HYBRID MICROCIRCUIT
RELIABILITY DATA

DEVICE SECTION

MANUFACTURER: HUGHES AIRCRAFT CO
TECHNOLOGY: THICK FILM

FUNCTIONAL CATEGORY: LINEAR
DEVICE FUNCTION: DEFLECTION AMPLIFIER

ENTRY NO.	PKG NO. PINS	SIZE OP TEMP	PKG MFG	PKG SEAL	SUBSTR MTL/BOND	SUBSTR SIZE	NO. COND LYR	SUBSTR METAL #BONDS	IC NO./TYPE	IC CHP ATCH/INTERCON	TRANSISTOR NO./TYPE	TRANSISTOR CHP ATCH/INTERCON	DIODE NO./TYPE	DIODE CHP ATCH/INTERCON	CAPACITOR NO./TYPE	CAPACITOR CHP ATCH/INTERCON	RESISTOR NO./TYPE	RESISTOR CHP ATCH/INTERCON	RES TOL (%)	ELM ATCH/INTERCON NO./TYPE
111	FPM1Cm 30	1.00x 1.13x 0.13/ -55/ 125C	Coors	Sldr	Al_2O_3 AgEpoxy	.75x .75	1	AuPst AuWire (24) AlWire (60)	1 OpAmp	AgEpoxy AlWire	4 SiPNP (2) SiNPN (2)	AgEpoxy AlWire	1 SiGp	AgEpoxy AlWire	2 Ceramic	Solder AuPst	13 Carbon	Fired AuPst	+1	

LIFE / ENVIRONMENTAL EXPERIENCE

DATA SRCE CLS	TST SRC	TEST TYP/ APP ENV	STR LVL/ EQP TYPE	TEST STD MTD/COND	NO. TSTD	TEST DUR.	PART HRS.	NO. FLD	FAILURE CLASSIFICATION IND; MODE; MECH; CAUSE (NO. FAILED / EVENT)	% DEF	TEST DATE
U	SSD Scr	Burn-In	150C	MS883 1008	4	72 Hrs	288	1	Intermittent OpAmp	25.0	3/69
U	SSD Env	LoPress	100C 100 cyc (0-70000 ft.)	1008	4			2	Leaks	50.0	
		ThrmShk	0/100C 5/5 min	MS883 1011	4			0			
		MechShk	1.5KGY$_1$	MS883	4			0			
		VbVrFrq	.02/2KHZ 20G X$_1$Y$_1$Z$_1$ 48 min	MS883 2007A	4			0			
U	SSD Env	TempCyc	-55/125C 10/10 min	MS883 1010B	4			0			
U	SSD Lab	StgLif	-65C	MS883 1008	4	6 Hrs	24	0			
U	SSD Env	Moistr	-10/65C 98%RH	MS202 106B	4			0			
		SltSpy	35C 5% NACL	MS202C 101C	4			0			
		FineLk	Tracer Gas		4			0			
U	SSD Env	GrossLk	Fluoro Carbon		4			0			

MALFUNCTION DATA

SYSTEM / EQUIPMENT	PART HISTORY	SCR CLS	DATE CODE	FAILURE ANALYSIS / CORRECTIVE ACTION

SYSTEM / EQUIPMENT	PART HISTORY	SCR CLS	DATE CODE	FAILURE ANALYSIS / CORRECTIVE ACTION

DEVICE SECTION

FUNCTIONAL CATEGORY: LINEAR

HYBRID MICROCIRCUIT
RELIABILITY DATA

MANUFACTURER: HUGHES AIRCRAFT CO

DEVICE FUNCTION: A/D CONVERTER

TECHNOLOGY: THIN FILM

RELIABILITY ANALYSIS CENTER

ENTRY NO.	PKG/ NO. PINS	SIZE OP TEMP	PKG MFG	PKG SEAL	SUBSTR MTL/ BOND	SUBSTR SIZE	NO. COND LYR	SUBSTR METAL #BONDS	IC NO./ TYPE	IC CHP ATCH/ INTERCON	TRANSISTOR NO./ TYPE	TRANSISTOR CHP ATCH/ INTERCON	DIODE NO./ TYPE	DIODE CHP ATCH/ INTERCON	CAPACITOR NO./ TYPE	CAPACITOR CHP ATCH/ INTERCON	RESISTOR NO./ TYPE	RESISTOR CHP ATCH/ INTERCON	RES TOL (%)	ELM ATCH/ INTERCON NO./ TYPE
112	FPMlCm 30	1.00x 1.13x 0.13 -55/ 125C	Coors	Sldr	Al₂O₃ AgEpoxy	.75x .75	1	AuCond 204	1 OpAmp	AgEpoxy AlWire	30 SiNPN (20) SiPNP (10)	AgEpoxy AlWire (10) AuWire (20)	0		14 Ceramic	AgEpoxy AuCond	60 N/R	Fired AuCond	±1	

LIFE / ENVIRONMENTAL EXPERIENCE

DATA SRCE	SCR CLS	TST SRC	TEST TYP/ APP ENV	STR LVL/ EQP TYPE	TEST STD MTD/COND	NO. TSTD	TEST DUR.	PART HRS.	NO. FLD	FAILURE CLASSIFICATION IND; MODE; MECH; CAUSE (NO. FAILED / EVENT)	% DEF	TEST DATE
U	SSD	Scr	Bake	150C	MS883 1008C	3	72 Hrs	216				2/69
U	SSD	Env	LoPress	100C; 100 cyc (0-70000) ft.								
			ThrmShk	0/100C 5/5min	MS883 1011A							
			MechShk	15 cyc 1.5KG	MS883 2007A							
			VbVrFrq	5 Blo Y .02/2KHZ Log 4 min X₁Y₁Z	MS883 2007A							
			TempCyc	-55/125C 10/10 min	MS883 1010B							
U	SSD	Lab	StgLif	-65C	MS883 1008		6 Hrs	18				
U	SSD	Env	Moistr	-10/65C 98%RH	MS202 106B							
			SltSpy	10 Days 35C 5% NACL	MS202 101C		48 Hrs	144				

MALFUNCTION DATA

SYSTEM / EQUIPMENT	PART HISTORY	SCR CLS	DATE CODE	FAILURE ANALYSIS / CORRECTIVE ACTION

SYSTEM / EQUIPMENT	PART HISTORY	SCR CLS	DATE CODE	FAILURE ANALYSIS / CORRECTIVE ACTION

REMARKS

DEVICE SECTION

MANUFACTURER: HUGHES AIRCRAFT CO.

TECHNOLOGY: THIN FILM

FUNCTIONAL CATEGORY: LINEAR

DEVICE FUNCTION: A/D CONVERTER

ENTRY NO.	PKG/ NO. PINS	SIZE OP TEMP	PKG MFG	PKG SEAL	SUBSTR MTL/ BOND	SUBSTR SIZE	NO. COND LYR	SUBSTR METAL #BONDS	IC NO./ TYPE	IC CHP ATCH/ INTERCON	TRANSISTOR NO./ TYPE	TRANSISTOR CHP ATCH/ INTERCON	DIODE NO./ TYPE	DIODE CHP ATCH/ INTERCON	CAPACITOR NO./ TYPE	CAPACITOR CHP ATCH/ INTERCON	RESISTOR NO./ TYPE	RESISTOR CHP ATCH/ INTERCON	RES TOL (%)	ELMT ATCH/ INTERCON NO./ TYPE
112 (Cnt'd)																				

LIFE / ENVIRONMENTAL EXPERIENCE (con't)

DATA SRCE	SCR CLS	TST SRC	TEST TYP/ APP ENV	STR LVL/ EQP TYPE	TEST STD MTD/COND	NO. TSTD	TEST DUR.	PART HRS.	NO. FLD	FAILURE CLASSIFICATION IND; MODE; MECH; CAUSE (NO. FAILED / EVENT)	% DEF	TEST DATE	REMARKS
U		SSD Env	FineLk GrossLk	Tracer Gas Fluoro Carbon	MS883 1014A MS883 1014C	3			0		0	2/69	

MALFUNCTION DATA

SYSTEM / EQUIPMENT	PART HISTORY	SCR CLS	DATE CODE	FAILURE ANALYSIS / CORRECTIVE ACTION	SYSTEM / EQUIPMENT	PART HISTORY	SCR CLS	DATE CODE	FAILURE ANALYSIS / CORRECTIVE ACTION

DEVICE SECTION

MANUFACTURER: INTERSIL INC.

TECHNOLOGY: THIN FILM

FUNCTIONAL CATEGORY: DIGITAL

DEVICE FUNCTION: DUAL FET GATE SWITCH

ENTRY NO.	PKG/ NO. PINS	SIZE/ OP TEMP	PKG MFG	PKG SEAL	SUBSTR MTL/ BOND	SUBSTR SIZE	NO. COND LYR	SUBSTR METAL #BONDS	IC NO./TYPE	IC CHP ATCH/ INTERCON	TRANSISTOR NO./TYPE	TRANSISTOR CHP ATCH/ INTERCON	DIODE NO./TYPE	DIODE CHP ATCH/ INTERCON	CAPACITOR NO./TYPE	CAPACITOR CHP ATCH/ INTERCON	RESISTOR NO./TYPE	RESISTOR CHP ATCH/ INTERCON	RES TOL (%)	ELMT ATCH/ INTERCON NO./TYPE
113	Can 12	TO-101 -55/ 125C		Weld	Al₂O₃ Eutect	.30D	1	N/R	0		4 S1NPN	Eutect AuWire	2 N/R	Eutect AuWire	0		N/R	N/R	N/R

LIFE / ENVIRONMENTAL EXPERIENCE

DATA SRCE	SCR CLS	TST SRC	STR LVL/ EQP TYPE	TEST TYP/ APP ENV	TEST STD MTD/COND	NO. TSTD	TEST DUR.	PART HRS.	NO. FLD	FAILURE CLASSIFICATION IND; MODE; MECH; CAUSE (NO. FAILED / EVENT)	% DEF	TEST DATE	REMARKS
V	SSD	Env		TempCyc	MS750 1051							8/68	
				ThrmShk	1056								
				Seal	1071	25			0				
				CnstAcc	2006								
				MechShk	2016	25			0				
				VibFtg	2046	10			0				
				SltAtm	1041								
				Barometric	1001.1								
				Press									
				InsRes	1016								
V	SSD	Env		TrmStr	2036								
U	SSD	Lab		Seal OpCnst	1071	10 25	2000 Hrs	50000	1 0	Gross Pkg Leak	10.0		
U	SSD	Lab		StgLif	1031.4	25	1000 Hrs	25000	0				
U	SSD	Env		Solder	2031	10			0				
				SldHt	2031.1	10			0				
				Seal	1071								

MALFUNCTION DATA

SYSTEM / EQUIPMENT	PART HISTORY	SCR CLS	DATE CODE	FAILURE ANALYSIS / CORRECTIVE ACTION

SYSTEM / EQUIPMENT	PART HISTORY	SCR CLS	DATE CODE	FAILURE ANALYSIS / CORRECTIVE ACTION

DEVICE SECTION

MANUFACTURER: INTERSIL INC.

TECHNOLOGY: THIN FILM

FUNCTIONAL CATEGORY: DIGITAL

DEVICE FUNCTION: DUAL FET GATE SWITCH

HYBRID MICROCIRCUIT RELIABILITY DATA

 RELIABILITY ANALYSIS CENTER

ENTRY NO.	PKG/ NO. PINS	SIZE OP TEMP	PKG MFG	PKG SEAL	SUBSTR MTL/ BOND	SUBSTR SIZE	NO. COND LYR	SUBSTR METAL #BONDS	IC NO./ TYPE	IC CHP ATCH/ INTERCON	TRANSISTOR NO./ TYPE	TRANSISTOR CHP ATCH/ INTERCON	DIODE NO./ TYPE	DIODE CHP ATCH/ INTERCON	CAPACITOR NO./ TYPE	CAPACITOR CHP ATCH/ INTERCON	RESISTOR NO./ TYPE	RESISTOR CHP ATCH/ INTERCON	RES TOL (%)	ELMT ATCH/ INTERCON NO./ TYPE
114	C-DIP 14	.79x .28x -20 -55/ 125C		Glass	Al_2O_3	.25x .25	1	N/A ≈33	0		16 SiNPN (2) SiPNP (10) Unij (4)	Eutect AuWire	1 SiGP	Eutect AuWire	4 Ceramic	Epoxy AuWire	10 N/R	Fired N/R	N/R	

LIFE / ENVIRONMENTAL EXPERIENCE

DATA SRCE	SCR CLS	TST SRC	TEST TYP/ APP ENV	STR LVL/ EQP TYPE	TEST STD MTD/COND	NO. TSTD	TEST DUR.	PART HRS.	NO. FLD	FAILURE CLASSIFICATION IND; MODE; MECH; CAUSE (NO. FAILED / EVENT)	% DEF	TEST DATE	REMARKS
V	A	Env	VisInsp	PreCap 150C		321			4	N/R	1.25	10/71	
V	SSD	Scr	Bake	150C		317			0				
V	SSD	Env	TempCyc MechShk CnstAcc	-65/150C 10/10 min 1.5KG .1-1.0 msec 30KG Y1 1 min			48 Hrs	15216					
V	SSD	Env	FineLk GrossLk	He.50psig FC-43		317 310			7 1	N/R N/R	2.21 .032		
V	SSD	Brn	OpCnst	125C 30sec 125C		237	168 Hrs	40000	3	N/R/1 Spec Reject/2	1.26		
V	SSD	Env	VisInsp X-Ray			235 235			3 49	N/R N/R	1.28 20.9		

MALFUNCTION DATA

SYSTEM / EQUIPMENT	PART HISTORY	SCR CLS	DATE CODE	FAILURE ANALYSIS / CORRECTIVE ACTION	SYSTEM / EQUIPMENT	PART HISTORY	SCR CLS	DATE CODE	FAILURE ANALYSIS / CORRECTIVE ACTION

DEVICE SECTION

MANUFACTURER: LOCKHEED ELECTRONICS

TECHNOLOGY: THICK FILM

FUNCTIONAL CATEGORY: DIGITAL

DEVICE FUNCTION: LOGIC MODULE

HYBRID MICROCIRCUIT
RELIABILITY DATA

ENTRY NO.	PKG/ NO. PINS	SIZE OP TEMP	PKG MFG	PKG SEAL	SUBSTR MTL/ BOND	SUBSTR SIZE	NO. COND LYR	SUBSTR METAL #BONDS	IC NO./ TYPE	IC CHP ATCH/ INTERCON	TRANSISTOR NO./ TYPE	TRANSISTOR CHP ATCH/ INTERCON	DIODE NO./ TYPE	DIODE CHP ATCH/ INTERCON	CAPACITOR NO./ TYPE	CAPACITOR CHP ATCH/ INTERCON	RESISTOR NO./ TYPE	RESISTOR CHP ATCH/ INTERCON	RES TOL (%)	LID NO./ TYPE	LID ELMT ATCH/ INTERCON
115	S-DIP 20	2.00x 0.75 0.50 0/70C	N/R	Silic	Al$_2$O$_3$ Eutect	0.50x	1	PtAu 26	0		3 SiNPN	Eutect AuWire	7 N/R	Eutect AuWire	0		N/R Cermet	Epoxy AuWire	N/R	10 Ceramic	Epoxy PtAu

LIFE / ENVIRONMENTAL EXPERIENCE

DATA SRCE	SCR CLS	TST SRC	TEST TYP/ APP ENV	STR LVL/ EQP TYPE	TEST STD MTD/COND	NO. TSTD	TEST DUR.	PART HRS.	NO. FLD	FAILURE CLASSIFICATION IND; MODE; MECH: CAUSE (NO. FAILED / EVENT)	% DEF	TEST DATE
U.	SSD	Env	ThrmShk	-55/150C 45 cyc		N/R			2	Cracked Substrate		1/71 -2/72
U	SSD	Lab	OpDyn	70C		25	10996 Hrs	2.75E5	0			
U	SSD	Lab	OpDyn	65C		65	3498 Hrs	2.27E5	0			

REMARKS

MALFUNCTION DATA

SYSTEM / EQUIPMENT	PART HISTORY	SCR CLS	DATE CODE	FAILURE ANALYSIS / CORRECTIVE ACTION	SYSTEM / EQUIPMENT	PART HISTORY	SCR CLS	DATE CODE	FAILURE ANALYSIS / CORRECTIVE ACTION

DEVICE SECTION

MANUFACTURER: MICRO NETWORK CORP
TECHNOLOGY: THIN FILM

FUNCTIONAL CATEGORY: DIGITAL
DEVICE FUNCTION: D/A LADDER SWITCH

HYBRID MICROCIRCUIT
RELIABILITY DATA

RELIABILITY ANALYSIS CENTER

ENTRY NO.	PKG/ NO. PINS	SIZE OP TEMP	PKG MFG	PKG SEAL	SUBSTR MTL/ BOND	SUBSTR SIZE	NO. COND LYR	SUBSTR METAL #BONDS	IC NO./ TYPE	CHP ATCH/ INTERCON	TRANSISTOR NO./ TYPE	CHP ATCH/ INTERCON	DIODE NO./ TYPE	CHP ATCH/ INTERCON	CAPACITOR NO./ TYPE	CHP ATCH/ INTERCON	RESISTOR NO./ TYPE	CHP ATCH/ INTERCON	RES TOL (%)	ELMT ATCH/ INTERCON NO./ TYPE
116	FPM1 10	TO-87 -55/ 125C		Weld	Header N/A	.30x .25	1	N/R 12	0		6 SiNPN (2) SiPNP (4)	Eutect AuWire	0		0		8 NiCr	Fired N/R	N/R	

LIFE / ENVIRONMENTAL EXPERIENCE

DATA SRCE	SCR CLS	TST SRC	TEST TYP/ APP ENV	STR LVL/ EQP TYPE	TEST STD MTD/COND	NO. TSTD	TEST DUR.	PART HRS.	NO. FLD	FAILURE CLASSIFICATION IND; MODE; MECH; CAUSE (NO. FAILED / EVENT)	% DEF	TEST DATE
v	SSD	Env	VisInsp		MSB3	45						
			Solder		2008B&A	22						
			ThmShk		2003	45						
			TempCyc		1011A							
			Moistr		1010C							
			MechShk		1004	45						
			VibFrq		2002B							
			VbVrFrq		2005A							
			CnstAcc		2007A							
			LeadInt		2001E							
					2004B₂	45						
			FineLk		1014A							
			GrossLk		1014B							
			SltAtm		1009A	45						
v	SSD	Env	BondStr		2011	100			0			10/70

MALFUNCTION DATA

SYSTEM / EQUIPMENT	PART HISTORY	SCR CLS	DATE CODE	FAILURE ANALYSIS / CORRECTIVE ACTION	SYSTEM / EQUIPMENT	PART HISTORY	SCR CLS	DATE CODE	FAILURE ANALYSIS / CORRECTIVE ACTION

PAGE 144

DEVICE SECTION

MANUFACTURER: MICRO NETWORKS CORP
TECHNOLOGY: SEMICONDUCTOR
FUNCTIONAL CATEGORY: DIGITAL
DEVICE FUNCTION: QUAD POWER DRIVER

HYBRID MICROCIRCUIT
RELIABILITY DATA

RELIABILITY ANALYSIS CENTER

ENTRY NO.	PKG/ NO. PINS	SIZE OP TEMP	PKG SEAL	PKG MFG	SUBSTR MTL/ BOND	SUBSTR SIZE	NO. COND LYR	SUBSTR METAL #BONDS	IC NO./TYPE	IC CHP ATCH/ INTERCON	TRANSISTOR NO./TYPE	TRANSISTOR CHP ATCH/ INTERCON	DIODE NO./TYPE	DIODE CHP ATCH/ INTERCON	CAPACITOR NO./TYPE	CAPACITOR CHP ATCH/ INTERCON	RESISTOR NO./TYPE	RESISTOR CHP ATCH/ INTERCON	RES TOL (%)	ELMT ATCH/INTERCON NO./TYPE	REMARKS
117	FPMl 14	.39x .27x .08 -55/ 125C	Weld		Header N/A	.30x .25	1	N/R 24	1 4 Gate	Eutect AuWire	4 SiNPN	Eutect AuWire	2 SiGP	Eutect AuWire	0		0			0	

LIFE / ENVIRONMENTAL EXPERIENCE

DATA SRCE NO.	SCR CLS	TST SRC	TEST TYP/ APP ENV	STR LVL/ EQP TYPE	TEST STD MTD/COND	NO. TSTD	TEST DUR.	PART HRS.	NO. FLD	FAILURE CLASSIFICATION IND; MODE; MECH; CAUSE (NO. FAILED / EVENT)	% DEF	TEST DATE
V	SSD	Env	VisInsp		MS883 2008B	18			0			10/70
			VisInsp		2008A	18			0			
			Solder		2003	18			0			
			ThrmShk		1011A							
			TempCyc		1010C							
			Moistr		1004	18			0			
			MechShk		2002B							
			VibFtg		2005A							
			VbVrFq		2007A							
			CnstAcc		2001E							
			LeadInt		2004B$_2$	18			0			
			FineLk		1014A							
			GrossLk		1014C							
V	SSD	Env	SltAtm	150C	1009	45	48		0			
V	SSD	Lab	StgLif		1008	35	1000	1.40E5	1	V(SAT) out of Tolerance	2.86	
V	SSD	Lab	OpCnst	25C 100%	1005	15	1000 Hrs	15000	0			
V	SSD	Env	BondStr		2011	100			0			

MALFUNCTION DATA

SYSTEM/ EQUIPMENT	PART HISTORY	SCR CLS	DATE CODE	FAILURE ANALYSIS / CORRECTIVE ACTION

SYSTEM/ EQUIPMENT	PART HISTORY	SCR CLS	DATE CODE	FAILURE ANALYSIS / CORRECTIVE ACTION

DEVICE SECTION

MANUFACTURER: MOTOROLA SEMICONDUCTORS
TECHNOLOGY: THIN FILM

FUNCTIONAL CATEGORY: DIGITAL
DEVICE FUNCTION: HYBRID SWITCH PAIR

HYBRID MICROCIRCUIT
RELIABILITY DATA

 RELIABILITY ANALYSIS CENTER

ENTRY NO.	PKG/NO. PINS	SIZE/OP TEMP	PKG MFG	PKG SEAL	SUBSTR MTL/BOND	SUBSTR SIZE	NO. COND LYR	SUBSTR METAL #BONDS	IC NO./TYPE	IC CHP ATCH/INTERCON	TRANSISTOR NO./TYPE	TRANSISTOR CHP ATCH/INTERCON	DIODE NO./TYPE	DIODE CHP ATCH/INTERCON	CAPACITOR NO./TYPE	CAPACITOR CHP ATCH/INTERCON	RESISTOR NO./TYPE	RESISTOR CHP ATCH/INTERCON	RES TOL (%)	ELMT ATCH/INTERCON NO./TYPE
118	Can 8	TO-5 -55/125C		Weld	Header N/A	N/A	1	Kov/Au N/R	0		2 Unij	Eutect AlWire	0		0		1 NiCr	Epoxy AlWire	N/R	

LIFE / ENVIRONMENTAL EXPERIENCE

DATA SRCE	SCR CLS	TST SRC	TEST TYP/APP ENV	STR LVL/EQP TYPE	TEST STD MTD/COND	NO. TSTD	TEST DUR.	PART HRS.	NO. FLD	FAILURE CLASSIFICATION IND; MODE; MECH; CAUSE (NO. FAILED / EVENT)	% DEF	TEST DATE	REMARKS
U	SSD	Env	VisInsp		MS883 2071	18			0				
			Moistr		MS883 1004	25			1	Package Failure	4.00	3/70	
			MechShk	1.5KG, 6 AXES (30B1o)	MS883 2002B								
			VibFtg	20G 6GHz 3 AXES	MS883 2005A								
U	SSD	Env	VbVrFrq	20G .1/2KHz	MS883 2007	25			0				
U	SSD	Lab	OpCnst	85C 100%	MS750 1026	52	1000 Hrs	52000	0				

MALFUNCTION DATA

SYSTEM / EQUIPMENT	PART HISTORY	SCR CLS	DATE CODE	FAILURE ANALYSIS / CORRECTIVE ACTION

SYSTEM / EQUIPMENT	PART HISTORY	SCR CLS	DATE CODE	FAILURE ANALYSIS / CORRECTIVE ACTION

RELIABILITY
ANALYSIS
CENTER

DEVICE SECTION

MANUFACTURER: MOTOROLA SEMICONDUCTOR **FUNCTIONAL CATEGORY:** LINEAR

TECHNOLOGY: THIN FILM **DEVICE FUNCTION:** DIFFERENTIAL AMPLIFIER

ENTRY NO.	PKG/ NO. PINS	SIZE OP TEMP	PKG MFG	PKG SEAL	SUBSTR MTL/ BOND	SUBSTR SIZE	NO. COND LYR	SUBSTR METAL #BONDS	IC NO./ TYPE	IC CHP ATCH/ INTERCON	TRANSISTOR NO./ TYPE	TRANSISTOR CHP ATCH/ INTERCON	DIODE NO./ TYPE	DIODE CHP ATCH/ INTERCON	CAPACITOR NO./ TYPE	CAPACITOR CHP ATCH/ INTERCON	RESISTOR NO./ TYPE	RESISTOR CHP ATCH/ INTERCON	RES TOL (%)	ELMT ATCH/ INTERCON NO./ TYPE
119	Can 10	TO-100 -55/ 125C		Weld	Al_2O_3 Eutect	.30D	1	AgPst N/R	0		5 SiNPN (3) SiPNP (2)	Eutect AlWire	0		0		3 TaO_2	Epoxy AlWire	N/R	

LIFE / ENVIRONMENTAL EXPERIENCE

DATA SRCE	SCR CLS	TST SRC	TEST TYP/ APP ENV	STR LVL/ EQP TYPE	TEST STD MTD/COND	NO. TSTD	TEST DUR.	PART HRS.	NO. FLD	FAILURE CLASSIFICATION IND; MODE; MECH; CAUSE (NO. FAILED / EVENT)	% DEF	TEST DATE
V	SSD	Lab	RevBias	25C 30% 100 mw		15		42400	0			1/68
			RevBias	125C 100% 300 mw		25	2784 Hrs	69600	2	N/R	8.0	
			RevBias	125C		66	992.4 Hrs	65500	1	N/R	1.51	
			OpDyn	125C 100%		25	980	24500	1	N/R	4.0	
			StgLif	150C		15	2866.6 Hrs	43000	2	N/R	13.3	
			RevBias	125C 30% 100 mw		25	2800	10000	3	N/R	12.0	
V	SSD	Lab	StgLif	125C		94	989.4	93000	2	N/R	2.12	
V	SSD	Env	SltAtm	35C 50gm/m²	MS750 1041.1	68	24 Hrs	1632	0			
V	SSD	Stp	Temp	150C 175C 200C 225C 250C 275C 300C 325C		15		0	0			
V	SSD	Env	SldHt	1 cyc	MS750 2031.1	15			3	N/R	20.0	
									6	N/R	40.0	
			TmpCyc	125C	MS750 1051.1B	N/R			3	N/R		

MALFUNCTION DATA

SYSTEM / EQUIPMENT	PART HISTORY	SCR CLS	DATE CODE	FAILURE ANALYSIS / CORRECTIVE ACTION

SYSTEM / EQUIPMENT	PART HISTORY	SCR CLS	DATE CODE	FAILURE ANALYSIS / CORRECTIVE ACTION

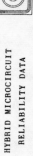

HYBRID MICROCIRCUIT
RELIABILITY DATA

DEVICE SECTION

MANUFACTURER: MOTOROLA SEMICONDUCTOR   FUNCTIONAL CATEGORY: LINEAR

TECHNOLOGY: THIN FILM   DEVICE FUNCTION: DIFFERENTIAL AMPLIFIER

ENTRY NO.	PKG/ NO. PINS	SIZE OP TEMP	PKG MFG	PKG SEAL	SUBSTR MTL/ BOND	SUBSTR SIZE	NO. COND LYR	SUBSTR METAL #BONDS	IC NO./ TYPE	IC CHP ATCH/ INTERCON	TRANSISTOR NO./ TYPE	TRANSISTOR CHP ATCH/ INTERCON	DIODE NO./ TYPE	DIODE CHP ATCH/ INTERCON	CAPACITOR NO./ TYPE	CAPACITOR CHP ATCH/ INTERCON	RESISTOR NO./ TYPE	RESISTOR CHP ATCH/ INTERCON	RES TOL (%)	ELM ATCH/ INTERCON NO./ TYPE
119 (Cntd)																				

LIFE / ENVIRONMENTAL EXPERIENCE (con't)

DATA SRCE	SCR CLS	TST SRC	TEST TYP/ APP ENV	STR LVL/ EQP TYPE	TEST STD MTD/COND	NO. TSTD	TEST DUR.	PART HRS.	NO. FLD	FAILURE CLASSIFICATION IND; MODE; MECH; CAUSE (NO. FAILED / EVENT)	% DEF	TEST DATE	REMARKS
V	SSD Env		ThrmShk		MS750 1056.1A	120			0				
			Moistr		MS750 1021.1								
			MechShk	50G 3 AXES 5 Blo	MS750 2016								
			VibFtg	10G	MS750 2046								
			VbVrFtg	10G	MS750 2056								
			CnstAcc	20KG	MS750 2006	70			4	N/R	5.71		
			MechShk	1.5KG 3 AXES 5 Blo	MS750 2016								
			VibFtg	10G	MS750 2046								
			VbVrFrq	10G	MS750 2056								
V	SSD Env		CnstAcc	20KG	MS750 2006	70			2	N/R	2.86		
V	SSD Env		TrmStr		MS750 2036	95			0				

MALFUNCTION DATA

SYSTEM / EQUIPMENT	PART HISTORY	SCR CLS	DATE CODE	FAILURE ANALYSIS / CORRECTIVE ACTION	SYSTEM / EQUIPMENT	PART HISTORY	SCR CLS	DATE CODE	FAILURE ANALYSIS / CORRECTIVE ACTION

DEVICE SECTION

MANUFACTURER: MOTOROLA SEMICONDUCTOR
TECHNOLOGY: THIN FILM

FUNCTIONAL CATEGORY: LINEAR
DEVICE FUNCTION: DIFFERENTIAL AMPLIFIER

ENTRY NO.	PKG/ NO. PINS	SIZE OP TEMP	PKG MFG	PKG SEAL	SUBSTR MTL/ BOND	SUBSTR SIZE	NO. COND LYR	SUBSTR METAL #BONDS	IC NO./ TYPE	IC CHP ATCH/ INTERCON	TRANSISTOR NO./ TYPE	TRANSISTOR CHP ATCH/ INTERCON	DIODE NO./ TYPE	DIODE CHP ATCH/ INTERCON	CAPACITOR NO./ TYPE	CAPACITOR CHP ATCH/ INTERCON	RESISTOR NO./ TYPE	RESISTOR CHP ATCH/ INTERCON	RES TOL (%)	ELMT ATCH/ INTERCON NO./ TYPE
119 (Cntd)																				

LIFE / ENVIRONMENTAL EXPERIENCE (con't)

DATA SRCE NO.	SCR CLS	TST SRC	TEST TYP/ APP ENV	STR LVL/ EQP TYPE	TEST STD MTD/COND	NO. TSTD	TEST DUR.	PART HRS.	NO. FLD	FAILURE CLASSIFICATION IND; MODE; MECH; CAUSE (NO. FAILED / EVENT)	% DEF	TEST DATE	REMARKS
V	SSD Stp			150C		15			0				
				175C		15			0				
				200C		15			0				
				225C		15			0				
				250C		15			1	N/R	6.67		
				275C		15			6	N/R	40.0		
				300C		15			3	N/R			
				325C		N/R							
V	SSD Stp		Power	100 mw		15			0				
				25C		15			0				
				900 mw		15			3	N/R			
				1000 mw		15			7	N/R			
				1100 mw		15			0				
V	SSD Stp		Power	100		15			0				
				200		15			0				
				300		15			0				
				400		15			1		6.66		
				500		15			0				
				600		15			3	N/R			
				700		N/R							

MALFUNCTION DATA

SYSTEM / EQUIPMENT	PART HISTORY	SCR CLS	DATE CODE	FAILURE ANALYSIS / CORRECTIVE ACTION	SYSTEM / EQUIPMENT	PART HISTORY	SCR CLS	DATE CODE	FAILURE ANALYSIS / CORRECTIVE ACTION

RELIABILITY ANALYSIS CENTER

HYBRID MICROCIRCUIT RELIABILITY DATA

DEVICE SECTION

MANUFACTURER: MOTOROLA SEMICONDUCTOR
TECHNOLOGY: THIN FILM

FUNCTIONAL CATEGORY: LINEAR
DEVICE FUNCTION: POWER DARLINGTON

ENTRY NO.	PKG/ NO. PINS	SIZE OP TEMP	SUBSTR MTL/ BOND	PKG SEAL	PKG MFG	SUBSTR SIZE	NO. COND LYR	SUBSTR METAL #BONDS	IC NO./ TYPE	IC CHP ATCH/ INTERCON	TRANSISTOR NO./ TYPE	TRANSISTOR CHP ATCH/ INTERCON	DIODE NO./ TYPE	DIODE CHP ATCH/ INTERCON	CAPACITOR NO./ TYPE	CAPACITOR CHP ATCH/ INTERCON	RESISTOR NO./ TYPE	RESISTOR CHP ATCH/ INTERCON	RES TOL (%)	ELMT ATCH/ INTERCON NO./ TYPE
120	Can 3	TO-5 -55/ 125C	Header N/A	Weld		N/A	1	Kov/Au N/R	0		? SiN/R	Eutect AlWire	0		0		1 NiCr	Eutect AlWire	N/R	

LIFE / ENVIRONMENTAL EXPERIENCE

DATA SRCE	SCR CLS	TST SRC	TEST TYP/ APP ENV	STR LVL/ EQP TYPE	TEST STD MTD/COND	NO. TSTD	TEST DUR.	PART HRS.	NO. FLD	% DEF	TEST DATE	REMARKS
U	C	Env	VisInsp		MS883 2008	25			0			
			Moistr	-10/65C 100%RH	MS883 1004						1/70	
			MechShk	1.5KG 1.0 msec 6 AXES	MS883 2002							
			VibFtg	20G 60HZ 3 AXES	MS883 2005							
U	C	Env	VbVrFrq	20G .1/2KHZ	MS883 2007	25			0			
U	C	Lab	OpCnst	25C 100%	MS750 1026	52	1000 Hrs	52000	0			
I	C	Env	CnstAcc	1KGY 1	MS750 2006	643			10	1.55		
			Hrmtc		MS750 1071	633			0			
			FineLk	He 5x10^{-7} ATM cc/sec	MS750 1071H							
			GrossLk	Fluoro Carbon	MS750 1071D							
			BurnIn	25C								
			BurnIn	25C			28 Hrs	17724	0			
I	C	Env	ElectMeas	25C		633	144 Hrs	91152	64	10.1		

MALFUNCTION DATA

SYSTEM/ EQUIPMENT	PART HISTORY	SCR CLS	DATE CODE	FAILURE ANALYSIS / CORRECTIVE ACTION

HYBRID MICROCIRCUIT
RELIABILITY DATA

RELIABILITY
ANALYSIS
CENTER

DEVICE SECTION

MANUFACTURER: MOTOROLA SEMICONDUCTOR

TECHNOLOGY: THICK FILM

FUNCTIONAL CATEGORY: LINEAR

DEVICE FUNCTION: PHASE INVERTER

ENTRY NO.	PKG/ NO. PINS	SIZE OP TEMP	PKG MFG	PKG SEAL	SUBSTR MTL/ BOND	SUBSTR SIZE	NO. COND LYR	SUBSTR METAL #BONDS	IC NO./ TYPE	IC CHP ATCH/ INTERCON	TRANSISTOR NO./ TYPE	TRANSISTOR CHP ATCH/ INTERCON	DIODE NO./ TYPE	DIODE CHP ATCH/ INTERCON	CAPACITOR NO./ TYPE	CAPACITOR CHP ATCH/ INTERCON	RESISTOR NO./ TYPE	RESISTOR CHP ATCH/ INTERCON	RES TOL (%)	ELMT ATCH/ INTERCON NO./ TYPE
h21.	Can 8	TO-99 -55/ 125C		Weld	Al₂O₃ Eutect	.30D	1	MoMn Au 34	0		2 SiN/R	Eutect AlWire	0		0		6 NiCr	Eutect AlWire	N/R	

LIFE / ENVIRONMENTAL EXPERIENCE

DATA SRCE	SCR CLS	TST SRC	TEST TYP/ APP ENV	STR LVL/ EQP TYPE	TEST STD MTD/COND	NO. TSTD	TEST DUR.	PART HRS.	NO. FLD	FAILURE CLASSIFICATION IND; MODE; MECH; CAUSE (NO. FAILED / EVENT)	% DEF	TEST DATE	REMARKS
U	SSD	Env	VisInsp VisInsp Moistr MechShk	1.5KG 1 msec 6 AXES	MS883 2027 2027 1004 2002B	25 18 25			0 0 0			3/70	
			VibFtg VbVrFrq CnstAcc	10KG 6 AXES	2005A 2007A 2001	25			0				
U	SSD	Env	OpCnst	25C 100%	1026	52	1000 Hrs	52000	0				

MALFUNCTION DATA

SYSTEM / EQUIPMENT	PART HISTORY	SCR CLS	DATE CODE	FAILURE ANALYSIS / CORRECTIVE ACTION	SYSTEM / EQUIPMENT	PART HISTORY	SCR CLS	DATE CODE	FAILURE ANALYSIS / CORRECTIVE ACTION

PAGE 151

DEVICE SECTION

MANUFACTURER: MOTOROLA SEMICONDUCTOR   FUNCTIONAL CATEGORY: LINEAR

TECHNOLOGY: SEMICONDUCTOR   DEVICE FUNCTION: OPERATIONAL AMPLIFIER

RELIABILITY
ANALYSIS
CENTER

HYBRID MICROCIRCUIT
RELIABILITY DATA

ENTRY NO.	PKG/ NO. PINS	SIZE OP TEMP	PKG SEAL	PKG MFG	SUBSTR MTL/ BOND	SUBSTR SIZE	NO. COND LYR	SUBSTR METAL #BONDS	IC NO./ TYPE	IC CHP ATCH/ INTERCON	TRANSISTOR NO./ TYPE	TRANSISTOR CHP ATCH/ INTERCON	DIODE NO./ TYPE	DIODE CHP ATCH/ INTERCON	CAPACITOR NO./ TYPE	CAPACITOR CHP ATCH/ INTERCON	RESISTOR NO./ TYPE	RESISTOR CHP ATCH/ INTERCON	RES TOL (%)	ELM ATCH/ INTERCON NO./ TYPE
122	Can 10	TO-100 -55/ 125C	Weld		Header Eutect	N/A	1	Kov/Au N/R	2 OpAmp	Eutect AlWire	0		0		0		0			

LIFE / ENVIRONMENTAL EXPERIENCE

DATA SRCE SCR CLS	TST SRC	TEST TYP/ APP ENV	STR LVL/ EQP TYPE	TEST STD MTD/COND	NO. TSTD	TEST DUR.	PART HRS.	NO. FLD	FAILURE CLASSIFICATION IND; MODE; MECH; CAUSE (NO. FAILED / EVENT)	% DEF	TEST DATE

REMARKS

MALFUNCTION DATA

SYSTEM / EQUIPMENT	PART HISTORY	SCR CLS	DATE CODE	FAILURE ANALYSIS / CORRECTIVE ACTION
	Bench Test Ambient	D		Thin Film Resistor Open at Interface Between Film and Aluminum Pad/1

SYSTEM / EQUIPMENT	PART HISTORY	SCR CLS	DATE CODE	FAILURE ANALYSIS / CORRECTIVE ACTION

DEVICE SECTION

MANUFACTURER: NATIONAL SEMICONDUCTOR

TECHNOLOGY: THICK FILM

FUNCTIONAL CATEGORY: DIGITAL

DEVICE FUNCTION: 2 Ø MOS CLOCK DRIVER

HYBRID MICROCIRCUIT
RELIABILITY DATA

RELIABILITY ANALYSIS CENTER

ENTRY NO.	PKG/ NO. PINS	SIZE OP TEMP	PKG MFG	PKG SEAL	SUBSTR MTL/ BOND	SUBSTR SIZE	NO. COND LYR	SUBSTR METAL/ #BONDS	IC NO./TYPE	IC CHP ATCH/ INTERCON	TRANSISTOR NO./TYPE	TRANSISTOR CHP ATCH/ INTERCON	DIODE NO./TYPE	DIODE CHP ATCH/ INTERCON	CAPACITOR NO./TYPE	CAPACITOR CHP ATCH/ INTERCON	RESISTOR NO./TYPE	RESISTOR CHP ATCH/ INTERCON	RES TOL (%)	ELM ATCH/ INTERCON NO./TYPE
123	Can 12	TO-8 -55/ 125C	N/R	Weld	Al$_2$O$_3$ Eutect	.50D	1	N/R 24	0		6 SiPNP	Eutect AuWire	6 SiGP	Eutect AuWire	0		6 Cermet	Fired N/R	N/R	

LIFE / ENVIRONMENTAL EXPERIENCE

DATA SRCE	SCR CLS	TST SRC	TEST TYP/ APP ENV	STR LVL/ EQP TYPE	TEST STD MTD/COND	NO. TSTD	TEST DUR.	PART HRS.	NO. FLD	FAILURE CLASSIFICATION IND; MODE; MECH; CAUSE (NO. FAILED / EVENT)	% DEF	TEST DATE
U	N	Scr/SSB	VisInsp			31			0			8/72
			FineLk	He 73psig 5x10-8 cc/sec		31			4	Package Failure	12.9	
			GrossLk	FC-78 73psig		31			3	Package Failure	9.68	
			Brn	125C OpCnst			168 Hrs					
			BondStr	MM Spec								
			ThrmShk	-65/150C 15 cyc	1011C							
			ThrmCyc	-65/150C 10 cyc	1011C							
			MechShk	1.5KG 4 AXES .5 msec	2002B							
			VibFtg	50Ω	2007							
			CnstAcc	30KG 5 AXES	2001E							
U	SSB	Lab	RngCnt	125C 100%	1005E	31	2000 Hrs	62000	0			

MALFUNCTION DATA

SYSTEM/ EQUIPMENT	PART HISTORY	SCR CLS	DATE CODE	FAILURE ANALYSIS / CORRECTIVE ACTION	SYSTEM/ EQUIPMENT	PART HISTORY	SCR CLS	DATE CODE	FAILURE ANALYSIS / CORRECTIVE ACTION

H.M.R.D.—F

RELIABILITY
ANALYSIS
CENTER

HYBRID MICROCIRCUIT
RELIABILITY DATA

DEVICE SECTION

MANUFACTURER: NATIONAL SEMICONDUCTOR
TECHNOLOGY: THICK FILM

FUNCTIONAL CATEGORY: LINEAR
DEVICE FUNCTION: OPERATIONAL AMPLIFIER

ENTRY NO.	PKG/ NO. PINS	SIZE/ OP TEMP	PKG MFG	PKG SEAL	SUBSTR MTL/ BOND	SUBSTR SIZE	NO. COND LYR	SUBSTR METAL #BONDS	IC NO./TYPE	IC CHP ATCH/INTERCON	TRANSISTOR NO./TYPE	TRANSISTOR CHP ATCH/INTERCON	DIODE NO./TYPE	DIODE CHP ATCH/INTERCON	CAPACITOR NO./TYPE	CAPACITOR CHP ATCH/INTERCON	RESISTOR NO./TYPE	RESISTOR CHP ATCH/INTERCON	RES TOL (%)	ELM ATCH/INTERCON NO./TYPE
124	Can 8	TO-5 -55/ 125C	N/R	Weld	Al$_2$O$_3$ Eutect	.30D	1	N/R 36	0		4 SiNPN (2) SiPNP (2)	Eutect AuWire	0		0		4 Cermet	Fired N/R	N/R	

LIFE / ENVIRONMENTAL EXPERIENCE

DATA SRCE CLS	TST SRC	TEST TYP/ APP ENV	STR LVL/ EQP TYPE	TEST STD MTD/COND	NO. TSTD	TEST DUR.	PART HRS.	NO. FLD	FAILURE CLASSIFICATION. IND; MODE; MECH; CAUSE; (NO. FAILED / EVENT)	% DEF	TEST DATE	REMARKS
V	SSD Lab	OpCnst	25C 100%	MS883 1005B	121	1000 Hrs	1.21E5	0			2/71	

MALFUNCTION DATA

SYSTEM / EQUIPMENT	PART HISTORY	SCR CLS	DATE CODE	FAILURE ANALYSIS / CORRECTIVE ACTION

SYSTEM / EQUIPMENT	PART HISTORY	SCR CLS	DATE CODE	FAILURE ANALYSIS / CORRECTIVE ACTION

HYBRID MICROCIRCUIT
RELIABILITY DATA

RELIABILITY
ANALYSIS
CENTER

DEVICE SECTION

MANUFACTURER: NATIONAL SEMICONDUCTOR

TECHNOLOGY: THICK FILM

FUNCTIONAL CATEGORY: LINEAR

DEVICE FUNCTION: OPERATIONAL AMPLIFIER

ENTRY NO.	PKG/NO. PINS	SIZE OP TEMP	PKG MFG	PKG SEAL	SUBSTR MTL/BOND	SUBSTR SIZE	NO. COND LYR	SUBSTR METAL #BONDS	IC NO./TYPE	IC CHP ATCH/INTERCON	TRANSISTOR NO./TYPE	TRANSISTOR CHP ATCH/INTERCON	DIODE NO./TYPE	DIODE CHP ATCH/INTERCON	CAPACITOR NO./TYPE	CAPACITOR CHP ATCH/INTERCON	RESISTOR NO./TYPE	RESISTOR CHP ATCH/INTERCON	RES TOL (%)	ELMT ATCH/INTERCON NO./TYPE
125	Can 8	TO-9 -55/125C	N/R	Weld	Al$_2$O$_3$ Eutect	.30D	1	N/R ≃44	2 OpAmp	Eutect AuWire	0		0		0		1 Cermet	Fired N/R	N/R	

LIFE / ENVIRONMENTAL EXPERIENCE

DATA SRCE	SCR CLS	PART HISTORY	DATE CODE	TST SRC	TEST TYP/APP ENV	STR LVL/EQP TYPE	TEST STD MTD/COND	NO. TSTD	TEST DUR.	PART HRS.	NO. FLD	FAILURE CLASSIFICATION IND; MODE; MECH; CAUSE (NO. FAILED / EVENT)	% DEF	TEST DATE	REMARKS
V				BSD Lab	OpCnst	25C 100%	MS883 1005B	121	1000 Hrs	1.21E5	0			2/71	

MALFUNCTION DATA

SYSTEM / EQUIPMENT	PART HISTORY	SCR CLS	DATE CODE	FAILURE ANALYSIS / CORRECTIVE ACTION	SYSTEM / EQUIPMENT	PART HISTORY	SCR CLS	DATE CODE	FAILURE ANALYSIS / CORRECTIVE ACTION

RELIABILITY
ANALYSIS
CENTER

HYBRID MICROCIRCUIT
RELIABILITY DATA

DEVICE SECTION

MANUFACTURER: NATIONAL SEMICONDUCTOR FUNCTIONAL CATEGORY: LINEAR

TECHNOLOGY: THICK FILM DEVICE FUNCTION: OPERATIONAL AMPLIFIER

ENTRY NO.	PKG/ NO. PINS	SIZE OP TEMP	PKG SEAL	PKG MFG	SUBSTR MTL/ BOND	SUBSTR SIZE	NO. COND LYR	SUBSTR METAL #BONDS	IC NO./TYPE	IC CHP ATCH/INTERCON	TRANSISTOR NO./TYPE	TRANSISTOR CHP ATCH/INTERCON	DIODE NO./TYPE	DIODE CHP ATCH/INTERCON	CAPACITOR NO./TYPE	CAPACITOR CHP ATCH/INTERCON	RESISTOR NO./TYPE	RESISTOR CHP ATCH/INTERCON	RES TOL (%)	ELMT ATCH/INTERCON NO./TYPE
126	Can 10	TO-5 -55/125C	Weld	N/R	Al₂O₃ Eutect	.30D	3	N/R 44	0		10 SiNPN (3) SiPNP (7)	Eutect AuWire	0		0		7 Cermet	Fired AuWire	N/R	

LIFE / ENVIRONMENTAL EXPERIENCE

DATA SRCE	SCR CLS	TST SRC	TEST TYP/ APP ENV	STR LVL/ EQP TYPE	TEST STD MTD/COND	NO. TSTD	TEST DUR.	PART HRS.	NO. FLD	FAILURE CLASSIFICATION IND; MODE; MECH; CAUSE (NO. FAILED / EVENT)	% DEF	TEST DATE
U	SSD	Env	VisInsp	N/R		6			0			
		Brn	X-Ray	N/R		6			3	Spec Reject	50.0	8/74
		Env	Temp	N/R		2			0			
			Vib	N/R								
			X-Ray	N/R								
		Env	FineLk	N/R		2						
		Brn	GrossLk RevBias	125C		8	168 Hrs	1344	5	Offset Volt/1	16.6	4/71
U	Scr/SSD		FineLk	He		6						
			GrossLk	Fluoro		6						
U	Scr/SSD		VisInsp			30						
		Brn	RevBias	125C		30	168 Hrs	5040	0	Gain Delta/4		8/69
U	Scr/SSD		Temp ThmCyc FineLk GrossLk			25	96 Hrs	2400	0		20.0	
			VisIns	10x								
U	SSD	Brn	RevBias	125C		25	168 Hrs	4200	0	Spec Reject/3 Def Test Socket/2		2/71
V	N	Lab	OpCnst	25C	MS883 1005B	242	1000 Hrs	2.42E5	0			

MALFUNCTION DATA

SYSTEM / EQUIPMENT	PART HISTORY	SCR CLS	DATE CODE	FAILURE ANALYSIS / CORRECTIVE ACTION	SYSTEM / EQUIPMENT	PART HISTORY	SCR CLS	DATE CODE	FAILURE ANALYSIS / CORRECTIVE ACTION
	Bench Test Internal Visual	B		Electrical, Broken Wedge Bond/1 Cracked Transistor/1					

DEVICE SECTION

MANUFACTURER: NATIONAL SEMICONDUCTOR

TECHNOLOGY: THICK FILM

FUNCTIONAL CATEGORY: LINEAR

DEVICE FUNCTION: OPERATIONAL AMPLIFIER

ENTRY NO.	PKG/ NO. PINS	SIZE OP TEMP		IC		SUBSTR METAL #BONDS	NO. COND LYR	SUBSTR SIZE	SUBSTR MTL/ BOND	TRANSISTOR		DIODE		CAPACITOR		RESISTOR		RES TOL (%)	ELMT ATCH/ INTERCON
			NO./ TYPE	CHP ATCH/ INTERCON	SUBSTR METAL #BONDS				NO./ TYPE	CHP ATCH/ INTERCON	NO./ TYPE	CHP ATCH/ INTERCON	NO./ TYPE	CHP ATCH/ INTERCON	NO./ TYPE	CHP ATCH/ INTERCON		NO./ TYPE
126 (Cnt'd]																			

LIFE / ENVIRONMENTAL EXPERIENCE (con't)

DATA SRCE	SCR CLS	TST SRC	TEST TYP/ APP ENV	STR LVL/ EQP TYPE	TEST STD MTD/COND	NO. TSTD	TEST DUR.	PART HRS.	NO. FLD	FAILURE CLASSIFICATION IND; MODE; MECH; CAUSE (NO. FAILED / EVENT)	% DEF	TEST DATE	REMARKS
I	N	Brn Scr/SSD	Temp TempCyc	125C -65/150C 10 cyc	MSB83 1008 1010	12	48 Hrs	576				8/72	
I	N		CnstAcc	20KG Y_1	2001D				0				
			FineLk	1×10^{-8} cc/sec	1014A				1	Package Leak	8.33		
I	N	Brn Scr/SSD	GrossLk RevBias X-Ray VisInsp	Fluoro 105C	1014C 1015 2012 2008	12	240 Hrs	2880	0				

MALFUNCTION DATA

SYSTEM/ EQUIPMENT	PART HISTORY	SCR CLS	DATE CODE	FAILURE ANALYSIS / CORRECTIVE ACTION	SYSTEM/ EQUIPMENT	PART HISTORY	SCR CLS	DATE CODE	FAILURE ANALYSIS / CORRECTIVE ACTION

DEVICE SECTION

MANUFACTURER: PHILCO FORD CORP
TECHNOLOGY: THIN FILM

FUNCTIONAL CATEGORY: DIGITAL
DEVICE FUNCTION: HIGH VOLTAGE GATE

HYBRID MICROCIRCUIT
RELIABILITY DATA

ENTRY NO.	PKG/ NO. PINS	SIZE OP TEMP	PKG MFG	PKG SEAL	SUBSTR MTL/ BOND	SUBSTR SIZE	NO. COND LYR	SUBSTR METAL #BONDS	IC NO./TYPE	IC CHP ATCH/ INTERCON	TRANSISTOR NO./TYPE	TRANSISTOR CHP ATCH/ INTERCON	DIODE NO./TYPE	DIODE CHP ATCH/ INTERCON	CAPACITOR NO./TYPE	CAPACITOR CHP ATCH/ INTERCON	RESISTOR NO./TYPE	RESISTOR CHP ATCH/ INTERCON	RES TOL (%)	ELMT ATCH/ INTERCON NO./TYPE
127	FPCm 14	TO-86 -55/ 125C	N/R	Glass Header N/A	N/A	1	Eutect Therm 44 Skip 4	2 8 Gate	Eutect AuWire	2 SiNPN	Eutect AuWire	0		0		0			

LIFE / ENVIRONMENTAL EXPERIENCE

DATA SRCE	SCR CLS	TST SRC	TEST TYP/ APP ENV	STR LVL/ EQP TYPE	TEST STD MTD/COND	NO. TSTD	TEST DUR.	PART HRS.	NO. FLD	FAILURE CLASSIFICATION IND; MODE; MECH; CAUSE (NO. FAILED / EVENT)	% DEF	TEST DATE
U	SSD	Brn		125C		460		77280	3	Skip Bond Failure		12/70
U	SSD	Env		20KGY 1					0		0.65	
U	SSD	Env	MechShk Vib	N/R N/R		22			0			
U	SSD	Env	CnstAcc	20KC 6 AXES					7	Skip Bond Failure	31.8	
U	SSD	Lab	OpLif	125C	1000 Hrs	84		84000	0			
U	SSD	Env	CnstAcc	20KGY 1		84			1	Skip Bond Failure	1.19	
U	SSD	Env	CnstAcc	30KG Y 1		38			1	Skip Bond Failure	2.63	
U	SSD	Env	CnstAcc	20KG 6 AXES		20			7	Skip Bond Failure	35.0	
U	SSD	Lab	StgLif	150C	1000 Hrs	52		52000	3	Skip Bond Failure	5.76	

MALFUNCTION DATA

SYSTEM / EQUIPMENT	PART HISTORY	SCR CLS	DATE CODE	FAILURE ANALYSIS / CORRECTIVE ACTION

SYSTEM / EQUIPMENT	PART HISTORY	SCR CLS	DATE CODE	FAILURE ANALYSIS / CORRECTIVE ACTION

DEVICE SECTION

MANUFACTURER: PHILCO FORD CORP

TECHNOLOGY: THIN FILM

FUNCTIONAL CATEGORY: LINEAR

DEVICE FUNCTION: VOLTAGE REGULATOR

HYBRID MICROCIRCUIT
RELIABILITY DATA

RELIABILITY ANALYSIS CENTER

ENTRY NO.	PKG/ NO. PINS	SIZE OP TEMP	PKG MFG	PKG SEAL	SUBSTR MTL/ BOND	SUBSTR SIZE	NO. COND LYR	SUBSTR METAL #BONDS	IC NO./ TYPE	IC CHP ATCH/ INTERCON	TRANSISTOR NO./ TYPE	TRANSISTOR CHP ATCH/ INTERCON	DIODE NO./ TYPE	DIODE CHP ATCH/ INTERCON	CAPACITOR NO./ TYPE	CAPACITOR CHP ATCH/ INTERCON	RESISTOR NO./ TYPE	RESISTOR CHP ATCH/ INTERCON	RES TOL (%)	ELMT ATCH/ INTERCON NO./ TYPE
128	Car 12	.38x .38D -55/ 125C	N/R	Weld	VitGl Eutect	.30D	1	AuCond 66	0		6 SiPNP 4 Unij 2	Eutect AuWire	1 ZenAv	Eutect AuWire	0		5 Cermet	Fired AuCond	± 5	

LIFE / ENVIRONMENTAL EXPERIENCE

DATA SRCE	SCR CLS	TST SRC	TEST TYP/ APP ENV	STR LVL/ EQP TYPE	TEST STD MTD/COND	NO. TSTD	TEST DUR.	PART HRS.	NO. FLD	FAILURE CLASSIFICATION IND; MODE; MECH; CAUSE (NO. FAILED / EVENT)	% DEF	TEST DATE
U	B	Env	VisInsp		MSB883 2008	25			0			9/69
			X-Ray		2012	25						
U	SSD	Scr	Bake	125C	1008B	18	72 Hrs	1296				
U	SSD	Env	TempCyc	-55/125C 10/10 min	1010B	18						
			CnstAcc	10KG 6 AXES	2001B	18			0			
U	SSD	Lab	OpCnst	125C 100%	1014	14	500 Hrs	7000	6	Poor Regulation and current drain	4.29	
U	SSD	Scr	Bake	150C	1004	14	72 Hrs	1008	0			
U	SSD	Env	ThrmShk	-55/125C 5/5 min	1011B	4						
			TmStr Moistr	-10/65C 98%RH	1014 1004							
			Solder FineLk MechShk	He 90psi 1.5KG 4 AXES	1014A 2002B							
U	SSD	Env	VbVrFrq	.02/.2KHz 20G	2007A	4			0			

MALFUNCTION DATA

SYSTEM/ EQUIPMENT	PART HISTORY	SCR CLS	DATE CODE	FAILURE ANALYSIS / CORRECTIVE ACTION

SYSTEM/ EQUIPMENT	PART HISTORY	SCR CLS	DATE CODE	FAILURE ANALYSIS / CORRECTIVE ACTION

DEVICE SECTION

MANUFACTURER: PRECISION MONOLITHICS

TECHNOLOGY: THIN FILM

FUNCTIONAL CATEGORY: LINEAR

DEVICE FUNCTION: D/A CURRENT CONVERTER

HYBRID MICROCIRCUIT
RELIABILITY DATA

RELIABILITY
ANALYSIS
CENTER

ENTRY NO.	PKG/ NO. PINS	SIZE OP TEMP	PKG MFG	PKG SEAL	SUBSTR MTL/ BOND	SUBSTR SIZE	NO. COND LYR	SUBSTR METAL #BONDS	IC NO./ TYPE	IC CHP ATCH/ INTERCON	TRANSISTOR NO./ TYPE	TRANSISTOR CHP ATCH/ INTERCON	DIODE NO./ TYPE	DIODE CHP ATCH/ INTERCON	CAPACITOR NO./ TYPE	CAPACITOR CHP ATCH/ INTERCON	RESISTOR NO./ TYPE	RESISTOR CHP ATCH/ INTERCON	RES TOL (%)	FET SWITCHES NO./ TYPE	FET SWITCHES ELMT ATCH/ INTERCON
129	CM-DIP 16	TO-116 -55/ 125C	N/R	Weld	Header Al$_2$O$_3$ Eutect	N/A	1	AlCond N/R	0	AlCond N/R	10 SiNPN	Eutect AuWire	0		0		21 N/R	Eutect AuWire	N/R	10 N/R	Eutect AuWire

LIFE / ENVIRONMENTAL EXPERIENCE

DATA SRCE NO.	SCR CLS	TST SRC	TEST TYP/ APP ENV	STR LVL/ EQP TYPE	TEST STD MTD/COND	NO. TSTD	TEST DUR.	PART HRS.	NO. FLD	FAILURE CLASSIFICATION IND; MODE; MECH; CAUSE (NO. FAILED / EVENT)	% DEF	TEST DATE	REMARKS
U	B	RelDemo		-55/55C 2.2G 27 cyc CMCTNS/ GrndMobl		8	500 Hrs	4000	0			12/73	

MALFUNCTION DATA

SYSTEM / EQUIPMENT	PART HISTORY	SCR CLS	DATE CODE	FAILURE ANALYSIS / CORRECTIVE ACTION	SYSTEM / EQUIPMENT	PART HISTORY	SCR CLS	DATE CODE	FAILURE ANALYSIS / CORRECTIVE ACTION

PAGE 160

DEVICE SECTION

MANUFACTURER: RAYTHEON CORPORATION
TECHNOLOGY: THICK FILM

FUNCTIONAL CATEGORY: DIGITAL
DEVICE FUNCTION: TEST DEVICE

HYBRID MICROCIRCUIT RELIABILITY DATA

RELIABILITY ANALYSIS CENTER

ENTRY NO.	PKG/NO. PINS	SIZE/OP TEMP	PKG MFG	PKG SEAL	SUBSTR MTL/BOND	NO. COND LYR	SUBSTR SIZE	SUBSTR METAL/#BONDS	IC NO./TYPE	IC CHP ATCH/INTERCON	TRANSISTOR NO./TYPE	TRANSISTOR CHP ATCH/INTERCON	DIODE NO./TYPE	DIODE CHP ATCH/INTERCON	CAPACITOR NO./TYPE	CAPACITOR CHP ATCH/INTERCON	RESISTOR NO./TYPE	RESISTOR CHP ATCH/INTERCON	RES TOL (%)	ELMT ATCH/INTERCON NO./TYPE
130	FPMlCm 40	1.3lx 1.3lx .03/ -55/ 125C	N/R	Weld	Al$_2$O$_3$ Eutect	1	1.0x	MoMn / 8	1 8 Gate	Eutect AuWire	1 SiNPN	Eutect AuWire	2 SiGP	Eutect AuWire	0		0			

LIFE / ENVIRONMENTAL EXPERIENCE

DATA SRCE NO.	SCR CLS	TST SRC	TEST TYP/APP ENV	STR LVL/EQP TYPE	TEST STD MTD/COND	NO. TSTD	TEST DUR.	PART HRS.	NO. FLD	FAILURE CLASSIFICATION IND; MODE; MECH; CAUSE (NO. FAILED / EVENT)	% DEF	TEST DATE
V	SSD	Env	TempCyc	-65/200C	MS883 1010D	50	96 Hrs	2112	0	Leak Rate	88.0	7/70
			Hrmtc	He Fluoro	1014A-C	50			44	Corrosion Pits on Plateau Area of Cover	100.	
			SltSpy	30K MGM/	1009C	22			22	and on Package Leads		
			Solder	260C	2003	22			0			
			MechShk	1.5KG; 6 AXES	2002	30			0			
			VbVrFrq	20-20KC 70G	2007	29			1	Leak Test	3.45	
			HiPress	1.3Hg 70K ft.	1001				0			
			Moistr	85C/98%RH	1002	29			0			
			VbVrFrq	20-20KC 70G	2007	31			1	Leak Rate	3.23	
			HiPress	1.3Hg 70K ft.	1001	30			1	Leak Rate	3.33	
			Moistr	85C/98%RH	1004	30			0			
			Moistr	85C/98%RH	1004	16			0			
			HiPress	1.3 Hg 70K ft.	1001	17			0			
V	SSD	Env	Moistr	85C/98%RH	1004	17			0	Leak Rate	3.45	
V	C	Env	ThrmShk	-65/150C	1011	29			1	Leak Rate	3.57	
			MechShk	1.5KG 5 AXES	2002	28			1			
			VbVrFrq	20-20K 70G	2007	24			4	Leak Rate	16.6	

REMARKS: Seal Test Performed after every Env. Test ($<1\times10^{-8}$ cc/s) Except SltSpy

MALFUNCTION DATA

SYSTEM/EQUIPMENT	PART HISTORY	SCR CLS	DATE CODE	FAILURE ANALYSIS / CORRECTIVE ACTION

SYSTEM/EQUIPMENT	PART HISTORY	SCR CLS	DATE CODE	FAILURE ANALYSIS / CORRECTIVE ACTION

RELIABILITY
ANALYSIS
CENTER

DEVICE SECTION

MANUFACTURER: RAYTHEON CORPORATION   FUNCTIONAL CATEGORY: DIGITAL

TECHNOLOGY: THICK FILM   DEVICE FUNCTION: TEST DEVICE

ENTRY NO.	PKG/ NO. PINS	SIZE OP TEMP	PKG MFG	PKG SEAL	SUBSTR MTL/ BOND	SUBSTR SIZE	NO. COND LYR	SUBSTR METAL #BONDS	IC NO./TYPE	IC CHP ATCH/INTERCON	TRANSISTOR NO./TYPE	TRANSISTOR CHP ATCH/INTERCON	DIODE NO./TYPE	DIODE CHP ATCH/INTERCON	CAPACITOR NO./TYPE	CAPACITOR CHP ATCH/INTERCON	RESISTOR NO./TYPE	RESISTOR CHP ATCH/INTERCON	RES TOL (%)	ELMT ATCH/INTERCON NO./TYPE
130 (Cnt'd)																				

LIFE / ENVIRONMENTAL EXPERIENCE (con't)

DATA SRCE	SCR CLS	TST SRC	TEST TYP/ APP ENV	STR LVL/ EQP TYPE	TEST STD MTD/COND	NO. TSTD	TEST DUR.	PART HRS.	NO. FLD	FAILURE CLASSIFICATION IND; MODE; MECH; CAUSE (NO. FAILED / EVENT)	% DEF	TEST DATE	REMARKS
			HiPress Moistr	1.3Hg 70K ft. 85C/98%RH	MSB83 1001 1004	24			0				
V	SSD	Lab Env	AccLif Hrmtc	400C	He Fluoro1014A&C Carbon	25	200 Hrs	5000	0				
									1	1st continunity (EM)	4.0	7/70	
		Lab Env	AccLif Hrmtc	400°C	He Fluoro1014A&C Carbon		300 Hrs	7500					
		Lab Env	AccLif Hrmtc	400°C	He Fluoro1014A&C Carbon		400 Hrs	10000	1	2nd Continunity (EM)	4.0		
		Lab Env	AccLif Hrmtc	400°C	He Fluoro1014A&C Carbon	25	500 Hrs	12500					
		Lab Env	AccLif Hrmtc	350°C	HeFluoro 1014A&C Carbon	25	200 Hrs	5000	0				
		Lab Env	AccLif Hrmtc	350°C	HeFluoro 1014A&C Carbon	5	300 Hrs	6000	0				
		Lab Env	AccLif Hrmtc	350°C	HeFluoro 1014A&C Carbon	20 5	500 Hrs	5000					All Units Subject to Electric Measure
V	SSD	Lab Env	AccLif Hrmtc		HeFluoro 1014A&C Carbon	10 10			0				

MALFUNCTION DATA

SYSTEM / EQUIPMENT	PART HISTORY	SCR CLS	DATE CODE	FAILURE ANALYSIS / CORRECTIVE ACTION					

SYSTEM / EQUIPMENT	PART HISTORY	SCR CLS	DATE CODE	FAILURE ANALYSIS / CORRECTIVE ACTION					

DEVICE SECTION

MANUFACTURER: RAYTHEON CORPORATION
FUNCTIONAL CATEGORY: DIGITAL
DEVICE FUNCTION: TEST DEVICE
TECHNOLOGY: THICK FILM

ENTRY NO.	PKG/ NO. PINS	SIZE OP TEMP	PKG MFG	PKG SEAL	SUBSTR MTL/ BOND	SUBSTR SIZE	NO. COND LYR	SUBSTR METAL #BONDS	IC NO./ TYPE	IC CHP ATCH/ INTERCON	TRANSISTOR NO./ TYPE	TRANSISTOR CHP ATCH/ INTERCON	DIODE NO./ TYPE	DIODE CHP ATCH/ INTERCON	CAPACITOR NO./ TYPE	CAPACITOR CHP ATCH/ INTERCON	RESISTOR NO./ TYPE	RESISTOR CHP ATCH/ INTERCON	RES TOL (%)	ELM ATCH/ INTERCON NO./ TYPE
130 (Cnt'd)																				

LIFE / ENVIRONMENTAL EXPERIENCE (con't)

DATA SRCE	SCR CLS	TST SRC	TEST TYP/ APP ENV	STR LVL/ EQP TYPE	TEST STD MTD/COND	NO. TSTD	TEST DUR.	PART HRS.	NO. FLD	FAILURE CLASSIFICATION IND; MODE; MECH; CAUSE (NO. FAILED / EVENT)	% DEF	TEST DATE	REMARKS
V	SSD	Lab Env	Acclif Hrmtc	300°C HeFluoro Carbon	MS883 1014A&C	25 4	200 Hrs	5000	0			7/70	
		Lab Env	Acclif Hrmtc	300°C HeFluoro Carbon	1014A&C	20 5	300 Hrs	6000					
		Lab Env	Acclif Hrmtc	300°C HeFluoro Carbon	1014A&C	15 2	400 Hrs	6000					
		Lab Env	Acclif Hrmtc	300°C HeFluoro Carbon	1014A&C	10 7	500 Hrs	5000					
		Lab Env	Acclif Hrmtc	200°C HeFluoro Carbon	1014A&C	25 5	200 Hrs	5000					
		Lab Env Lab Env	Acclif Hrmtc Acclif Hrmtc	200°C HeFluoro 200°C HeFluoro Carbon	1014A&C 1014A&C	20 5 15 3	300 Hrs 400 Hrs	6000 6000					All Units Subject to Electric Measure
V	SSD	Lab Env	Acclif Hrmtc	200°C HeFluoro Carbon	1014A&C	10 9	500 Hrs	5000	0				

MALFUNCTION DATA

SYSTEM / EQUIPMENT	PART HISTORY	SCR CLS	DATE CODE	FAILURE ANALYSIS / CORRECTIVE ACTION

SYSTEM / EQUIPMENT	PART HISTORY	SCR CLS	DATE CODE	FAILURE ANALYSIS / CORRECTIVE ACTION

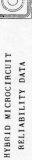
RELIABILITY ANALYSIS CENTER

HYBRID MICROCIRCUIT
RELIABILITY DATA

DEVICE SECTION

MANUFACTURER: RAYTHEON CORPORATION   FUNCTIONAL CATEGORY: DIGITAL

TECHNOLOGY: THICK FILM   DEVICE FUNCTION: TEST DEVICE

ENTRY NO.	PKG/ NO. PINS	SIZE OP TEMP	PKG MFG	PKG SEAL	SUBSTR MTL/ BOND	SUBSTR SIZE	NO. COND LYR	SUBSTR METAL #BONDS	IC NO./ TYPE	IC CHP ATCH/ INTERCON	TRANSISTOR NO./ TYPE	TRANSISTOR CHP ATCH/ INTERCON	DIODE NO./ TYPE	DIODE CHP ATCH/ INTERCON	CAPACITOR NO./ TYPE	CAPACITOR CHP ATCH/ INTERCON	RESISTOR NO./ TYPE	RESISTOR CHP ATCH/ INTERCON	RES TOL (%)	ELMT ATCH/ INTERCON NO./ TYPE
131	FPMlCm 40	1.3lx 1.3lx .03 -55/ 125C	N/R	Weld	Al₂O₃ Eutect	1.0x 1.0	3	MoMn 8	1 8 Gate	Eutect AuWire	1 SiNPN	Eutect AuWire	2 SiGP	Eutect AuWire	0		0			

LIFE / ENVIRONMENTAL EXPERIENCE

DATA SRCE	SCR CLS	TST SRC	TEST TYP/ APP ENV	STR LVL/ EQP TYPE	TEST STD MTD/COND	NO. TSTD	TEST DUR.	PART HRS.	NO. FLD	FAILURE CLASSIFICATION IND; MODE; MECH: CAUSE (NO. FAILED / EVENT)	% DEF	TEST DATE	REMARKS
V	SSD	Env	HiPress	1.3Hg 70K ft.	MS883 1001	23			2	N/R	8.6	7/70	Seal Test Performed after every Env. Test (< 1x10⁻⁸ cc/s) Except SltSpy
			Moistr	N/R	1004	21			0				
			VbVrFrq	20-20KC 70G	2007	26							
			HiPress	1.3Hg 70K ft	1001	26			0				
			Moistr	N/R	1004	3			1	Electrical	33.3		
			TempCyc	-65/200C	1010D	42			0				
			Hrmtc	HeFluoro Carbon	1014A&C	42			2	Leak Rate	4.76		
			ThrmShk	-65/150C	1011	31			1	N/R			
			MechShk	1.5KG 6 AXES	2002								
			VbVrFrq	20-20KC 70G	2007								
			HiPress	1.31 Hg 70K ft.	1001	31			0	Corrosion Pits in Plateau Area of Cover 100.			
			Moistr	50mgm/m² per day	1004	22	96 Hrs		22	and on Leads			
			SltSpy	260C	1009C								
V	SSD	Env	Solder		2003	22			0				
			MechShk	1.5KG 6 AXES	2002	29			0				

MALFUNCTION DATA

SYSTEM / EQUIPMENT	PART HISTORY	SCR CLS	DATE CODE	FAILURE ANALYSIS / CORRECTIVE ACTION	SYSTEM / EQUIPMENT	PART HISTORY	SCR CLS	DATE CODE	FAILURE ANALYSIS / CORRECTIVE ACTION

DEVICE SECTION

MANUFACTURER: RAYTHEON CORPORATION

TECHNOLOGY: THICK FILM

FUNCTIONAL CATEGORY: DIGITAL

DEVICE FUNCTION: TEST DEVICE

HYBRID MICROCIRCUIT

RELIABILITY DATA

RELIABILITY ANALYSIS CENTER

ENTRY NO.	PKG/ NO. PINS	SIZE OP TEMP	PKG MFG	PKG SEAL	SUBSTR MTL/ BOND	SUBSTR SIZE	NO. COND LYR	SUBSTR METAL #BONDS	NO./ TYPE	CHP ATCH/ INTERCON	NO./ TYPE	CHP ATCH/ INTERCON	NO./ TYPE	CHP ATCH/ INTERCON	NO./ TYPE	CHP ATCH/ INTERCON	RES TOL (%)	NO./ TYPE	ELMT ATCH/ INTERCON
									IC		TRANSISTOR		DIODE		CAPACITOR		RESISTOR		
131 (Cntd)																			

LIFE / ENVIRONMENTAL EXPERIENCE (con't)

DATA SRCE	SCR CLS	TST SRC	TEST TYP/ APP ENV	STR LVL/ EQP TYPE	TEST STD MTD/COND	NO. TSTD	TEST DUR.	PART HRS.	NO. FLD	FAILURE CLASSIFICATION IND; MODE; MECH; CAUSE (NO. FAILED / EVENT)	% DEF	TEST DATE	REMARKS
V	SSD Env	VbVrFrq	20-20KC 70G	MS883 2007	29			0				
V	SSD Env	HiPress	1.31 Hg 70K ft	1001	29			0				
V	SSD Env	Moistr SltSpy	N/R 50Kmgm/m2 per day	1004 1009C	29 10			8	Corrosion Pits in Plateau Area of Cover on Leads			

MALFUNCTION DATA

SYSTEM / EQUIPMENT	PART HISTORY	SCR CLS	DATE CODE	FAILURE ANALYSIS / CORRECTIVE ACTION	CORRECTIVE ACTION
SYSTEM / EQUIPMENT	PART HISTORY	SCR CLS	DATE CODE	FAILURE ANALYSIS / CORRECTIVE ACTION	CORRECTIVE ACTION

DEVICE SECTION

RELIABILITY
ANALYSIS
CENTER

HYBRID MICROCIRCUIT
RELIABILITY DATA

MANUFACTURER: SCS MICRO SYSTEMS
TECHNOLOGY: SEMICONDUCTOR
FUNCTIONAL CATEGORY: DIGITAL
DEVICE FUNCTION: DRIVER STEERING

ENTRY NO.	PKG/ NO. PINS	SIZE OP TEMP	PKG MFG	PKG SEAL	SUBSTR MTL/ BOND	SUBSTR SIZE	NO. COND LYR	SUBSTR METAL #BONDS	IC NO./ TYPE	IC CHP ATCH/ INTERCON	TRANSISTOR NO./ TYPE	TRANSISTOR CHP ATCH/ INTERCON	DIODE NO./ TYPE	DIODE CHP ATCH/ INTERCON	CAPACITOR NO./ TYPE	CAPACITOR CHP ATCH/ INTERCON	RESISTOR NO./ TYPE	RESISTOR CHP ATCH/ INTERCON	RES TOL (%)	ELMT ATCH/ INTERCON NO./ TYPE
132	C-DIP 16	.190x .10x .063 0/70C	N/R	Epoxy	Al_2O_3 AuPste	.19x .10	1	AuPste 13	0	0	0		13 SiGP	Eutect AlWire	0		5 Cermet	Fired AuPste		

LIFE / ENVIRONMENTAL EXPERIENCE

DATA SRCE NO.	SCR CLS	TST SRC	TEST TYP/ APP ENV	STR LVL/ EQP TYPE	TEST STD MTD/COND	NO. TSTD	TEST DUR.	PART HRS.	NO. FLD	FAILURE CLASSIFICATION IND; MODE; MECH; CAUSE (NO. FAILED / EVENT)	% DEF	TEST DATE	REMARKS
I	SSD	Scr/SSD	TempCyc brn ExtVis EM	-35/85C 10/10 min 70C 25C		4318 4316	168 Hrs	725424	0 2 207	N/R N/R	4.79	10/73 4/74	

MALFUNCTION DATA

SYSTEM / EQUIPMENT	PART HISTORY	SCR CLS	DATE CODE	FAILURE ANALYSIS / CORRECTIVE ACTION

SYSTEM / EQUIPMENT	PART HISTORY	SCR CLS	DATE CODE	FAILURE ANALYSIS / CORRECTIVE ACTION

DEVICE SECTION

MANUFACTURER: SCS MICRO SYSTEMS

TECHNOLOGY: SEMICONDUCTOR

FUNCTIONAL CATEGORY: DIGITAL

DEVICE FUNCTION: DRIVER

HYBRID MICROCIRCUIT
RELIABILITY DATA

RELIABILITY ANALYSIS CENTER

ENTRY NO.	PKG/ NO. PINS	SIZE OP TEMP	PKG MFG	PKG SEAL	SUBSTR MTL/ BOND	SUBSTR SIZE	NO. COND LYR	SUBSTR METAL #BONDS	IC NO./ TYPE	IC CHP ATCH/ INTERCON	TRANSISTOR NO./ TYPE	TRANSISTOR CHP ATCH/ INTERCON	DIODE NO./ TYPE	DIODE CHP ATCH/ INTERCON	CAPACITOR NO./ TYPE	CAPACITOR CHP ATCH/ INTERCON	RESISTOR NO./ TYPE	RESISTOR CHP ATCH/ INTERCON	RES TOL (%)	ELMT ATCH/ INTERCON NO./ TYPE
133	S-DIP 20	.260x .190x .05 15/55C	N/R	Silic	Al_2O_3 N/A	.26x .19	1	AgCond 20	0		6 SiNPN	Eutect AlWire	4 SiGP	Eutect AlWire	0		28 Cermet	Fired AgCond	N/R	

LIFE / ENVIRONMENTAL EXPERIENCE

DATA SRCE NO.	SCR CLS	TST SRC	TEST TYP/ APP ENV	STR LVL/ EQP TYPE	TEST STD MTD/COND	NO. TSTD	TEST DUR.	PART HRS.	NO. FLD	FAILURE CLASSIFICATION IND; MODE; MECH; CAUSE (NO. FAILED / EVENT)	% DEF	TEST DATE	REMARKS
I	SSD	Scr/SSD	TempCyc	-35/85C 10/10 min 70C		20973			0			10/73	
			Brn				168 Hrs	3523464	0			4/74	
			ExtVis										
			EM	25C		20973			145	N/R/140 Electrical Measurement Reject/5	5.69		

MALFUNCTION DATA

SYSTEM / EQUIPMENT	PART HISTORY	SCR CLS	DATE CODE	FAILURE ANALYSIS / CORRECTIVE ACTION	SYSTEM / EQUIPMENT	PART HISTORY	SCR CLS	DATE CODE	FAILURE ANALYSIS / CORRECTIVE ACTION

DEVICE SECTION

MANUFACTURER: SILICONIX

TECHNOLOGY: THIN FILM

FUNCTIONAL CATEGORY: DIGITAL

DEVICE FUNCTION: HIGH VOLTAGE HIGH CURRENT DRIVER

RELIABILITY
ANALYSIS
CENTER

HYBRID MICROCIRCUIT
RELIABILITY DATA

ENTRY NO.	PKG/ NO. PINS	SIZE OP TEMP	PKG SEAL	PKG MFG	SUBSTR MTL/ BOND	SUBSTR SIZE	NO. COND LYR	SUBSTR METAL #BONDS	IC NO./TYPE	IC CHP ATCH/INTERCON	TRANSISTOR NO./TYPE	TRANSISTOR CHP ATCH/INTERCON	DIODE NO./TYPE	DIODE CHP ATCH/INTERCON	CAPACITOR NO./TYPE	CAPACITOR CHP ATCH/INTERCON	RESISTOR NO./TYPE	RESISTOR CHP ATCH/INTERCON	RES TOL (%)	NO./TYPE	ELMT ATCH/INTERCON
134	Can 12	.375x .375D -55/ 125C	Weld	N/R	Header N/A	N/A	1	Kov/Au 4	0		2 SiNPN	Eutect AlWire	0		0		0				

LIFE / ENVIRONMENTAL EXPERIENCE

DATA SRCE	SCR CLS	TST SRC	TEST TYP/ APP ENV	STR LVL/ EQP TYPE	TEST STD MTD/COND (user)	NO. TSTD	TEST DUR.	PART HRS.	NO. FLD	FAILURE CLASSIFICATION IND; MODE; MECH; CAUSE (NO. FAILED / EVENT)	% DEF	TEST DATE	REMARKS
U		SSD Env	VisInsp Intern	100x		45			0			6/70	
			ThrmShk	50/100C		2			0				
			VbVrFrq	1/1 min 15HZ/2KHZ 20G 3 Axe		16			0				
			MechShk	3 AXES 1.5KG .5 msec		16			0				
			HiPress	3 AXES RmTemp 75 psig/		16			0				
			Moistr	RM 40 min -10/65C 98%RH	MS202 106	16			0				
			LeadFtg	3 cyc/ 90° ARC 30G 2-5 sec/ARC		3 Leads 16			0				
			SldHt	230°C 10 sec		16			0				
			FineLk	50 psig He/N2		16			0				
U		SSD Env	GrossLk	50 psig He/EthGl		16			0				

MALFUNCTION DATA

SYSTEM / EQUIPMENT	PART HISTORY	SCR CLS	DATE CODE	FAILURE ANALYSIS / CORRECTIVE ACTION		SYSTEM / EQUIPMENT	PART HISTORY	SCR CLS	DATE CODE	FAILURE ANALYSIS / CORRECTIVE ACTION

PAGE 168

DEVICE SECTION

FUNCTIONAL CATEGORY: DIGITAL

DEVICE FUNCTION: HIGH VOLTAGE HIGH CURRENT DRIVER

MANUFACTURER: SILICONIX

TECHNOLOGY: THIN FILM

RELIABILITY ANALYSIS CENTER

ENTRY NO.	PKG/ NO. PINS	SIZE OP TEMP	PKG MFG	PKG SEAL	SUBSTR MTL/ BOND	SUBSTR SIZE	NO. COND LYR	SUBSTR METAL #BONDS	IC NO./ TYPE	IC CHP ATCH/ INTERCON	TRANSISTOR NO./ TYPE	TRANSISTOR CHP ATCH/ INTERCON	DIODE NO./ TYPE	DIODE CHP ATCH/ INTERCON	CAPACITOR NO./ TYPE	CAPACITOR CHP ATCH/ INTERCON	RESISTOR NO./ TYPE	RESISTOR CHP ATCH/ INTERCON	RES TOL (%)	ELMT ATCH/ INTERCON NO./ TYPE
134 (Cntd)																				

LIFE / ENVIRONMENTAL EXPERIENCE (con't)

DATA SRCE	SCR CLS	TST SRC	TEST TYP/ APP ENV	STR LVL/ EQP TYPE	TEST STD MTD/COND (user)	NO. TSTD	TEST DUR.	PART HRS.	NO. FLD	FAILURE CLASSIFICATION IND; MODE; MECH; CAUSE (NO. FAILED / EVENT)	% DEF	TEST DATE	REMARKS
U	SSD	Lab	OpCnst	125C 100%		10	500 Hrs	5000	0				
U	SSD	Env	FineLk	50 psig He/N$_2$		10			0				
			GrossLk	50 psig He/EthGl								6/70	
U	SSD	Lab	StgLif	125C		10	500 Hrs	5000	0				

MALFUNCTION DATA

SYSTEM / EQUIPMENT	PART HISTORY	SCR CLS	DATE CODE	FAILURE ANALYSIS / CORRECTIVE ACTION

SYSTEM / EQUIPMENT	PART HISTORY	SCR CLS	DATE CODE	FAILURE ANALYSIS / CORRECTIVE ACTION

RELIABILITY ANALYSIS CENTER

HYBRID MICROCIRCUIT
RELIABILITY DATA

DEVICE SECTION

MANUFACTURER: SPRAGUE ELECTRIC CO   FUNCTIONAL CATEGORY: DIGITAL

TECHNOLOGY: SEMICONDUCTOR   DEVICE FUNCTION: DRIVER

ENTRY NO.	PKG/ NO. PINS	SIZE OP TEMP	PKG SEAL	PKG MFG	SUBSTR MTL/ BOND	SUBSTR SIZE	NO. COND LYR	SUBSTR METAL #BONDS	IC NO./TYPE	IC CHP ATCH/INTERCON	TRANSISTOR NO./TYPE	TRANSISTOR CHP ATCH/INTERCON	DIODE NO./TYPE	DIODE CHP ATCH/INTERCON	CAPACITOR NO./TYPE	CAPACITOR CHP ATCH/INTERCON	RESISTOR NO./TYPE	RESISTOR CHP ATCH/INTERCON	RES TOL (%)	ELMT ATCH/INTERCON NO./TYPE
135	Can 10	TO-5 -55/ 125C	Weld	N/R	Header N/A	N/A	1	Kov/Au 32	2 8 Gate	Eutect AuWire	4 SiNPN	Eutect AuWire	0		0		0			

LIFE / ENVIRONMENTAL EXPERIENCE

DATA SRCE	SCR CLS	TST SRC	TEST TYP/ APP ENV	STR LVL/ EQP TYPE	TEST STD MTD/COND	NO. TSTD	TEST DUR.	PART HRS.	NO. FLD	FAILURE CLASSIFICATION IND; MODE; MECH; CAUSE (NO. FAILED / EVENT)	REMARKS	TEST DATE	% DEF
U	SSD	Env	MechShk	1.5KG 3 AXES 30G	MS883 2002	10			0		12/69 Date CD 6941		
		Env	VbVrFrq		MS883 2007								
		Lab	Stglif	150C		10	1000 Hrs	10000	0				
		Lab	OpCnst	85C 100%	MS883 1008	15	1000 Hrs	15000	0				
U	B	Fld	StlOrbt	Combin/ Operate		78	35641 Hrs	2.78E6	0			4/70– 5/74	
U	B	Fld	StlOrbt	Combin/ Operate		86	35697 Hrs	3.07E6	0				
U	B	Fld	StlOrbt	Combin/ Operate		52	35769 Hrs	1.86E6	0				

MALFUNCTION DATA

SYSTEM / EQUIPMENT	PART HISTORY	SCR CLS	DATE CODE	FAILURE ANALYSIS / CORRECTIVE ACTION	SYSTEM / EQUIPMENT	PART HISTORY	SCR CLS	DATE CODE	FAILURE ANALYSIS / CORRECTIVE ACTION
	Acceptance Test Vibration	A		N/R/1				4/72	
	Bench Test Ambient	B		Incorrect Readings, Poor Chip Bond/1				6/69	

PAGE 170

RELIABILITY
ANALYSIS
CENTER

DEVICE SECTION

MANUFACTURER: SPRAGUE. ELECTRIC CO

FUNCTIONAL CATEGORY: DIGITAL

DEVICE FUNCTION: LADDER SWITCH

TECHNOLOGY: SEMICONDUCTOR

ENTRY NO.	PKG/ NO. PINS	SIZE OP TEMP	PKG MFG	PKG SEAL	SUBSTR MTL/ BOND	SUBSTR SIZE	NO. COND LYR	SUBSTR METAL #BONDS	IC NO./ TYPE	IC CHP ATCH/ INTERCON	TRANSISTOR NO./ TYPE	TRANSISTOR CHP ATCH/ INTERCON	DIODE NO./ TYPE	DIODE CHP ATCH/ INTERCON	CAPACITOR NO./ TYPE	CAPACITOR CHP ATCH/ INTERCON	RESISTOR NO./ TYPE	RESISTOR CHP ATCH/ INTERCON	RES TOL (%)	ELMT ATCH/ INTERCON NO./ TYPE
136	FPG1 10	TO-86 -55/ 125C	N/R	Glass	Header N/A	N/A	1	Eutect 32	0		8 SiNPN	Eutect AuWire	0							

LIFE / ENVIRONMENTAL EXPERIENCE

DATA SRCE CLS	SCR CLS	TST SRC	TEST TYP/ APP ENV	STR LVL/ EQP TYPE	TEST STD MTD/COND	NO. TSTD	TEST DUR.	PART HRS.	NO. FLD	FAILURE CLASSIFICATION IND; MODE; MECH; CAUSE (NO. FAILED / EVENT)	% DEF	TEST DATE	REMARKS
U	N/R	Rel	Grnd Lbty	Cmctns		12	7178 Hrs	86136	0			10/72	

MALFUNCTION DATA

SYSTEM / EQUIPMENT	PART HISTORY	SCR CLS	DATE CODE	FAILURE ANALYSIS / CORRECTIVE ACTION

SYSTEM/ EQUIPMENT	PART HISTORY	SCR CLS	DATE CODE	FAILURE ANALYSIS / CORRECTIVE ACTION

DEVICE SECTION

MANUFACTURER: SPRAGUE ELECTRIC CO
TECHNOLOGY: SEMICONDUCTOR

FUNCTIONAL CATEGORY: DIGITAL
DEVICE FUNCTION: QUAD POWER DRIVER

HYBRID MICROCIRCUIT
RELIABILITY DATA

RELIABILITY
ANALYSIS
CENTER

ENTRY NO.	PKG/ NO. PINS	SIZE OP TEMP	PKG MFG	PKG SEAL	SUBSTR MTL/ BOND	SUBSTR SIZE	NO. COND LYR	SUBSTR METAL/ #BONDS	IC NO./ TYPE	IC CHP ATCH/ INTERCON	TRANSISTOR NO./ TYPE	TRANSISTOR CHP ATCH/ INTERCON	DIODE NO./ TYPE	DIODE CHP ATCH/ INTERCON	CAPACITOR NO./ TYPE	CAPACITOR CHP ATCH/ INTERCON	RESISTOR NO./ TYPE	RESISTOR CHP ATCH/ INTERCON	RES TOL (%)	ELMT ATCH/ INTERCON NO./ TYPE
137	FPM1Cm 14	TO-86 -55/ 125C	N/R	Weld	Al₂O₃ Eutect	.25x .35	1	N/R 43	4 8 Gate	Eutect AuWire	4 SiNPN	Eutect AuWire	0		0		0			

LIFE / ENVIRONMENTAL EXPERIENCE

DATA SRCE	SCR CLS	TST SRC	TEST TYP/ APP ENV	STR LVL/ EQP TYPE	TEST STD MTD/COND	NO. TSTD	TEST DUR.	PART HRS.	NO. FLD	FAILURE CLASSIFICATION IND; MODE; MECH; CAUSE (NO. FAILED / EVENT)	% DEF	TEST DATE	REMARKS
U	N/R	Brn	OpDyn	125C 100%		1	76 Hrs	76	0			1/73- 5/75	

MALFUNCTION DATA

SYSTEM / EQUIPMENT	PART HISTORY	SCR CLS	DATE CODE	FAILURE ANALYSIS / CORRECTIVE ACTION	SYSTEM / EQUIPMENT	PART HISTORY	SCR CLS	DATE CODE	FAILURE ANALYSIS / CORRECTIVE ACTION

PAGE 172

RELIABILITY ANALYSIS CENTER

HYBRID MICROCIRCUIT
RELIABILITY DATA

FUNCTIONAL CATEGORY: DIGITAL
DEVICE FUNCTION: QUAD DRIVER

DEVICE SECTION

MANUFACTURER: SPRAGUE ELECTRIC CO
TECHNOLOGY: SEMICONDUCTOR

ENTRY NO.	PKG/ NO. PINS	SIZE OP TEMP	PKG MFG	PKG SEAL	SUBSTR MTL/ BOND	SUBSTR SIZE	NO. COND LYR	SUBSTR METAL #BONDS	IC NO./ TYPE	IC CHP ATCH/ INTERCON	TRANSISTOR NO./ TYPE	TRANSISTOR CHP ATCH/ INTERCON	DIODE NO./ TYPE	DIODE CHP ATCH/ INTERCON	CAPACITOR NO./ TYPE	CAPACITOR CHP ATCH/ INTERCON	RESISTOR NO./ TYPE	RESISTOR CHP ATCH/ INTERCON	RES TOL (%)	ELMT ATCH/ INTERCON NO./ TYPE
138	FPCm 14	TO-86 -55/ 125C	N/R	Glass Header N/A	N/A		1	Eutect 44	4 8 Gate	Eutect AuWire	8 SiNPN	Eutect AuWire	0		0		0			

LIFE / ENVIRONMENTAL EXPERIENCE

DATA SRCE	SCR CLS	TST SRC	TEST TYP/ APP ENV	STR LVL/ EQP TYPE	TEST STD MTD/COND	NO. TSTD	TEST DUR.	PART HRS.	NO. FLD	FAILURE CLASSIFICATION IND; MODE; MECH; CAUSE (NO. FAILED / EVENT)	% DEF	TEST DATE	REMARKS
U	SSD	Env	MechShk	1.5KG 3 AXES 30G	MS883 2002	10			0			12/69	Date Code 6940
		Env	VbVrFrq	30G	MS883 2007								
		Lab	StgLif	150C	MS883 1008	10	1000 Hrs	10000	0				
		Lab	OpCnst	85C 100%	MS883 1008	15	1000	15000	0				
U	B	Fld	StLOrbt	Combin/ Operate		324		1.50E7	0			4/70- 5/74	

MALFUNCTION DATA

SYSTEM/ EQUIPMENT	PART HISTORY	SCR CLS	DATE CODE	FAILURE ANALYSIS / CORRECTIVE ACTION	SYSTEM/ EQUIPMENT	PART HISTORY	SCR CLS	DATE CODE	FAILURE ANALYSIS / CORRECTIVE ACTION
	Bench Test Vibration	B	1/68 9/69	Open, Bond Lifted/1 Open Metallization Broke Loose/1		Bench Test Ambient	A	7/71	Diode has Defective Output; Process Procedure; Lifted Resistor Block/1
	Acceptance Test, Vibration	A	1/71	Excessive Current Flow After Final Pack; Floating Conductive Particle Inside Diode/1		Bench Test Temperature	A	7/71	Loss of Channel - Diode Replaced; Process Procedure; Bad Ball Bond/1

DEVICE SECTION

MANUFACTURER: SPRAGUE ELECTRIC CO   FUNCTIONAL CATEGORY: DIGITAL

TECHNOLOGY: SEMICONDUCTOR   DEVICE FUNCTION: QUAD DRIVER

RELIABILITY
ANALYSIS
CENTER

HYBRID MICROCIRCUIT
RELIABILITY DATA

ENTRY NO.	PKG/ NO. PINS	SIZE OP TEMP	PKG MFG	PKG SEAL	SUBSTR MTL/ BOND	SUBSTR SIZE	NO. COND LYR	SUBSTR METAL #BONDS	IC NO./ TYPE	IC CHP ATCH/ INTERCON	TRANSISTOR NO./ TYPE	TRANSISTOR CHP ATCH/ INTERCON	DIODE NO./ TYPE	DIODE CHP ATCH/ INTERCON	CAPACITOR NO./ TYPE	CAPACITOR CHP ATCH/ INTERCON	RESISTOR NO./ TYPE	RESISTOR CHP ATCH/ INTERCON	RES TOL (%)	ELMT ATCH/ INTERCON NO./ TYPE
138 (Cntd)																				

LIFE / ENVIRONMENTAL EXPERIENCE

DATA SRCE	SCR CLS	TST SRC	TEST TYP/ APP ENV	STR LVL/ EQP TYPE	TEST STD MTD/COND	NO. TSTD	TEST DUR.	PART HRS.	NO. FLD	FAILURE CLASSIFICATION IND; MODE; MECH; CAUSE (NO. FAILED / EVENT)	REMARKS	% DEF	TEST DATE

MALFUNCTION DATA   (con't)

SYSTEM / EQUIPMENT	PART HISTORY	SCR CLS	DATE CODE	FAILURE ANALYSIS / CORRECTIVE ACTION	SYSTEM / EQUIPMENT	PART HISTORY	SCR CLS	DATE CODE	FAILURE ANALYSIS / CORRECTIVE ACTION
	Bench Test Ambient	A	4/71	Output Pin 7, Failed to Respond to Command; Defective Transistor/1					
	Bench Test Ambient	B	1/68- 9/69	Collector Resistor of Transistor 4 open/1 Internal Short, Pin Identification Oriented incorrectly/1 Shorted, Lifted Bond at Collector/1 Open, Chip Loose in Case/1					

PAGE 174

DEVICE SECTION

MANUFACTURER: SPRAGUE ELECTRIC CO

TECHNOLOGY: SEMICONDUCTOR

FUNCTIONAL CATEGORY: DIGITAL

DEVICE FUNCTION: QUAD POWER DRIVER

ENTRY NO.	PKG/ NO. PINS	SIZE OP TEMP	PKG MFG	PKG SEAL	SUBSTR MTL/ BOND	SUBSTR SIZE	NO. COND LYR	SUBSTR METAL #BONDS	IC NO./ TYPE	IC CHP ATCH/ INTERCON	TRANSISTOR NO./ TYPE	TRANSISTOR CHP ATCH/ INTERCON	DIODE NO./ TYPE	DIODE CHP ATCH/ INTERCON	CAPACITOR NO./ TYPE	CAPACITOR CHP ATCH/ INTERCON	RESISTOR NO./ TYPE	RESISTOR CHP ATCH/ INTERCON	RES TOL (%)	ELMT ATCH/ INTERCON NO./ TYPE
139	FPG1 14	TO-86 -55/ 125C	N/R	Glass Header N/A	N/A	N/A	1	Eutect 43	1 8 Gate	Eutect AuWire	4 SiNPN		0		0		0			

LIFE / ENVIRONMENTAL EXPERIENCE

DATA SRCE	SCR CLS	TST SRC	TEST TYP/ APP ENV	STR LVL/ EQP TYPE	TEST STD MTD/COND	NO. TSTD	TEST DUR.	PART HRS.	NO. FLD	FAILURE CLASSIFICATION IND; MODE; MECH; CAUSE (NO. FAILED / EVENT)	% DEF	TEST DATE
U	C	Chk		30C 90/110%	781A	3	571.66	1715	0			10/70
U	C	Rel		70C .2.2G 20/60HZ 90/110%	781A	3	571.66	1715	0			
U	C	Chk		30C 90/110%	781A	3	1715	5145	0			
U	C	Rel		70C .2.2G 20/60HZ 90/110%	781A	3	1715	5145	0			

REMARKS

MALFUNCTION DATA

SYSTEM/ EQUIPMENT	PART HISTORY	SCR CLS	DATE CODE	FAILURE ANALYSIS / CORRECTIVE ACTION	SYSTEM/ EQUIPMENT	PART HISTORY	SCR CLS	DATE CODE	FAILURE ANALYSIS / CORRECTIVE ACTION

HYBRID MICROCIRCUIT
RELIABILITY DATA

DEVICE SECTION

MANUFACTURER: SPRAGUE ELECTRIC CO   FUNCTIONAL CATEGORY: LINEAR

TECHNOLOGY: THIN FILM   DEVICE FUNCTION: BUFFER AMPLIFIER

ENTRY NO.	PKG/ NO. PINS	SIZE OP TEMP	PKG MFG	PKG SEAL	SUBSTR MTL/ BOND	SUBSTR SIZE	NO. COND LYR	SUBSTR METAL #BONDS	IC NO./ TYPE	IC CHP ATCH/ INTERCON	TRANSISTOR NO./ TYPE	TRANSISTOR CHP ATCH/ INTERCON	DIODE NO./ TYPE	DIODE CHP ATCH/ INTERCON	CAPACITOR NO./ TYPE	CAPACITOR CHP ATCH/ INTERCON	RESISTOR NO./ TYPE	RESISTOR CHP ATCH/ INTERCON	RES TOL (%)	ELMT ATCH/ INTERCON NO./ TYPE
140	FPG1 10	TO-86 -55/ 125C	N/R	Glass Header	N/A	N/A	1	N/R 36	0		4 SiNPN	Eutect AuWire	0		0		12 Cermet	Fired N/R		

LIFE / ENVIRONMENTAL EXPERIENCE

DATA SRCE SRCE	SCR CLS	TST SRC	TEST TYP/ APP ENV	STR LVL/ EQP TYPE	TEST STD MTD/COND	NO. TSTD	TEST DUR.	PART HRS.	NO. FLD	FAILURE CLASSIFICATION IND; MODE; MECH; CAUSE (NO. FAILED / EVENT)	% DEF	TEST DATE	REMARKS
U	N/R	Rel	GrndLbty	Cnnctns		12	7178 Hrs	86136	0			10/72	

MALFUNCTION DATA

SYSTEM / EQUIPMENT	PART HISTORY	SCR CLS	DATE CODE	FAILURE ANALYSIS / CORRECTIVE ACTION	SYSTEM / EQUIPMENT	PART HISTORY	SCR CLS	DATE CODE	FAILURE ANALYSIS / CORRECTIVE ACTION

HYBRID MICROCIRCUIT
RELIABILITY DATA

DEVICE SECTION

MANUFACTURER: SPRAGUE ELECTRIC CO

TECHNOLOGY: THIN FILM

FUNCTIONAL CATEGORY: N/A

DEVICE FUNCTION: RESISTOR NETWORK

ENTRY NO.	PKG/ NO. PINS	SIZE OP TEMP	PKG MFG	PKG SEAL	SUBSTR MTL/ BOND	SUBSTR SIZE	NO. COND LYR	SUBSTR METAL #BONDS	IC NO./ TYPE	IC CHP ATCH/ INTERCON	TRANSISTOR NO./ TYPE	TRANSISTOR CHP ATCH/ INTERCON	DIODE NO./ TYPE	DIODE CHP ATCH/ INTERCON	CAPACITOR NO./ TYPE	CAPACITOR CHP ATCH/ INTERCON	RESISTOR NO./ TYPE	RESISTOR CHP ATCH/ INTERCON	RES TOL (%)	ELMT ATCH/ INTERCON NO./ TYPE
141	FPG1 10	TO-86 -55/ 125C	N/R	Glass	Al_2O_3 Eutect	.20x .20	1	AlCond N/A	0		0		0		0		12 TaNi/ NiCr	Fired AlCond	±10	

LIFE / ENVIRONMENTAL EXPERIENCE

DATA SRCE	SCR CLS	TST SRC	TEST TYP/ APP ENV	STR LVL/ EQP TYPE	TEST STD MTD/COND	NO. TSTD	TEST DUR.	PART HRS.	NO. FLD	FAILURE CLASSIFICATION IND; MODE; MECH; CAUSE (NO. FAILED / EVENT)	% DEF	TEST DATE	REMARKS
U	N/R	Rel	GrndLbty	Cnnctns		12	7178	86136	0			10/72	

MALFUNCTION DATA

SYSTEM / EQUIPMENT	PART HISTORY	SCR CLS	DATE CODE	FAILURE ANALYSIS / CORRECTIVE ACTION

SYSTEM / EQUIPMENT	PART HISTORY	SCR CLS	DATE CODE	FAILURE ANALYSIS / CORRECTIVE ACTION

RELIABILITY ANALYSIS CENTER

H.M.R.D.—G

DEVICE SECTION

MANUFACTURER: SYLVANIA ELECTRIC PROD   **FUNCTIONAL CATEGORY:** DIGITAL

TECHNOLOGY: SEMICONDUCTOR   **DEVICE FUNCTION:** TEST DEVICE

ENTRY NO.	PKG/ NO. PINS	SIZE OP TEMP	SUBSTR MTL/ BOND	SUBSTR SIZE	NO. COND LYR	SUBSTR METAL #BONDS	IC NO./ TYPE	IC CHP ATCH/ INTERCON	TRANSISTOR NO./ TYPE	TRANSISTOR CHP ATCH/ INTERCON	DIODE NO./ TYPE	DIODE CHP ATCH/ INTERCON	CAPACITOR NO./ TYPE	CAPACITOR CHP ATCH/ INTERCON	RESISTOR NO./ TYPE	RESISTOR CHP ATCH/ INTERCON	RES TOL (%)	ELMT ATCH/ INTERCON NO./ TYPE
142	N/A	N/A	Al$_2$O$_3$ N/A	2.22x 2.22	4	PdAg N/R	9 8 Gate (8) 9 Gate (1)	Pin Weld PdAg	0		0		0		0	0		

LIFE / ENVIRONMENTAL EXPERIENCE

DATA SRCE NO.	SCR CLS	TST SRC	TEST TYP/ APP ENV	STR LVL/ EQP TYPE	TEST STD MTD/COND (user)	NO. TSTD	TEST DUR.	PART HRS.	NO. FLD	FAILURE CLASSIFICATION IND; MODE; MECH; CAUSE (NO. FAILED / EVENT)	% DEF	TEST DATE
U	N/R	Env/SSD	VibFtg	500 HZ 10G	A1002	10			0			10/69
			MechShk	18 Blo 20G	AH003							
			ThrmShk	-55/150C 5 cyc	AJ018							
			TempCyc	0/100C 5 cyc	AJ019							
			Moistr	100C 95%RH	AA048	10			0			

                        REMARKS

MALFUNCTION DATA

SYSTEM / EQUIPMENT	PART HISTORY	SCR CLS	DATE CODE	FAILURE ANALYSIS / CORRECTIVE ACTION	SYSTEM / EQUIPMENT	PART HISTORY	SCR CLS	DATE CODE	FAILURE ANALYSIS / CORRECTIVE ACTION

HYBRID MICROCIRCUIT
RELIABILITY DATA

FUNCTIONAL CATEGORY: LINEAR
DEVICE FUNCTION: OPERATIONAL AMPLIFIER

DEVICE SECTION

MANUFACTURER: TELEDYNE PHILBRICK
TECHNOLOGY: THIN FILM

ENTRY NO.	PKG/ NO. PINS	SIZE OP TEMP	PKG MFG	PKG SEAL	SUBSTR MTL/ BOND	SUBSTR SIZE	NO. COND LYR	SUBSTR METAL #BONDS	IC NO./ TYPE	IC CHP ATCH/ INTERCON	TRANSISTOR NO./ TYPE	TRANSISTOR CHP ATCH/ INTERCON	DIODE NO./ TYPE	DIODE CHP ATCH/ INTERCON	CAPACITOR NO./ TYPE	CAPACITOR CHP ATCH/ INTERCON	RESISTOR NO./ TYPE	RESISTOR CHP ATCH/ INTERCON	RES TOL (%)	ELM ATCH/ INTERCON NO./ TYPE
143	Can 14	.88x .52x -.20 -55/ 125C	N/R	Weld	Al$_2$O$_3$ Eutect	.80x .50	1	AuCond 124	0		10 SiNPN	Eutect AuWire	7 SiGP	Eutect AuWire	5 N/R	AgEpoxy AuWire	2 N/R 1 N/R	Fired AuCond AgEpoxy AuWire	N/R	

LIFE / ENVIRONMENTAL EXPERIENCE

DATA SRCE	SCR CLS	TST SRC	TEST TYP/ APP ENV	STR LVL/ EQP TYPE	TEST STD MTD/COND	NO. TSTD	TEST DUR.	PART HRS.	NO. FLD	FAILURE CLASSIFICATION IND; MODE; MECH; CAUSE (NO. FAILED / EVENT)	% DEF	TEST DATE	REMARKS
U	C	Scr/SSB	Burn-In	70C		2057			184	N/R	8.94	8/72– 3/74	

MALFUNCTION DATA

SYSTEM / EQUIPMENT	PART HISTORY	SCR CLS	DATE CODE	FAILURE ANALYSIS / CORRECTIVE ACTION

SYSTEM / EQUIPMENT	PART HISTORY	SCR CLS	DATE CODE	FAILURE ANALYSIS / CORRECTIVE ACTION

DEVICE SECTION

RELIABILITY
ANALYSIS
CENTER

HYBRID MICROCIRCUIT RELIABILITY DATA

MANUFACTURER: TELEDYNE SEMICONDUCTOR (AMELCO)

FUNCTIONAL CATEGORY: THIN FILM

TECHNOLOGY:

DEVICE FUNCTION: N/R

ENTRY NO.	PKG/ NO. PINS	SIZE OP TEMP	PKG MFG	PKG SEAL	SUBSTR MTL/ BOND	SUBSTR SIZE	NO. COND LYR	SUBSTR METAL #BONDS	IC NO./ TYPE	IC CHP ATCH/ INTERCON	TRANSISTOR NO./ TYPE	TRANSISTOR CHP ATCH/ INTERCON	DIODE NO./ TYPE	DIODE CHP ATCH/ INTERCON	CAPACITOR NO./ TYPE	CAPACITOR CHP ATCH/ INTERCON	RESISTOR NO./ TYPE	RESISTOR CHP ATCH/ INTERCON	RES TOL (%)	ELMT ATCH/ INTERCON NO./ TYPE
144	Can 12	TO-8 -55/ 125C	N/R	Weld	Al₂O₃	.50D	1	AuPst	0		6 SiNPN	Eutect AuWire	2 ZenAv	Eutent AuWire	1	N/R	9 NiCr	Alloy/ AuWire	N/R	
								N/R					3 SiGP	Eutect AuWire	N/R	N/R				

LIFE / ENVIRONMENTAL EXPERIENCE

DATA SRCE	SCR CLS	TST SRC	TEST TYP/ APP ENV	STR LVL/ EQP TYPE	TEST STD MTD/COND	NO. TSTD	TEST DUR.	PART HRS.	NO. FLD	FAILURE CLASSIFICATION IND; MODE; MECH; CAUSE (NO. FAILED / EVENT)	TEST DATE % DEF	REMARKS
U	SSD	Env	VisInsp			25			0			
		Env	X-Ray			25			0			
U	SSD	Brn	Temp	125C 72 hr	MS883 1008B	23			1	Spec Reject	4.35	TTF 4.35 Hrs
U	SSD	Env	TempCyc	-55/125C 10/10 min 10KG	MS883 1010B	23			0			
			CnstAcc	6 Axes	MS883 2001B	23			0			
U	SSD	Lab	OpCnst	125C 100%		15	500	7500	3	Spec Rej	20.0	TTF 2.0 Hrs
U	SSD	Stp	MechShk	5 stp 500G/stp 2.5KG init	MS883 2002	3			1	Out of Register; shorted Res, Scratch	33.3	
U	SSD	Env	ThrmShk	-55/125C 5/5 min	MS883 1011B	4			0			
			TrmStr Moistr	-10/65C 98% RH	MS883 1004B	4			0			
U	SSD	Env	Solder		MS883 1014A	4			0			

MALFUNCTION DATA

SYSTEM / EQUIPMENT	PART HISTORY	SCR CLS	DATE CODE	FAILURE ANALYSIS / CORRECTIVE ACTION	SYSTEM / EQUIPMENT	PART HISTORY	SCR CLS	DATE CODE	FAILURE ANALYSIS / CORRECTIVE ACTION

MANUFACTURER: TELEDYNE SEMICONDUCTOR
(AMELCO) (Con't)
TECHNOLOGY: THIN FILM

FUNCTIONAL CATEGORY:
DEVICE FUNCTION: N/R

HYBRID MICROCIRCUIT
RELIABILITY DATA

RELIABILITY ANALYSIS CENTER

ENTRY NO.	PKG/ NO. PINS	SIZE OP TEMP	PKG MFG	PKG SEAL	SUBSTR MTL/ BOND	SUBSTR SIZE	NO. COND LYR	SUBSTR METAL #BONDS	IC		TRANSISTOR		DIODE		CAPACITOR		RESISTOR		RES TOL (%)	ELMT ATCH/ INTERCON
									NO./ TYPE	CHP ATCH/ INTERCON	NO./ TYPE	CHP ATCH/ INTERCON	NO./ TYPE	CHP ATCH/ INTERCON	NO./ TYPE	CHP ATCH/ INTERCON	NO./ TYPE	CHP ATCH/ INTERCON		NO./ TYPE
144 (Cnt'd)																				

LIFE / ENVIRONMENTAL EXPERIENCE

DATA SRCE	SCR CLS	TST SRC	TEST TYP/ APP ENV	STR LVL/ EQP-ᵀYPE	TEST STD MTD/COND	NO. TSTD	TEST DUR.	PART HRS.	NO. FLD	FAILURE CLASSIFICATION IND; MODE; MECH: CAUSE (NO. FAILED / EVENT)	% DEF	TEST DATE	REMARKS
U	SSD	Env	MechShk	1.5KG 6 Axes	MS883 2002B	4			0				
			VbVrFg	.02/2KHZ .2G	MS883 2007A	4			0				

MALFUNCTION DATA

SYSTEM / EQUIPMENT	PART HISTORY	SCR CLS	DATE CODE	FAILURE ANALYSIS / CORRECTIVE ACTION	SYSTEM / EQUIPMENT	PART HISTORY	SCR CLS	DATE CODE	FAILURE ANALYSIS / CORRECTIVE ACTION

DEVICE SECTION

MANUFACTURER: TELEDYNE SEMICONDUCTOR (AMELCO)
TECHNOLOGY: THIN FILM

FUNCTIONAL CATEGORY: LINEAR
DEVICE FUNCTION: OPERATIONAL AMPLIFIER

HYBRID MICROCIRCUIT
RELIABILITY DATA

ENTRY NO.	PKG/NO. PINS	SIZE/OP TEMP	PKG MFG	PKG SEAL	SUBSTR MTL/BOND	SUBSTR SIZE	NO. COND LYR	SUBSTR METAL #BONDS	IC NO./TYPE	IC CHP ATCH/INTERCON	TRANSISTOR NO./TYPE	TRANSISTOR CHP ATCH/INTERCON	DIODE NO./TYPE	DIODE CHP ATCH/INTERCON	CAPACITOR NO./TYPE	CAPACITOR CHP ATCH/INTERCON	RESISTOR NO./TYPE	RESISTOR CHP ATCH/INTERCON	RES TOL (%)	ELMT ATCH/INTERCON NO./TYPE
145	Can 12	TO-8 -55/125C	N/R	Weld	Header	N/A	N/A	Kov/Au N/R	0		8 Unij 8 SiNPN	Eutect AuWire Eutect AuWire	3 SiGp	Eutect AuWire	1 N/R	N/R N/R	12 Ta	N/A Au	N/R	

LIFE / ENVIRONMENTAL EXPERIENCE

DATA SRCE	SCR CLS	TST SRC	TEST TYP/APP ENV	STR LVL/EQP TYPE	TEST STD MTD/COND	NO. TSTD	TEST DUR.	PART HRS.	NO. FLD	% DEF	TEST DATE
I	SSD	Env	VisInsp		MS750 2071	159			0		9/69
I	SSD	Env	VisInsp		MS750 2066	22			0		
I	SSD	Env	TempCyc	-65/200C 5 cyc	MS750 1051	22			0		
			ThrmShk	0/100C 5/5 min	MS750 1056A						
			Moistr	-10/65C 98% RH	MS750 1021	22			0		
I	SSD	Env	MechShk	1.5 KG 0.5 msec	MS750 2016						
			VbFtg	60HZ 20G 3 Axes	MS750 2016						
			VbVrFq	.1/2 KHZ 20G	MS750 2016						
			CnstAcc	20KG 6 Axes	MS750 2006						
I	SSD	Env	SltAtm	35C	MS750 1041	11			0		

FAILURE CLASSIFICATION IND; MODE; MECH; CAUSE (NO. FAILED / EVENT) — REMARKS

MALFUNCTION DATA

SYSTEM/EQUIPMENT	PART HISTORY	SCR CLS	DATE CODE	FAILURE ANALYSIS / CORRECTIVE ACTION	SYSTEM/EQUIPMENT	PART HISTORY	SCR CLS	DATE CODE	FAILURE ANALYSIS / CORRECTIVE ACTION

DEVICE SECTION

MANUFACTURER: TELEDYNE SEMICONDUCTOR (AMELCO) (Con't)
TECHNOLOGY: THIN FILM

FUNCTIONAL CATEGORY: LINEAR
DEVICE FUNCTION: OPERATIONAL AMPLIFIER

 RELIABILITY ANALYSIS CENTER

HYBRID MICROCIRCUIT
RELIABILITY DATA

ENTRY NO.	PKG/ NO. PINS	SIZE OP TEMP	PKG MFG	PKG SEAL	SUBSTR MTL/ BOND	SUBSTR SIZE	NO. COND LYR	SUBSTR METAL /#BONDS	IC NO./TYPE	IC CHP ATCH/ INTERCON	TRANSISTOR NO./TYPE	TRANSISTOR CHP ATCH/ INTERCON	DIODE NO./TYPE	DIODE CHP ATCH/ INTERCON	CAPACITOR NO./TYPE	CAPACITOR CHP ATCH/ INTERCON	RESISTOR NO./TYPE	RESISTOR CHP ATCH/ INTERCON	RES TOL (%)	ELMT ATCH/ INTERCON NO./TYPE
145 (Cntd)																				

LIFE / ENVIRONMENTAL EXPERIENCE

DATA SRCE	SCR CLS	TST SRC	TEST TYP/ APP ENV	STR LVL/ EQP TYPE	TEST STD MTD/COND	NO. TSTD	TEST DUR.	PART HRS.	NO. FLD	FAILURE CLASSIFICATION IND; MODE; MECH; CAUSE (NO. FAILED / EVENT)	% DEF	TEST DATE	REMARKS
I	SSD	Env	TrmStr	MS750	MS750 2036E	11			0				
I	SSD	Lab	StgLife		MS750 1031	38		38000	0				
I	SSD	Lab	StgLife										
I	SSD	Lab	OpCnst	MS750	MS750 1026	77		77000	0				
I	SSD	Env	Solder	MS	MS750 1026	22			0				All Leads Immersed

MALFUNCTION DATA

SYSTEM / EQUIPMENT	PART HISTORY	SCR CLS	DATE CODE	FAILURE ANALYSIS / CORRECTIVE ACTION	SYSTEM / EQUIPMENT	PART HISTORY	SCR CLS	DATE CODE	FAILURE ANALYSIS / CORRECTIVE ACTION

DEVICE SECTION

MANUFACTURER: TEXAS INSTRUMENTS
TECHNOLOGY: THIN FILM

FUNCTIONAL CATEGORY: DIGITAL
DEVICE FUNCTION: EMITTER FOLLOWER

HYBRID MICROCIRCUIT RELIABILITY DATA

RELIABILITY ANALYSIS CENTER

ENTRY NO.	PKG/ NO. PINS	SIZE OP TEMP	PKG MFG	PKG SEAL	SUBSTR MTL/ BOND	SUBSTR SIZE	NO. COND LYR	SUBSTR METAL #BONDS	IC NO./ TYPE	IC CHP ATCH/ INTERCON	TRANSISTOR NO./ TYPE	TRANSISTOR CHP ATCH/ INTERCON	DIODE NO./ TYPE	DIODE CHP ATCH/ INTERCON	CAPACITOR NO./ TYPE	CAPACITOR CHP ATCH/ INTERCON	RESISTOR NO./ TYPE	RESISTOR CHP ATCH/ INTERCON	RES TOL (%)	ELM ATCH/ INTERCON NO./ TYPE
146	Can 12	TO-5 / -55/ 125C	N/R	Weld	Al₂O₃ Au BmLd	.50D	1	AuCond 47	0		10 SiNPN	BmLd AuCond	1 SiGP	BmLd AuCond	3 Ceramic	BmLd AuCond	6 Thin	BmLd AuCond		

LIFE / ENVIRONMENTAL EXPERIENCE

DATA SRCE	SCR CLS	TST SRC	TEST TYP/ APP ENV	STR LVL/ EQP TYPE	TEST STD MTD/COND	NO. TSTD	TEST DUR.	PART HRS.	NO. FLD	FAILURE CLASSIFICATION IND; MODE; MECH; CAUSE (NO. FAILED / EVENT)	% DEF	TEST DATE	REMARKS
U	C	Rel	GrndLbty	25C 100% 90/100%	MS781B	124	9193.5 Hrs	1.14E6	0			5/73- 9/73	MS781B (Plan IV Leve A-1)
U	C	Chk	GrndLbty	25C/100%	MS781B	124	168 Hrs	20852	0				

MALFUNCTION DATA

SYSTEM / EQUIPMENT	PART HISTORY	SCR CLS	DATE CODE	FAILURE ANALYSIS / CORRECTIVE ACTION	SYSTEM / EQUIPMENT	PART HISTORY	SCR CLS	DATE CODE	FAILURE ANALYSIS / CORRECTIVE ACTION

HYBRID MICROCIRCUIT
RELIABILITY DATA

RELIABILITY ANALYSIS CENTER

DEVICE SECTION

MANUFACTURER: TEXAS INSTRUMENTS

TECHNOLOGY: THIN FILM

FUNCTIONAL CATEGORY: LINEAR

DEVICE FUNCTION: POWER DARLINGTON

ENTRY NO.	PKG/ NO. PINS	SIZE OP TEMP	PKG MFG	PKG SEAL	SUBSTR MTL/ BOND	SUBSTR SIZE	NO. COND LYR	SUBSTR METAL #BONDS	IC NO./ TYPE	IC CHP ATCH/ INTERCON	TRANSISTOR NO./ TYPE	TRANSISTOR CHP ATCH/ INTERCON	DIODE NO./ TYPE	DIODE CHP ATCH/ INTERCON	CAPACITOR NO./ TYPE	CAPACITOR CHP ATCH/ INTERCON	RESISTOR NO./ TYPE	RESISTOR CHP ATCH/ INTERCON	RES TOL (%)	ELMT ATCH/INTERCON NO./ TYPE	ELMT ATCH/ INTERCON
147	Can 3	TO-5 -55/ 125C	N/R	Weld	Header N/A	N/A	1	Kov/Au N/R	0		2 SiNPN	Eutect AuWire	0		0		1 Thin	N/R AuWire	N/R		

LIFE / ENVIRONMENTAL EXPERIENCE

DATA SRCE	SCR CLS	TST SRC	TEST TYP/ APP ENV	STR LVL/ EQP TYPE	TEST STD MTD/COND	NO. TSTD	TEST DUR.	PART HRS.	NO. FLD	FAILURE CLASSIFICATION IND; MODE; MECH; CAUSE (NO. FAILED / EVENT)	% DEF	TEST DATE	REMARKS
U	SSD	Env	VisInsp VisIns MechShk	1.5KG 1.0msec 3 Blo	2017 2008A 2002B	32 25			0			1/70	
			VibFtg VbVrFrq	20G 60HZ 20G .02/2KHZ	2005A 2007A		96 Hrs	2400					
U	SSD	Env	CnstAcc	10KG 6 AXES	2001	25			0				
U	SSD	Lab	OpCnst	25C 100%	1005B	52	340 Hrs	17680	0				

MALFUNCTION DATA

SYSTEM / EQUIPMENT	PART HISTORY	SCR CLS	DATE CODE	FAILURE ANALYSIS / CORRECTIVE ACTION

SYSTEM / EQUIPMENT	PART HISTORY	SCR CLS	DATE CODE	FAILURE ANALYSIS / CORRECTIVE ACTION

DEVICE SECTION

MANUFACTURER: TEXAS INSTRUMENTS
TECHNOLOGY: THIN FILM

FUNCTIONAL CATEGORY: LINEAR
DEVICE FUNCTION: CLAMPED DIFFERENTIAL

HYBRID MICROCIRCUIT
RELIABILITY DATA

RELIABILITY ANALYSIS CENTER

ENTRY NO.	PKG/ NO. PINS	SIZE OP TEMP	PKG MFG	PKG SEAL	SUBSTR MTL/ BOND	SUBSTR SIZE	NO. COND LYR	SUBSTR METAL #BONDS	IC NO./ TYPE	IC CHP ATCH/ INTERCON	TRANSISTOR NO./ TYPE	TRANSISTOR CHP ATCH/ INTERCON	DIODE NO./ TYPE	DIODE CHP ATCH/ INTERCON	CAPACITOR NO./ TYPE	CAPACITOR CHP ATCH/ INTERCON	RESISTOR NO./ TYPE	RESISTOR CHP ATCH/ INTERCON	RES TOL (%)	CROSSOVER NO./ TYPE	CROSSOVER ELM/ATCH/ INTERCON
148	Can 12	TO-8 -55/ 125C	N/R	Weld	Al₂O₃ Eutect	.50D	1	AuCond 47 BmLd	0		3 N/R	BmLd AuCond	10 N/R	BmLd AuCond	2 N/R	BmLd AuCond	7 Thin	BmLd AuCond	N/R	3 Thin	Dep AuCond

LIFE / ENVIRONMENTAL EXPERIENCE

DATA SRCE	SCR CLS	TST SRC	TEST TYP/ APP ENV	STR LVL/ EQP TYPE	TEST STD MTD/COND	NO. TSTD	TEST DUR.	PART HRS.	NO. FLD	FAILURE CLASSIFICATION IND; MODE; MECH; CAUSE (NO. FAILED / EVENT)	% DEF	TEST DATE	REMARKS
U	C	Chk	GrndLbty	25C 100%	MS781B	124	168 Hrs	20852	0			5/73	MS781B; Plan IV, Level A-1
U	C	Rel	GrndLbty	25C/90% 100%,110%	MS781B	124	9193 Hrs	1.14E6	0			9/73	

MALFUNCTION DATA

SYSTEM / EQUIPMENT	PART HISTORY	SCR CLS	DATE CODE	FAILURE ANALYSIS / CORRECTIVE ACTION	SYSTEM / EQUIPMENT	PART HISTORY	SCR CLS	DATE CODE	FAILURE ANALYSIS / CORRECTIVE ACTION

DEVICE SECTION

MANUFACTURER: TRW ELECTRONICS

TECHNOLOGY: THICK FILM

FUNCTIONAL CATEGORY: DIGITAL

DEVICE FUNCTION: DUAL LEVEL SHIFT GATE

HYBRID MICROCIRCUIT
RELIABILITY DATA

RELIABILITY ANALYSIS CENTER

ENTRY NO.	PKG/ NO. PINS	SIZE OP TEMP	PKG MFG	PKG SEAL	SUBSTR MTL/ BOND	SUBSTR SIZE	NO. COND LYR	SUBSTR METAL #BONDS	IC NO./ TYPE	IC CHP ATCH/ INTERCON	TRANSISTOR NO./ TYPE	TRANSISTOR CHP ATCH/ INTERCON	DIODE NO./ TYPE	DIODE CHP ATCH/ INTERCON	CAPACITOR NO./ TYPE	CAPACITOR CHP ATCH/ INTERCON	RESISTOR NO./ TYPE	RESISTOR CHP ATCH/ INTERCON	RES TOL (%)	ELM ATCH/ INTERCON NO./ TYPE
149	FPM1 14	.18x .38D -55/ 125C	N/R	Soldr	Glass Epoxy	.35D	1	AuCond 70	1 6 Gate	AgEpoxy AuWire	4 SiNPN	AgEpoxy AuWire	0		0		20 Cermet	Fired AuCond	N/R	

LIFE / ENVIRONMENTAL EXPERIENCE

DATA SRCE NO.	SCR CLS	TST SRC	TEST TYP/ APP ENV	STR LVL/ EQP TYPE	TEST STD MTD/COND	NO. TSTD	TEST DUR.	PART HRS.	NO. FLD	FAILURE CLASSIFICATION IND; MODE; MECH; CAUSE (NO. FAILED / EVENT)	% DEF	TEST DATE	REMARKS
U	B	Env	VisInsp		MS883	21			0			9/69	
			X-Ray			21			0				
U	SSD	Brn	Temp	125C	1008B	19	72 Hrs	1368	0				
U	SSD	Env	TempCyc	-55/125C 10/10 min	1010B				0				
			CnstAcc	10KG 6 AXES	2001B	19			0				
U	SSD	Lab	OpCnst	125C 100%	1011C	11	500 Hrs	5500	2	"O" $V_{OLmax} >$ Spec	18.2		
U	SSD	Stp	ThrmShk	-65/150C OIL 15cyc	1011B	4			0				
U	SSD	Env	ThrmShk	-55/125C 5/5 min									
			TrmStr	-10/65C 98%RH					0				
			Moistr		1004B				2	Bond (Chip) Failure			
U	SSD	Env	Solder	1.5KG 6 AXES	1014A	4			0		0.5		
			MechShk		2002B	4							
			VbVrFrq	.02/2KHZ 20G	2007A	2			0				

SYSTEM / EQUIPMENT	PART HISTORY	SCR CLS	DATE CODE	FAILURE ANALYSIS / CORRECTIVE ACTION

MALFUNCTION DATA

SYSTEM / EQUIPMENT	PART HISTORY	SCR CLS	DATE CODE	FAILURE ANALYSIS / CORRECTIVE ACTION

DEVICE SECTION

RELIABILITY ANALYSIS CENTER

MANUFACTURER: PROPRIETARY

FUNCTIONAL CATEGORY: DIGITAL

HYBRID MICROCIRCUIT
RELIABILITY DATA

TECHNOLOGY: THICK FILM

DEVICE FUNCTION: FET SWITCH

ENTRY NO.	PKG/ NO. PINS	SIZE OP TEMP	PKG MFG	PKG SEAL	SUBSTR MTL/ BOND	SUBSTR SIZE	NO. COND LYR	SUBSTR METAL #BONDS	IC NO./TYPE	IC CHP ATCH/ INTERCON	TRANSISTOR NO./TYPE	TRANSISTOR CHP ATCH/ INTERCON	DIODE NO./TYPE	DIODE CHP ATCH/ INTERCON	CAPACITOR NO./TYPE	CAPACITOR CHP ATCH/ INTERCON	RESISTOR NO./TYPE	RESISTOR CHP ATCH/ INTERCON	RES TOL (%)	ELM ATCH/ INTERCON NO./TYPE
150	Can 12	TO-8 -55/ 125C	N/R	Weld	Al₂O₃ Eutect	.50D	1	PdAg 26	0		4 N/R	Eutect AuWire	2 N/R	Eutect AuWire	2 Thick	Dep AuCond	6 Cermet	Fired AuWire	N/R	

LIFE / ENVIRONMENTAL EXPERIENCE

DATA SRCE	SCR CLS	TST SRC	TEST TYP/ APP ENV	STR LVL/ EQP TYPE	TEST STD MTD/COND	NO. TSTD	TEST DUR.	PART HRS.	NO. FLD	FAILURE CLASSIFICATION IND; MODE; MECH; CAUSE (NO. FAILED / EVENT)	% DEF	TEST DATE	REMARKS
U	B	Fld	AirInhab	AirInhab/ Cmctns 500 sys/ 91 per	Combin	45500	384.6 Hrs	17.5E6	5	N/R	0.01	1/71- 6/72	

MALFUNCTION DATA

SYSTEM / EQUIPMENT	PART HISTORY	SCR CLS	DATE CODE	FAILURE ANALYSIS / CORRECTIVE ACTION

SYSTEM / EQUIPMENT	PART HISTORY	SCR CLS	DATE CODE	FAILURE ANALYSIS / CORRECTIVE ACTION

HYBRID MICROCIRCUIT
RELIABILITY DATA

DEVICE SECTION

MANUFACTURER: PROPRIETARY

TECHNOLOGY: THICK FILM

FUNCTIONAL CATEGORY: DIGITAL

DEVICE FUNCTION: MEMORY SWITCH

ENTRY NO.	PKG/ NO. PINS	SIZE OP TEMP	PKG MFG	PKG SEAL	SUBSTR MTL/ BOND	SUBSTR SIZE	NO. COND LYR	SUBSTR METAL #BONDS	IC NO./ TYPE	IC CHP ATCH/ INTERCON	TRANSISTOR NO./ TYPE	TRANSISTOR CHP ATCH/ INTERCON	DIODE NO./ TYPE	DIODE CHP ATCH/ INTERCON	CAPACITOR NO./ TYPE	CAPACITOR CHP ATCH/ INTERCON	RESISTOR NO./ TYPE	RESISTOR CHP ATCH/ INTERCON	RES TOL (%)	ELMT ATCH/ INTERCON NO./ TYPE
151	FPM1 14	TO-87 -55/ 125C	N/R	Weld	Al₂O₃ Eutect	.35x .25	1	AuPst 38	0		4 SiNPN (2) SiPNP (2)	Eutect AuWire	2 SiGP	Eutect AuWire	0		4 Cermet	Fired AuPst	N/R	

LIFE / ENVIRONMENTAL EXPERIENCE

DATA SRCE	SCR CLS	TST SRC	TEST TYP/ APP ENV	STR LVL/ EQP TYPE	TEST STD MTD/COND	NO. TSTD	TEST DUR.	PART HRS.	NO. FLD	FAILURE CLASSIFICATION IND; MODE; MECH; CAUSE (NO. FAILED / EVENT)	% DEF	TEST DATE
U	A	Env	VisInsp		MS883 2008	448			3	Ext. Lead Missing	0.66	5/71
			GrossLk		1014C	306			1	Package Leak	0.33	
			Temp	150C	1008	305		14640	2	Tp out of ±	0.66	
			TempCyc	-65/150C	1010C							
			CnstAcc	30KG	2001				0			
				6 AXES								
			FineLk		1014A					Exploded/1; Loose Ceramic Substrate/1		
			GrossLk		1014C	305			5	Unkown/1; External Lead Off/1;	1.64	
										Au Ball Bond/1		
U	A	Brn	ThmShk	125C	1015D	300	168 Hrs	50400	1	Q2 CE Short	0.33	
U	A	Env		-65/150C	1011C	299			2	N/R	0.67	
			MechShk	20KG Y₁	2002F	297			48	N/R/28; Subst Broken/3; Loose Ceramic	16.2	
				1 Blo						Subst/3; Tp > Spec/1 Loose Au Wedge		
										Bd to Au Post/6; Loose Transistor		
										Chip/2 Au Ball		
U	A	Env	CnstAcc	30KG Y₂	2001E	249			8	Shorted Q₂ Elongated Wire/3; Cover off/3	33.21	
										Loose Ceramic Subst/1; Lead Short,		
U	A	Brn	RevBias	125C	1015D	241	72 Hrs	17352	2	Erroneous Wire Bonding/1	0.83	
			CnstAcc	125C	1015A	238			1	Broken Package/1; N/R/1	0.42	
				40KG Y₁	2001	237	72 Hrs	17136	1	N/R	0.42	
		Brn	FineLk		1014A	236			0	Cover Lifted	0	
		Env	GrossLk		1014C	236			100	Package Leak	42.3	

MALFUNCTION DATA

SYSTEM / EQUIPMENT	PART HISTORY	SCR CLS	DATE CODE	FAILURE ANALYSIS / CORRECTIVE ACTION

DEVICE SECTION

MANUFACTURER: PROPRIETARY
TECHNOLOGY: THICK FILM

FUNCTIONAL CATEGORY: DIGITAL
DEVICE FUNCTION: MEMORY SWITCH

HYBRID MICROCIRCUIT
RELIABILITY DATA

 RELIABILITY ANALYSIS CENTER

ENTRY NO.	PKG/ NO. PINS	SIZE OP TEMP	PKG MFG	PKG SEAL	SUBSTR MTL/ BOND	SUBSTR SIZE	NO. COND LYR	SUBSTR METAL #BONDS	TRANSISTOR NO./TYPE	TRANSISTOR CHP ATCH/INTERCON	DIODE NO./TYPE	DIODE CHP ATCH/INTERCON	CAPACITOR NO./TYPE	CAPACITOR CHP ATCH/INTERCON	RESISTOR NO./TYPE	RESISTOR CHP ATCH/INTERCON	RES TOL (%)	ELMT ATCH/INTERCON NO./TYPE
151 (Cnt'd)																		

REMARKS (con't):
Broken Case/2; Ceramic Substrate Broken/10; Loose Au Ball on Semi Chip/10; Looser Ceramic Substrate/8; Diode I_{LK} > Spec/1; Wedge Bond to Cond. Loose/3; N/R/2

LIFE / ENVIRONMENTAL EXPERIENCE   (con't)

DATA SRCE NO.	SCR CLS	TST SRC	TEST TYP/ APP ENV	STR LVL/ EQP TYPE	TEST STD MTD/COND	NO. TSTD	TEST DUR.	PART HRS.	NO. FLD	FAILURE CLASSIFICATION — IND; MODE; MECH; CAUSE (NO. FAILED / EVENT)	% DEF	TEST DATE
	A		X-Ray		MS883 1012	20			0			
			VisInsp		2009	113			0			
			TempCyc	-65/150C	1010C	38						
U		Env	VisIns	150C	1008C	171	48 Hrs	8208	0			
			Temp	-65/150C	1010C				1	Q1 CE Short	0.58	
			TempCyc	30KG	2001							
			CnstAcc	6 AXES								
			FineLk		1014A	171			7	Package Leak/2; External Lead Missing/2; Loose Au Ball to Diode/1; Loose Ceramic Subst/1; N/R/1	4.09	
			GrossLk		1014C							
U	A	Brn	ThrmShk	125C	1015D	164	168 Hrs	27600	1	I_{LK} > Spec	0.61	
		Env		-65/150C	1011C	164			1	I_{LK} > Spec	0.61	
			MechShk	20KG Y1	2002F	163			33	Ext.; Pin 8 Missing	20.2	
				1 BLo								
U	A	Env	CnstAcc	30KG Y2	2001E	130	72 Hrs	8350	14	Loose Ceramic Subst/8; Broken Ceramic Subst/2; N/R/4	10.8	
U	A	Brn	RevBias	125C	1015D	116	72 Hrs	8350	0			
U	A	Brn	CnstAcc	125C	1015A	116			0			
U	A	Brn	FineLk	40KGY2-Y1	2001	115			2	Cover Off; Package Fell Apart	1.74	
		Env	GrossLk		1014A	114			0			
					1014C	114			1	I_{LK} > Spec	0.88	

MALFUNCTION DATA

SYSTEM / EQUIPMENT	PART HISTORY	SCR CLS	DATE CODE	FAILURE ANALYSIS / CORRECTIVE ACTION	CORRECTIVE ACTION

SYSTEM / EQUIPMENT	PART HISTORY	SCR CLS	DATE CODE	FAILURE ANALYSIS / CORRECTIVE ACTION

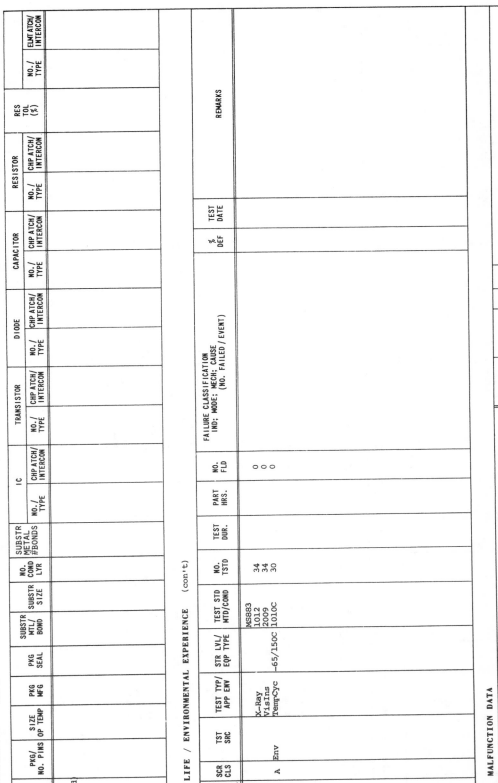

DEVICE SECTION

FUNCTIONAL CATEGORY: DIGITAL

MANUFACTURER: PROPRIETARY

DEVICE FUNCTION: MEMORY SWITCH

TECHNOLOGY: THICK FILM

HYBRID MICROCIRCUIT
RELIABILITY DATA

ENTRY NO.	PKG/ NO. PINS	SIZE OP TEMP	PKG MFG	PKG SEAL	SUBSTR MTL/ BOND	SUBSTR SIZE	NO. COND LYR	SUBSTR METAL #BONDS	IC NO./ TYPE	IC CHP ATCH/ INTERCON	TRANSISTOR NO./ TYPE	TRANSISTOR CHP ATCH/ INTERCON	DIODE NO./ TYPE	DIODE CHP ATCH/ INTERCON	CAPACITOR NO./ TYPE	CAPACITOR CHP ATCH/ INTERCON	RESISTOR NO./ TYPE	RESISTOR CHP ATCH/ INTERCON	RES TOL (%)	ELMT ATCH/ INTERCON NO./ TYPE
151 (Cntd)																				

LIFE / ENVIRONMENTAL EXPERIENCE (con't)

DATA SRCE	SCR CLS	TST SRC	TEST TYP/ APP ENV	STR LVL/ EQP TYPE	TEST STD MTD/COND	NO. TSTD	TEST DUR.	PART HRS.	NO. FLD	FAILURE CLASSIFICATION IND; MODE; MECH; CAUSE (NO. FAILED / EVENT)	% DEF	TEST DATE	REMARKS
U	A	Env	X-Ray VisIns TempCyc	-65/150C	MS883 1012 2009 1010C	34 34 30			0 0 0				

MALFUNCTION DATA

SYSTEM/ EQUIPMENT	PART HISTORY	SCR CLS	DATE CODE	FAILURE ANALYSIS / CORRECTIVE ACTION	SYSTEM/ EQUIPMENT	PART HISTORY	SCR CLS	DATE CODE	FAILURE ANALYSIS / CORRECTIVE ACTION

DEVICE SECTION

MANUFACTURER: PROPRIETARY
TECHNOLOGY: THIN FILM

FUNCTIONAL CATEGORY: DIGITAL
DEVICE FUNCTION: LADDER SWITCH AND DRIVER

HYBRID MICROCIRCUIT RELIABILITY DATA

RELIABILITY ANALYSIS CENTER

ENTRY NO.	PKG/ NO. PINS	SIZE/ OP TEMP	PKG MFG	PKG SEAL	SUBSTR MTL/ BOND	SUBSTR SIZE	NO. COND LYR	SUBSTR METAL #BONDS	IC NO./ TYPE	IC CHP ATCH/ INTERCON	TRANSISTOR NO./ TYPE	TRANSISTOR CHP ATCH/ INTERCON	DIODE NO./ TYPE	DIODE CHP ATCH/ INTERCON	CAPACITOR NO./ TYPE	CAPACITOR CHP ATCH/ INTERCON	RESISTOR NO./ TYPE	RESISTOR CHP ATCH/ INTERCON	RES TOL (%)	ELMT ATCH/ INTERCON NO./ TYPE
152	FPCm 10	TO-86 -55/ 125C	N/R	Glass Header N/A	N/A		1	Eutect N/R	0		3 SiNPN	Eutect AuWire	0		0		5 NiCr	Eutect AuWire	N/R	

LIFE / ENVIRONMENTAL EXPERIENCE

DATA SRCE	SCR CLS	TST SRC	TEST TYP/ APP ENV	STR LVL/ EQP TYPE	TEST STD MTD/COND	NO. TSTD	TEST DUR.	PART HRS.	NO. FLD	FAILURE CLASSIFICATION IND; MODE; MECH; CAUSE (NO. FAILED / EVENT)	% DEF	TEST DATE	REMARKS
U	A	Env	VisIns GrossLk Temp TempCyc CnstAcc	150C -65/150C 30KG 6 AXES	MS883 1014C 1008C 1010C 2001	193	48 Hrs	9300	0 1	Failed R_S Max	0.52	5/71	
U	A	Env	FineLk		1014A				19	Package Fail	9.84		
U	A	Brn	GrossLk	125C	1014C 1015D		168 Hrs	32400	12 3	Loose R Chips/11; Package Fail/1 $V_{IO} >$ Max Limit/1; $I_I >$ Max Limit/1; $I_{LK} >$ Max Limit/1	6.21 1.55		
U	A	Env	ThrmShk MechShk	-65/150C 20KG Y_1 1 Blo	1011C 2002F	193			7	Loose Subst/3; Loose R Chip/1; Loose Xister Chip/1; Loose Wedge Bond to Conductor/2	3.63		
U	A	Env	CnstAcc	30KG Y_2	2001E	186			1	Loose Wedge Bond to Conductor	0.54		
U	A	Brn	RevBias	125C	1015D	185	72 Hrs	13300	0	Foreign Material Solidified/1;			Missing from Test/1
U	A	Brn		125C	1015A	184	72 Hrs	13250	5	$R_{LK} >$ Max Limit/3; $R_S >$ Max Limit/1	2.72		
U	A	Env	ConstAcc FineLk GrossLk	40KG Y_1	2001 1014A 1014C	184 183 183			1 7	EXK. Pin 1 Off/1 Int. Leads Drooped Shorting Semichips and Conductor/3 Int. Leads Drooped @125C only/1; N/R/3	0.54 3.83		

MALFUNCTION DATA

SYSTEM/ EQUIPMENT	PART HISTORY	SCR CLS	DATE CODE	FAILURE ANALYSIS / CORRECTIVE ACTION	SYSTEM/ EQUIPMENT	PART HISTORY	SCR CLS	DATE CODE	FAILURE ANALYSIS / CORRECTIVE ACTION

DEVICE SECTION

MANUFACTURER: PROPRIETARY
TECHNOLOGY: THIN FILM

FUNCTIONAL CATEGORY: DIGITAL
DEVICE FUNCTION: LADDER SWITCH AND DRIVER

HYBRID MICROCIRCUIT
RELIABILITY DATA

RELIABILITY ANALYSIS CENTER

ENTRY NO.	PKG/ NO. PINS	SIZE OP TEMP	PKG MFG	PKG SEAL	SUBSTR MTL/ BOND	SUBSTR SIZE	NO. COND LYR	SUBSTR METAL #BONDS	IC NO./ TYPE	IC CHP ATCH/ INTERCON	TRANSISTOR NO./ TYPE	TRANSISTOR CHP ATCH/ INTERCON	DIODE NO./ TYPE	DIODE CHP ATCH/ INTERCON	CAPACITOR NO./ TYPE	CAPACITOR CHP ATCH/ INTERCON	RESISTOR NO./ TYPE	RESISTOR CHP ATCH/ INTERCON	RES TOL (%)	ELMT ATCH/ INTERCON NO./ TYPE
152 (Cnt'd)																				

LIFE / ENVIRONMENTAL EXPERIENCE (con't)

DATA SRCE	SCR CLS	TST SRC	TEST TYP/ APP ENV	STR LVL/ EQP TYPE	SUBSTR MTL/ BOND	TEST STD MTD/COND	NO. TSTD	TEST DUR.	PART HRS.	NO. FLD	FAILURE CLASSIFICATION IND; MODE; CAUSE (NO. FAILED / EVENT)	% DEF	TEST DATE
U	A		X-Ray			MSB83	20			0			5/71
			VisIns			1012	141			0			
			TempCyc	-65/15uC		2009	38			0			
			VisIns			1010C	499						
			GrossLk										
U	A	Env	Temp	150C		1014C 1008C	499	48 Hrs	24000	14	R_S > Max Limit/4; V_{IO} > Max Limit/4; I_{CC} > Max Limit/2; I_{LK} > Max Limit/5	2.80	
			TempCyc	-65/150C		1010C	499			16	I_{LK} > Max Limit/2; Intern. CB Short/1; Switch Time Over Max Limit/1; CB Short; Al Metal Scratch/1; Electrical Rejects from Previous Tests/1	3.21	
			CnstAcc	30KG 6 AXES		2001	498			0			
U	A	Env	FineLk			1014A	498			4	Package Fail	0.80	
U	A	Brn	GrossLk	125C		1014C	498	168 Hrs	83160	42	Package Fail/40; Loose R Chip/2	8.43	
U	A	Env	ThrmShk	-65/150C		1015D 1011C	495			1	Res Short; Holes in Oxide	0.20	
							494			1	I_{LK} > Max Limit	0.20	
			MechShk	20KG Y1		2002F	494			2	Loose R Chip	0.40	
U	A	Env	ConstAcc	1 Blo 30KG Y2		2001E	491			4	Loose Au Ball to Base of Q2/1; Shorted Lead to Xistor Chip/1; EB Leads of Q1 Shorted/1; Elongated Wire Shorted to Film Pad/1	0.81	

MALFUNCTION DATA

SYSTEM/ EQUIPMENT	PART HISTORY	SCR CLS	DATE CODE	FAILURE ANALYSIS / CORRECTIVE ACTION	SYSTEM/ EQUIPMENT	PART HISTORY	SCR CLS	DATE CODE	FAILURE ANALYSIS / CORRECTIVE ACTION

DEVICE SECTION

MANUFACTURER: PROPRIETARY   FUNCTIONAL CATEGORY: DIGITAL

TECHNOLOGY: THIN FILM   DEVICE FUNCTION: LADDER SWITCH AND DRIVER

RELIABILITY ANALYSIS CENTER

HYBRID MICROCIRCUIT
RELIABILITY DATA

ENTRY NO.	PKG/ NO. PINS	SIZE OP TEMP		IC		SUBSTR METAL #BONDS	NO. COND LYR	SUBSTR SIZE	SUBSTR MTL/ BOND		TRANSISTOR			DIODE			CAPACITOR		RESISTOR		RES TOL (%)		ELMT ATCH/ INTERCON
				NO./ TYPE	CHP ATCH/ INTERCON						NO./ TYPE	CHP ATCH/ INTERCON		NO./ TYPE	CHP ATCH/ INTERCON		NO./ TYPE	CHP ATCH/ INTERCON	NO./ TYPE	CHP ATCH/ INTERCON		NO./ TYPE	
152 (Cntd)																							

LIFE / ENVIRONMENTAL EXPERIENCE (con't)

DATA SRCE	SCR CLS	TST SRC	TEST TYP/ APP ENV	STR LVL/ EQP TYPE	SUBSTR MTL/ BOND	TEST STD MTD/COND	NO. TSTD	TEST DUR.	PART HRS.	NO. FLD	FAILURE CLASSIFICATION IND; MODE; MECH; CAUSE (NO. FAILED / EVENT)	% DEF	TEST DATE	REMARKS
U	A	Brn	RevBias	125C		MS883 1015D	487	72 Hrs	35064	1	Unknown	0.21		
U	A	Brn		125C		1015A	486	72 Hrs	34992	23	$R_S >$ Max Limits/21; $I_{LK}>$ Max Limits/1	4.73		
U	A	Env	CnstAcc	40KG Y_1		2001	484			0	$P_D >$ Max Limits/1			
			FineLk	1014C		1014A	484			12		2.48		
			GrossLk			1014C	484			19	Package Leak	3.92		
			X-Ray			1012	20			0				
			VisIns			2009	367			0				Date Codes 7028, 7026, 7032, 7034
U	A	Env	TempCyc	-65/150C		1010C	45			0				98 Failed Initial Elect. Measure
			VisIns			1014C	718			0				
			GrossLk			1008C	718			0				
			Temp	150C		1010C	620	48 Hrs	2976	3	R_S Out of $\pm$	0.48		
			TempCyc	-65/150C		2001	619			1	Loose Au Ball Bond to Al on Xistor	0.16		
			CnstAcc	30KG 6 AXES			618			0				
U	A	Brn	FineLk	125C		1014A	618			0				
			GrossLk			1014C	618			4	Xistor Chip Loose/2; Res Chip Loose/2	0.65		
U	A	Env	ThrmShk	-65/150C		1015D	614	168 Hrs	1.03E5	3	Loose Xistor Chip/1; R_S Spec/1; N/R/1	0.49		
			MechShk	20KG Y_1 1 Blo		1011C 2002F	607			0				
U	A	Env	CnstAcc	30KG Y_2 125C		2001E	432/594			133/7	Shorted; Elongated Leads/97; Destroyed Auto. Tester Malfunction/20; EB Leads Shorted on Q3/8; Leads Shorting to Edge of Chip/3; Shorted; Drooping Wires & Loose Wedge Bond/2; Q1 Cracked/1;	30.8/ 1.17		

MALFUNCTION DATA

SYSTEM / EQUIPMENT	PART HISTORY	SCR CLS	DATE CODE	FAILURE ANALYSIS / CORRECTIVE ACTION	SYSTEM / EQUIPMENT	PART HISTORY	SCR CLS	DATE CODE	FAILURE ANALYSIS / CORRECTIVE ACTION

DEVICE SECTION

FUNCTIONAL CATEGORY: DIGITAL

HYBRID MICROCIRCUIT
RELIABILITY DATA

RELIABILITY ANALYSIS CENTER

MANUFACTURER: PROPRIETARY

TECHNOLOGY: THIN FILM

DEVICE FUNCTION: LADDER SWITCH AND DRIVER

ENTRY NO.	PKG/ NO. PINS	SIZE OP TEMP	PKG MFG	PKG SEAL	SUBSTR MTL/ BOND	SUBSTR SIZE	NO. COND LYR	SUBSTR METAL #BONDS	IC NO./ TYPE	IC CHP ATCH/ INTERCON	TRANSISTOR NO./ TYPE	TRANSISTOR CHP ATCH/ INTERCON	DIODE NO./ TYPE	DIODE CHP ATCH/ INTERCON	CAPACITOR NO./ TYPE	CAPACITOR CHP ATCH/ INTERCON	RESISTOR NO./ TYPE	RESISTOR CHP ATCH/ INTERCON	RES TOL (%)	ELM ATCH/ INTERCON NO./ TYPE
152 (Cnt'd)																			

LIFE / ENVIRONMENTAL EXPERIENCE (con't)

DATA SRCE	SCR CLS	TST SRC	TEST TYP/ APP ENV	STR LVL/ EQP TYPE	TEST STD MTD/COND	NO. TSTD	TEST DUR.	PART HRS.	NO. FLD	FAILURE CLASSIFICATION IND; MODE; MECH; CAUSE (NO. FAILED / EVENT)	% DEF	TEST DATE
					MS883					Loose Au Ball to Resistor Chip/1; V_{IO} Spec/1//		
										EB Leads Shorted due to Moving from Previous Y_2/3; Loose Wedge on Resistor Chip/1; Open Wedge Bond/1; Open Au Ball Bond/1; Open Au Ball on Xistor Chip/1		
U	A	Brn	RevBias	125C	1015D	544	72 Hrs	39200	1	CB Short; Silicon Particle	0.18	
U	A	Brn	CnstAcc	125C	1015A	534	72 Hrs	38500	1	Q1 or Q2 Channeled	0.19	
U	A	Env	FineLk	40KG Y_1	2001	534			0			
			GrossLk		1014A	164			1	Package Failure	0.61	
					1014C	164			12	Package Failure/2; V_{IO} Spec @ -55C/1; Open Au Wire Bond R_S Spec @ -55C/2; Open Au Wedge Bond to R to R chip/1; Open Au Wedge Bond to R chip/2; R_S Spec @ 125C/4	7.32	
			X-Ray		1012	60			0			
			VisIns		2009	486			0			
			TempCyc	-65/150C	1010C	115						

REMARKS

FAILURE ANALYSIS / CORRECTIVE ACTION

MALFUNCTION DATA

SYSTEM / EQUIPMENT	PART HISTORY	SCR CLS	DATE CODE	FAILURE ANALYSIS / CORRECTIVE ACTION

SYSTEM / EQUIPMENT	PART HISTORY	SCR CLS	DATE CODE	FAILURE ANALYSIS / CORRECTIVE ACTION

HYBRID MICROCIRCUIT
RELIABILITY DATA

DEVICE SECTION

MANUFACTURER: PROPRIETARY
TECHNOLOGY: THIN FILM

FUNCTIONAL CATEGORY: DIGITAL
DEVICE FUNCTION: LADDER SWITCH AND DRIVER

ENTRY NO.	PKG / NO. PINS	SIZE OP TEMP	PKG SEAL	PKG MFG	SUBSTR MTL/ BOND	SUBSTR SIZE	NO. COND LYR	SUBSTR METAL #BONDS	IC NO./ TYPE	IC CHP ATCH/ INTERCON	TRANSISTOR NO./ TYPE	TRANSISTOR CHP ATCH/ INTERCON	DIODE NO./ TYPE	DIODE CHP ATCH/ INTERCON	CAPACITOR NO./ TYPE	CAPACITOR CHP ATCH/ INTERCON	RESISTOR NO./ TYPE	RESISTOR CHP ATCH/ INTERCON	RES TOL (%)	ELM ATCH/ INTERCON NO./ TYPE
153	FPM1 10	TO-86 -55/ 125C	Glass Header N/A	N/R	N/A	N/A	1	Kov/Au N/R	0		3 SiNPN	Eutect AuWire	0		0		3 Cermet 2 Thin N/R	N/R AuPste Eutect AuWire	N/R	

LIFE / ENVIRONMENTAL EXPERIENCE

DATA SRCE	SCR CLS	TST SRC	TEST TYP/ APP ENV	STR LVL/ EQP TYPE	TEST STD MTD/COND	NO. TSTD	TEST DUR.	PART HRS.	NO. FLD	FAILURE CLASSIFICATION IND; MODE; MECH; CAUSE (NO. FAILED / EVENT)	% DEF	TEST DATE	REMARKS
U	A	Env	VisIns GrossLk		MSBBJ	307			0				5/71 Date Code 7011
			Temp	150C	1014C								
			TempCyc	-65/150C	1008C								
			CnstAcc	30KG	1010C								
				6 AXES	2001		48 Hrs	14700					
U	A	Env	FineLk	125C	1014A	307	168 Hrs	51400	21	Package Leak	6.84		
U	A	Brn	GrossLk	125C	1014A	306	168 Hrs	51400	15	Package Leak/14; V_{IO} > Spec, Package	4.89		
U	A	Brn	ThrmShk	-65/150C	1015D	306			5	Leak/1	1.63		
U	A	Env	MechShk	20KG Y1	1011C	306			5	Elect. Rejects			
				1 BLo	2002F				1	Loose Wedge Bond/1	0.33		
U	A	Env	CnstAcc	30KG Y2	2001E	305	72 Hrs	22000	0	Elect. Rejects			
U	A	Brn	RevBias	125C	1015D		72 Hrs	22000	1	R_S > Spec/2; V_{IO} > Spec/1	0.33		
U	A	Brn	CnstAcc	125C	1015A				3		0.98		
U	A	Env	FineLk	40KG Y1	2001				0	Package Leak			
			GrossLk		1014A	305			1	Ball Bond to Al Metal/1; Wedge Bond to	0.33		
					1014C				11	Au Post/2; V_{IO} & R_S Max Limits/4	3.61		
			X-Ray		1012	20			0				
			VisIns		2009	258			0				
			TempCyc	-65/150C	1010C	40			0				

MALFUNCTION DATA

SYSTEM / EQUIPMENT	PART HISTORY	SCR CLS	DATE CODE	FAILURE ANALYSIS / CORRECTIVE ACTION	SYSTEM / EQUIPMENT	PART HISTORY	SCR CLS	DATE CODE	FAILURE ANALYSIS / CORRECTIVE ACTION

DEVICE SECTION

FUNCTIONAL CATEGORY: DIGITAL

HYBRID MICROCIRCUIT
RELIABILITY DATA

MANUFACTURER: PROPRIETARY

DEVICE FUNCTION: DIODE ARRAY

TECHNOLOGY: SEMICONDUCTOR

ENTRY NO.	PKG/ NO. PINS	SIZE OP TEMP	PKG MFG	PKG SEAL	SUBSTR MTL/ BOND	SUBSTR SIZE	NO. COND LYR	SUBSTR METAL #BONDS	IC NO./ TYPE	IC CHP ATCH/ INTERCON	TRANSISTOR NO./ TYPE	TRANSISTOR CHP ATCH/ INTERCON	DIODE NO./ TYPE	DIODE CHP ATCH/ INTERCON	CAPACITOR NO./ TYPE	CAPACITOR CHP ATCH/ INTERCON	RESISTOR NO./ TYPE	RESISTOR CHP ATCH/ INTERCON	RES TOL (%)	ELMT ATCH/ INTERCON NO./ TYPE
154	MC-DIP 14	TO-116 -55/ 125C	N/R	Glass Header N/A		.25x .25	1	AuCond 36	0		0		16 SiGP	Eutect AuWire	0		0			

LIFE / ENVIRONMENTAL EXPERIENCE

DATA SRCE	SCR CLS	TST SRC	TEST TYP/ APP ENV	STR LVL/ EQP TYPE	TEST STD MTD/COND	NO. TSTD	TEST DUR.	PART HRS.	NO. FLD	FAILURE CLASSIFICATION IND; MODE; MECH; CAUSE (NO. FAILED / EVENT)	% DEF	TEST DATE	REMARKS
U	C	Fld	AirInhab	Navgtn/ Operate 30C		24	25416	6.1E5	1	Malfunction	4.17	3/72	
U	C		AirInhab	Navgtn/ Operate 30C		24	141250	3.39E6	1	Malfunction	4.17	5/73	

MALFUNCTION DATA

SYSTEM / EQUIPMENT	PART HISTORY	SCR CLS	DATE CODE	FAILURE ANALYSIS / CORRECTIVE ACTION

SYSTEM / EQUIPMENT	PART HISTORY	SCR CLS	DATE CODE	FAILURE ANALYSIS / CORRECTIVE ACTION

RELIABILITY ANALYSIS CENTER

RELIABILITY ANALYSIS CENTER

FUNCTIONAL CATEGORY: LINEAR
DEVICE FUNCTION: IF AMPLIFIER

DEVICE SECTION

MANUFACTURER: PROPRIETARY
TECHNOLOGY: THICK FILM

ENTRY NO.	PKG/ NO. PINS	SIZE OP TEMP	PKG SEAL	SUBSTR MTL/ BOND	SUBSTR SIZE	NO. COND LYR	SUBSTR METAL #BONDS	IC NO./ TYPE	IC CHP ATCH/ INTERCON	TRANSISTOR NO./ TYPE	TRANSISTOR CHP ATCH/ INTERCON	DIODE NO./ TYPE	DIODE CHP ATCH/ INTERCON	CAPACITOR NO./ TYPE	CAPACITOR CHP ATCH/ INTERCON	RESISTOR NO./ TYPE	RESISTOR CHP ATCH/ INTERCON	RES TOL (%)	TOROID NO./ TYPE	TOROID ELMT ATCH/ INTERCON
155	CmInLn 15	1.00x 1.00	Epoxy	Al_2O_3 Epoxy	1.00x	1	PtCond AuCond 80	0	PtCond AuCond	2 SiNPN	AgEpoxy PtCond AuCond	0		11 MOS	AgEpoxy PtCond	15 $TaNi_3$	AgEpoxy AuCond		2	Epoxy PtCond

LIFE / ENVIRONMENTAL EXPERIENCE

DATA SRCE SRC	SCR CLS	TST SRC	TEST TYP/ APP ENV	STR LVL/ EQP TYPE	TEST STD MTD/COND	NO. TSTD	TEST DUR.	PART HRS.	NO. FLD	FAILURE CLASSIFICATION IND; MODE; MECH; CAUSE (NO. FAILED / EVENT)	% DEF	TEST DATE	REMARKS
U	N/R	Env	FineLk	He 30psi	MS883 1014A	52	2 Hrs	104	0			7/71	
			GrossLk	Fluoro He 30psi	1014C	52			52	Gross Leak	100.		
		Lab	OpDyn	100C 100%	1005	20	2000 Hrs	4.0E4	0				
		Env	Moistr/ RevBias	25/65C 85%	1004	10			2	Elect. Deg./1; Gross Leak/1	0.20		
		Stp	TempCyc	-55/85C 20 cyc -55/125C 20 cyc	1010A&B	10			10	Low AGC/1; Fine Leak/1; Gross Leak/1	100.		
		Env	HiPress	127C 22psi		7			7	Gross Leak	100.		
		Stp	ThrmShk	-55/85C* 15 cyc -55/125C 15 cyc 5/5 min	1011	5			5	Elect. Deg/Gross Leak Fine Leak/1 Gross Leak/4	100.		*Dow Corning 704(+85 & 125) Aceton (-55)

MALFUNCTION DATA

SYSTEM / EQUIPMENT	PART HISTORY	SCR CLS	DATE CODE	FAILURE ANALYSIS / CORRECTIVE ACTION

SYSTEM / EQUIPMENT	PART HISTORY	SCR CLS	DATE CODE	FAILURE ANALYSIS / CORRECTIVE ACTION

DEVICE SECTION

FUNCTIONAL CATEGORY: LINEAR

DEVICE FUNCTION: VOLTAGE REGULATOR

MANUFACTURER: PROPRIETARY

TECHNOLOGY: THICK FILM

HYBRID MICROCIRCUIT
RELIABILITY DATA

RELIABILITY ANALYSIS CENTER

ENTRY NO.	PKG/ NO. PINS	SIZE OP TEMP	PKG MFG	PKG SEAL	SUBSTR MTL/ BOND	SUBSTR SIZE	NO. COND LYR	SUBSTR METAL #BONDS	IC NO./ TYPE	IC CHP ATCH/ INTERCON	TRANSISTOR NO./ TYPE	TRANSISTOR CHP ATCH/ INTERCON	DIODE NO./ TYPE	DIODE CHP ATCH/ INTERCON	CAPACITOR NO./ TYPE	CAPACITOR CHP ATCH/ INTERCON	RESISTOR NO./ TYPE	RESISTOR CHP ATCH/ INTERCON	RES TOL (%)	ELMT ATCH/ INTERCON NO./ TYPE
156	Can 3	TO-3 -55/ 125C	N/R	Weld	Al_2O_3 Solder	N/R	3	AuCond 36	1 OpAmp	Eutect AuWire	4 SiNPN (3) SiPNP (1)	Solder (3) Eutect (1) AuWire	3 ZeAv (2) FET Reg (1)	Eutect AuWire	3 N/R	AgEpoxy AuWire	16 N/R	N/R AuCond	N/R	

LIFE / ENVIRONMENTAL EXPERIENCE

DATA SRCE	SCR CLS	TST SRC	TEST TYP/ APP ENV	STR LVL/ EQP TYPE	TEST STD MTD/COND	NO. TSTD	TEST DUR.	PART HRS.	NO. FLD	FAILURE CLASSIFICATION IND; MODE; MECH; CAUSE (NO. FAILED / EVENT)	% DEF	TEST DATE	REMARKS

MALFUNCTION DATA

DATA SRCE	PART HISTORY	SCR CLS	DATE CODE	FAILURE ANALYSIS / CORRECTIVE ACTION	SYSTEM / EQUIPMENT	PART HISTORY	SCR CLS	DATE CODE	FAILURE ANALYSIS / CORRECTIVE ACTION
G	Srce Bench Test Ambient	N/R	1/72 9/73	Output Falls to Zero, Electrical Overstress, Resistor Trimming Fault/1 No Output, Broken Lead & Lifted Die Metallization Pads, Assembly Fault-Poor Workmanship/1 Output Follows Input, Failure Caused By Cl Contamination of AuWire/1					

PAGE 199

RELIABILITY ANALYSIS CENTER

HYBRID MICROCIRCUIT
RELIABILITY DATA

DEVICE SECTION

MANUFACTURER: PROPRIETARY

TECHNOLOGY: THICK FILM

FUNCTIONAL CATEGORY: LINEAR

DEVICE FUNCTION: 10 BIT D/A CONVERTER

ENTRY NO.	PKG/ NO. PINS	SIZE OP TEMP	PKG MFG	PKG SEAL	SUBSTR MTL/ BOND	SUBSTR SIZE	NO. COND LYR	SUBSTR METAL #BONDS	IC NO./ TYPE	IC CHP ATCH/ INTERCON	TRANSISTOR NO./ TYPE	TRANSISTOR CHP ATCH/ INTERCON	DIODE NO./ TYPE	DIODE CHP ATCH/ INTERCON	CAPACITOR NO./ TYPE	CAPACITOR CHP ATCH/ INTERCON	RESISTOR NO./ TYPE	RESISTOR CHP ATCH/ INTERCON	RES TOL (%)	ELMT ATCH/ INTERCON NO./ TYPE
157.	C-DIP 18	TO-116 -55/ 125C	N/R	Glass	Al₂O₃ N/R	.21x .75	1	AuCond 160	6 Cermet Switch (3) OpAmp (3)	Eutect AuWire	0		1 SiSig	Eutect AuWire	0		21 N/R	Epoxy AuWire	N/R	

LIFE / ENVIRONMENTAL EXPERIENCE

DATA SRCE	SCR CLS	TST SRC	TEST TYP/ APP ENV	STR LVL/ EQP TYPE	TEST STD MTD/COND	NO. TSTD	TEST DUR.	PART HRS.	NO. FLD	FAILURE CLASSIFICATION IND; MODE; MECH; CAUSE (NO. FAILED / EVENT)	% DEF	TEST DATE	REMARKS

MALFUNCTION DATA

SYSTEM / EQUIPMENT	PART HISTORY	SCR CLS	DATE CODE	FAILURE ANALYSIS / CORRECTIVE ACTION	SYSTEM / EQUIPMENT	PART HISTORY	SCR CLS	DATE CODE	FAILURE ANALYSIS / CORRECTIVE ACTION
Data Src G	Bench Test Ambient	N/R	1/72- 9/73	Erroneous Output Voltage at Elevated Temperatures Due to Excessive Leakage Currents Poor Design/4					

PAGE 200

HYBRID MICROCIRCUIT
RELIABILITY DATA

FUNCTIONAL CATEGORY: LINEAR
DEVICE FUNCTION: IF AMPLIFIER

DEVICE SECTION

MANUFACTURER: PROPRIETARY
TECHNOLOGY: THIN FILM

ENTRY NO.	PKG/ NO. PINS	SIZE OP TEMP	PKG MFG	PKG SEAL	SUBSTR MTL/ BOND	SUBSTR SIZE	NO. COND LYR	SUBSTR METAL #BONDS	IC NO./TYPE	IC CHP ATCH/ INTERCON	TRANSISTOR NO./TYPE	TRANSISTOR CHP ATCH/ INTERCON	DIODE NO./TYPE	DIODE CHP ATCH/ INTERCON	CAPACITOR NO./TYPE	CAPACITOR CHP ATCH/ INTERCON	RESISTOR NO./TYPE	RESISTOR CHP ATCH/ INTERCON	RES TOL (%)	INDUCTOR NO./TYPE	INDUCTOR ELMT ATCH/ INTERCON
158	Ml-InLn 15	1.00x 1.00 -55/ 125C	N/R	Weld	Al_2O_3 Epoxy	1.00x 1.00	1	AlCond 80	0		2 SiNPN	Eutect/ Epoxy AuWire AlWire	0		11 MOS	AgEpoxy AuWire/ AlWire	15 TaNi3			2 MOS	AgEpoxy AlCond

LIFE / ENVIRONMENTAL EXPERIENCE

DATA SRCE NO.	SCR CLS	TST SRC	TEST TYP/ APP ENV	STR LVL/ EQP TYPE	TEST STD MTD/COND	NO. TSTD	TEST DUR.	PART HRS.	NO. FLD	FAILURE CLASSIFICATION IND; MODE; MECH; CAUSE (NO. FAILED / EVENT)	% DEF	TEST DATE	REMARKS
U	N/R	Env	FineLk	He 30psi	MSB83 1014A	52	2 Hrs	104	0				
		Env	GrossLk	Fluoro He 30psi 100C	1014C	52			1	Open Lid	1.92	7/21	
		Lab	OpDyn	100C	1005	20	2000 Hrs	4E4	0				
		Env	Moister/ RevBias	25/65C 85%	1004	10			2	Elect. Deg./1; Package Leak/1	0.2		
		Stp	TempCyc	-55/85C -55/125C 20 cyc	1010A&B	10			0				
		Env	HiPress	127C 22psi		7			4	Severe Corrosion, Package Leak	57.1		Dow Corning (+85 & 125) Acetone (-55)
		Stp	ThrmShk	-55/85C 15 cyc -55/125C 15 cyc 5/5 min	1011	5			0				

MALFUNCTION DATA

SYSTEM/ EQUIPMENT	PART HISTORY	SCR CLS	DATE CODE	FAILURE ANALYSIS / CORRECTIVE ACTION	SYSTEM/ EQUIPMENT	PART HISTORY	SCR CLS	DATE CODE	FAILURE ANALYSIS / CORRECTIVE ACTION

DEVICE SECTION

MANUFACTURER: PROPRIETARY
TECHNOLOGY: THIN FILM

FUNCTIONAL CATEGORY: LINEAR
DEVICE FUNCTION: IF AMPLIFIER

HYBRID MICROCIRCUIT
RELIABILITY DATA

RELIABILITY ANALYSIS CENTER

ENTRY NO.	PKG/ NO. PINS	SIZE/ OP TEMP	PKG MFG	PKG SEAL	SUBSTR MTL/ BOND	SUBSTR SIZE	NO. COND LYR	SUBSTR METAL/ #BONDS	IC NO./ TYPE	IC CHP ATCH/ INTERCON	TRANSISTOR NO./ TYPE	TRANSISTOR CHP ATCH/ INTERCON	DIODE NO./ TYPE	DIODE CHP ATCH/ INTERCON	CAPACITOR NO./ TYPE	CAPACITOR CHP ATCH/ INTERCON	RESISTOR NO./ TYPE	RESISTOR CHP ATCH/ INTERCON	RES TOL (%)	TORROID NO./ TYPE	TORROID ELMT ATCH/ INTERCON
159	CmInLn 15	1.00x 1.00 -55/ 125C	N/R	Epoxy	Glass Epoxy	1.00x 1.00	1	AuNi 80	0		2 SiNPN (LID)	Eutect/ Epoxy AuNi	0		11 Pt	AgEpoxy AlWire	15 NiCr	AgEpoxy AuNi	N/R	2	Epoxy AuNi

LIFE / ENVIRONMENTAL EXPERIENCE

DATA SRCE SRC	SCR CLS	TST SRC	TEST TYP/ APP ENV	STR LVL/ EQP TYPE	TEST STD MTD/COND	NO. TSTD	TEST DUR.	PART HRS.	NO. FLD	FAILURE CLASSIFICATION IND; MODE; MECH; CAUSE (NO. FAILED / EVENT)	% DEF	TEST DATE	REMARKS
U	N/R	Env	FineLk	H_2 30psi	MSB3 1014A	52			0				
		Env	GrossLk	Fluoro/ H_2 30pis 100c	1014C	52			0			7/1	
		Lab	OpDyn	100c	1005	20	2000 Hrs	4.0E4	0				
		Env	Moistr/ RevBias	25/65 85%	1004	10			7	Elect. Deg/2; Fine Leak/5	70.0		
		Stp	TempCyc	-55/85C 20 cyc -55/125C 20 cyc	1010A&B	10			5	N/R	50.0		
		Env	HiPress	127C 22 psi		7			2	N/R	28.6		Dow Corning (85 & 125)
		Stp	ThrmShk	-55/85C 15 cyc -55/125C 15 cyc 5/5 min	1011	5			5	N/R	100.		Acetone (-55)

MALFUNCTION DATA

SYSTEM / EQUIPMENT	PART HISTORY	SCR CLS	DATE CODE	FAILURE ANALYSIS / CORRECTIVE ACTION

SYSTEM / EQUIPMENT	PART HISTORY	SCR CLS	DATE CODE	FAILURE ANALYSIS / CORRECTIVE ACTION

APPENDIX

HYBRID MICROCIRCUIT

DESCRIPTOR CODE INTERPRETATIONS

TECHNOLOGY

Thick:	thick film
Thin:	thin film
Semi:	semiconductor only

Functional Category

Digital
Linear

Device Function

Digital

Switch
Driver
Gates
FlipFlop
Adder
Counter
Divider
Encoder
Filter
Mixer
Shift Register
Checker
Converter

Linear

Regulator
Comparator
IF Amp
Squelch Control
Modulator
AGC Circuits

Pkg/ Pins : Package/Number of Pins

Can:	hermetically sealed metal can
FPMI:	flat pack metal
FPCm:	flat pack ceramic
FPGI:	flat pack plastic
FPMIGI:	flat pack metal glass
FPMICm:	flat pack metal ceramic
FP:	flat pack, unspecified
C-DIP:	ceramic dual in line
CM-DIP:	ceramic metal dual in line
S-DIP:	silicone dual in line
E-DIP:	epoxy dual in line
P-DIP:	phenolic dual in line
-DIP:	unencapsulated dual in line
PILn:	plastic in line

Pkg/ Pins: Package/Number of Pins (con't)

Plstc:	plastic encapsulated (non-DIF)
Modul:	module
MdulP:	module, plastic encapsulated
E-ILn:	epoxy in line
Subst/Lids:	substrate with Lids
Subst/Cover:	substrate with Cover
Subst/PtCvr:	substrate with Partial Cover

Size/Op Temp: Size/Operating Temperature

A JEDEC package number will appear here but if not known a dimension will be shown. The Operating Temperature will be reported as given by the source document or vendor specification.

Pkg Mfg: Package Manufacturer

Pkg Seal: Package Seal

Substr Mtl/Bond   Substrate Material/Bond

Vit:	vitreous glass
DeVit:	devitreous glass
Al_2O_3:	aluminum oxide
BeO:	beryllia
BaTi:	barium titanate
Saph:	sapphire
Glass	
$GlAl_2O_3$:	glazed alumina
Si:	silicon
Eutect:	eutectic
Gold	
Glass	
Epoxy	
Sylgard	
AgEpoxy:	silver epoxy

Substr Size: Substrate Size

length/width
diameter

No. Cod Lyr: Number Conductive Layers

Substr Metal/#Bonds   Substrate Metallization/Number of Bonds

Ag:	silver
PtAu:	platinum gold
AuDep:	gold deposit
PdAu:	palladium gold
AuCond:	gold conductor

Substr Metal: Substrate Metallization

PtPdAu:	platinum palladium gold
PdAuAg:	palladium gold silver
Solder	
MoMn:	molybdenum manganese
CrAu:	chrome gold
Al:	aluminum
MoAu:	molybdenum gold
PdAg:	palladium silver

IC: Integrated Circuit

No./Type: Number/Type

Digital
Simple Gates (n=number of inputs)

n Gate:	single n gate
n Buffer:	single n buffer
2-n Gate:	dual n gate
2-n Buffer:	dual n buffer
n Expander:	single n expander
2-n Inverter:	dual n inverter

Complex Gates Simple Multivibrator

3-n Gate:	triple n gate
Exclusive OR:	single exclusive OR
Adder	
4-n Gate	quad n driver
n Flip Flop	single n flip flop
Pulse Exclusive OR	

Complex Multivibrator

JK Flip Flop	single JK flip flop
2-n Exclusive OR:	dual n exclusive OR
One Shot Multivibrator	
JK/RS Flip Flop	
2-n Flip Flop:	dual n flip flop
RS Flip Flop	
Ripple Counter	
2-JK Flip Flop:	dual JK flip flop

Linear

Regulator
Comparator
Amplifiers
  IF
  RF
  Video
  Audio
  Sense
  Operational
  Differential
Duals

Chp Atch/Intercon: Chip Attach/Interconnection

Eutect	eutectic
Epoxy	
Solder	
Glass	
BmLd:	beam lead
FlChp:	flip chip
AlGe:	aluminum germanium
AgEpoxy:	silver epoxy

Interconnection: Chip to Chip/
Chip to Post

AuWire	
AlWire	
AlBumps	
AuDep:	gold deposited
Sldr Tab:	solder tab
AuBmLd:	gold beam leads
CuSpdr:	copper spider
AlSpdr	aluminum spider
CuSldr:	copper wire terminal
AuPaste:	gold paste
AuElect:	gold electrode

Transistor

No./Type: Number/Type

SiNPN:	silicon npn.
SiPNP:	silicon pnp
GePNP:	germanium pnp
GeNPN:	germanium npn
FET:	field effect transistor
Unij:	unijunction

Chp Atch/Intecon: Chip Attach/Interconnection

(see IC Chp attach & interconnects)

Diode

No./Type: Number / Type

SiGP:	silicon general purpose
GeGP:	germanium general purpose
ZenAv:	zener avalanche
Thyris:	thyristor
Micro:	microwave
GeDet:	germanium detector
SiDet:	silicon detector
GeMix:	germanium mixer
SiMix:	silicon mixer
Varact:	varactor
Recvy:	recovery Tunnel

Chp Atch/Intercon: Chip Attach/Interconnection

(see IC Chip attach and interconnection)

Capacitor

No./Type: Number/Type

AlO:	aluminum oxide
TaO:	tantalum oxide
WO:	tungsten oxide
TiO:	titanium oxide
MetO:	metal oxide
Ceramic:	ceramic chip
CerDep:	ceramic deposited
$BaTi_3$:	barium titanate

Chp Atch/Intercon: Chip Attach/Interconnection

(see IC Chip attach and interconnection)

Resistor

No./Type: Number/Type
(Films and Oxides)

Al:	aluminum
Carbon	
Cermet	
Cr:	chromium
Ir:	iridium
Mo:	molybdenum
Ni:	nickel
NiA:	nickel alloy
NiCr:	nickel chromium
NitCr:	nitrided chromium
Pd:	palladium
Pt:	platinum
PtIr:	platinum iridium
PtNi:	platinum nickel
Rh:	rhenium
SiCr:	silicon chromium
Ta:	tantalum
TaO:	tantalum oxide
Ti:	titanium
Thick	
Thin	
W:	tungsten
Zr:	zirconium

Chp Atch/Intercon: Chip Attach/Interconnection

(see IC Chp attach and interconnection)

Res Tol (%): Resistor Tolerance
(Data shown in percent)

Inductor
No./Type: Number/Type

AuFilm	
Ferrite	
Alloy	
AuFilm	
Toroid	
Wire Wnd:	miniature transformer
LC:	inductance capacitance chip combinations
TIT:	tuneable inductor transformer

Elmatch/Intercon: Element Attach/Interconnection
(see IC Chp attach and interconnection)

Data Srce: Test Data Source

u:	user
v:	vendor
I:	independent test laborato
O:	completed test signed by qualified agency
G:	government agency

Scr Cls: Screen Class

A, B, C	per MIL-STD-883 Method 5004
SSA, SSB, SSC	equivalent to MIL-STD-88: Method 5004
SSD	single stress or sequence no equivalent to any Method 5004 class
N	no screening beyond manu- facturers regular quality assurance practices
N/R	not reported

Tst Src: Test Source

Lab:	laboratory life test
Env:	environmental
Scr/x:	screening procedure/class
Brn:	burn-in procedure
Stp:	step stress
AGR :	AGREE sequence
Chk:	equipment checkout
Rel:	reliability demonstration
Fld:	field use of equipment

Evaluation		Commonly Employed Test Conditions		
		Mil Std 883	Mil Std 750	Mil Std 202
StgLif:	storage life test	1008	1031.4	108A
OpCnst:	operating life test with constant (dc) stress	1005B	1025.3	
OpDyn:	operating life test with dynamic (ac) stress	1005D		
RngCnt:	ring counter life test	1005E		
RevBias:	reverse bias test	1005A		
IntLif:	intermittent life	1006	1036.3	
HumLif:	humidity life			
AccLif:	accelerated life	1005F		
Quality Factors				
BndStr:	bond strength	2011		
Hrmtc:	hermetic seal	1014		112
FineLk:	fine leak			
GrossLk:	gross leak			
InsRes:	insulation resistance	1003	1016	
SldHt:	solder heat			
Solder:	solderability		2031	210
TrmStr:	terminal strength	2004	2036	211
LeadFtg:	lead fatigue			
BondStr:	bond strength			
VisIns:	visual inspection, external	2008	2071	
VisIns:	visual inspection, internal	2010		
X-Ray:	X-Ray (Radiography)	2012		210
Mechanical Environment				
CnstAcc:	constant acceleration	2001	2006	
MechShk:	mechanical shock	2002	2016	202B
VbVrFrq:	vibration variable frequency	2007	2056	204A
VibFtg:	vibration fatigue	2005	2046	201A
VibRdm:	vibration random	2006	2051	
Atmospheric Environment				
Immrsn:	immersion	1012	1011	104A
Moistr:	moisture resistance	1004	1021	106B
Temp:	temperature			
ThrmShk:	thermal shock	1011	1056	107B
TmpCyc:	temperature	1010	1051	102A
SltAtm:	salt atmosphere	1009	1041	
SltSpy:	salt spray		1046	101B
Physical Environment				
Flmbty:	flammability			111
HiPress:	high pressure			
LoPress:	low pressure			
Rdtn:	radiation	1001	1001	105C
Screening		**5004.1**		
Burn-In		**1015**		

AGREE

CHECKOUT

RELIABILITY DEMONSTRATION

StrLvl/EqpType: Stress Level/Equipment Type

Coded stress levels are reported by standard symbols as described in the applicable Military Standard Test methods

Equipment Type

Cmctns:	communications
SgProc:	signal processing
Comput:	computation
Navgtn:	navigation
IDspy:	instrumentation and display
Contrl:	control
Radar:	radar system
Power:	power supply
Combin:	combination and others not otherwise classified
Unspc:	unspecified

Test Std Mtd/Cond: Test Standard Method/Condition

(Test standards are described under TEST TYPE/APP ENV)

No./Tstd: Number Tested

Test Dur: Test Duration

Part Hrs: Part Hours

No. Fld: Number failed

Failure Classification

Ind:	indicator
Mode	
Mech:	mechanism
Cause	

% Def: Percent Defective

$$\% \text{ Def} = 100 \left(\frac{r}{n}\right)$$

where r = number of observed failures
       n = number tested

Test Date: Test Time Frame

System/Equipment: System, Equipment, Subsystem in which the Device Failed

Part History: Application Environment in which the devices failed

ScrCls: Screen Class
Device was screened to this level

Failure Analysis/Corrective Action: Narrative

MIL STD 883/1007
MIL STD 781 LEVELS E, F,G,H,J
MIL STD 781A or B
MIL STD 781A or B

☆U.S. GOVERNMENT PRINTING OFFICE: 1975-614-070/224